Family Law Arbitration – Practice and Precedents

Third Edition

Dennis Sheridan, Solicitor
Suzanne Kingston, Solicitor

Bloomsbury Professional
LONDON • DUBLIN • EDINBURGH • NEW YORK • NEW DELHI • SYDNEY

BLOOMSBURY PROFESSIONAL
Bloomsbury Publishing Plc
50 Bedford Square, London, WC1B 3DP, UK
1385 Broadway, New York, NY 10018, USA
29 Earlsfort Terrace, Dublin 2, Ireland

British Library Cataloguing-in-Publication Data

A catalogue record for this book is available from the British Library.

ISBN:	PB:	978-152652-207-8
	ePDF:	978-152652-209-2
	ePub:	978-152652-208-5

Typeset by Evolution Design & Digital Ltd (Kent)
Printed and bound by CPI Group (UK) Ltd, Croydon, CRO 4YY

Family Law Arbitration – Practice and Precedents

Foreword

In his Foreword to the second edition of this valuable book, published five years ago, Lord Falconer described it 'a very timely and useful guide to arbitration in family matters'. That was an entirely accurate description in 2016, and it is even more valid today, given the attractions of arbitration in almost all family dispute cases, and the increasing challenges faced by the family courts system.

Thanks to the hard work and commitment of the of the Institute of Family Law Arbitrators, IFLA, there is an increasing number of well qualified and experienced lawyers who are very well trained to act as arbitrators in each of the main types of private family law disputes – namely those concerned with children and those concerned with money. And also thanks to IFLA, there are rules which are tailor-made for arbitrations concerned with such issues.

The availability of appropriate individuals to act as family dispute arbitrators and an appropriate set of rules for the conduct of such arbitrations is of enormous benefit to individuals who find themselves caught up in family law disputes. At a time when the family courts are under greater pressure than ever, arbitration offers a very attractive alternative. It can be quick: particularly if both parties want their dispute resolved fast, an arbitrator should be able to accommodate their wish. It is reliable, in the sense that, save if one or both of the parties require or need it, appointments are not cancelled, and the same arbitrator will (save in case of illness or the like) deal with their dispute from start to finish. And arbitration is a confidential process, with the proceedings being conducted in private throughout.

Family law arbitration is not only a benefit to parties involved in family law disputes: it is also a benefit to the public. The very fact that a dispute which would otherwise be conducted in court goes to arbitration helps to reduce the great pressure on the courts. Hence, both for the benefit of the parties and for the benefit of the courts, Judges are prepared to encourage parties involved in family law litigation to consider alternative dispute resolution mechanisms. In some cases, for various reasons, parties need to fight out their dispute rather than to settle it: the only way to achieve that out of court is to arbitrate.

Any arbitration or litigation system benefits enormously from an authoritative guide on the currently applicable law and the currently applicable rules and practice, and which can be consulted with both ease and confidence by those who practice in that system. When it comes to family law arbitrations, Suzanne Kingston and Dennis Sheridan have produced such a book, and as busy practitioners that is a real achievement – and their involvement in practice makes this book all the more authoritative.

I strongly recommend this book. it gives user-friendly, up-to-date, full and practical guidance as to the law, rules and practice which apply to family arbitration, and it also includes a very useful set of precedents.

David Neuberger
One Essex Court
Temple
London

Preface

The launch of family arbitration ten years ago was to some extent a leap of faith by the stakeholders in IFLA – the Chartered Institute of Arbitrators, the Family Law Bar Association, Resolution and the Centre for Child and Family Law Reform of City University. In this jurisdiction it was novel. Whilst its potential was clear, no one could be sure that it would be taken up. The jurisprudential basis and procedural context were the subject of some debate.

Nevertheless, rules were drawn up, together with a training scheme, and IFLA was formed as a not-for-profit company. Now, ten years on the uncertainty has gone and the confidence of IFLA's founders has been justified. That this is the third edition of this useful work to no small extent testifies to that.

The take-up of family arbitration grew slowly at first as its usefulness began to be appreciated but, as with so many game-changing innovations, the Covid-19 pandemic proved a very considerable spur. It was also a happy coincidence that at about the same time a definitive and supportive decision of the Court of Appeal was handed down, sweeping away some of the uncertainty which had caused a conservative profession to be slow to embrace a form of dispute resolution which was novel to family professionals.

In 2020, in the case of *Haley v Haley* [2020] EWCA Civ 1369 the Court of Appeal for the first time considered and approved the enforcement of an IFLA financial award and explained how it was that such awards might effectively be appealed in the same way as a first instance judgment. Then on 9 July 2021 Mr Justice Mostyn handed down judgment in *A v A (Arbitration: Guidance)* [2021] EWHC 1889 (Fam), in which, with the President of the Family Division's agreement and approval, he promulgated guidance concerning the procedure for challenging and/or implementing an arbitral award. All this firmly established confidence in the efficacy of IFLA arbitrations among professionals and parties.

Even more recently, in the case of *BT v CU* [2021] EWFC 87 Mr Justice Mostyn promulgated the implementation of a new approach in financial remedy cases in which the long-established policy of maintaining privacy through anonymity has been abandoned as the norm. This is bound to prove a further incentive to those wishing to avoid the full glare of publicity following a financial remedy judgment in the Family Court, and lead them to resolve their family's financial disputes privately, through an IFLA arbitration.

These decisions and other changes clearly justified a third edition of this work and I was very pleased to be invited to write a third preface. It enables me to acknowledge the work of the members of the IFLA Advisory Committee, including one of the co-authors of this book, Suzanne Kingston, who have done so much to support IFLA, by updating its rules on a regular basis and overseeing its training of arbitrators, an area again where Suzanne Kingston and her colleague, Jonathan Tecks, are the driving force.

Since its inception IFLA has trained and the Chartered Institute of Arbitrators has accredited 210 arbitrators in its Financial Scheme, and 91 in its Children's Scheme, of those 41 are dual qualified. The demand for further training has increased since the Covid-19 pandemic and further training courses are in prospect. Arbitrators are available around the country and for a very wide range of cases. I am particularly pleased to note that it is now understood that family arbitration is not just for the rich in "big money" cases.

The scope of the IFLA Children's Scheme has been expanded since the second edition of this book. IFLA was encouraged by a paper prepared by Janet Bazely QC to include relocation cases in the Scheme. Such cases often require much faster decisions than can be achieved in the Family Court and with Brexit and the pandemic stimulating family relocation such a change was timely. The revision of the rules of the Children's Scheme by a subcommittee of the Advisory Committee chaired by Michael Horowitz QC is helpfully covered in this edition.

The Covid-19 pandemic has presented challenges at every level and I am pleased to see that the authors have included the good practice protocol for remote hearings prepared by Suzanne Kingston and a group of leading practitioners. Whilst it has not been formally adopted by IFLA, it is certainly a very useful and practical guide to those engaged in remote arbitrations, as so many will be from now on regardless of the post-pandemic recovery.

The Rules and a basic guide can be found on the IFLA website, but this book provides much more material besides and will prove a very useful guide to both new and seasoned practitioners who will increasingly be asked to advise their clients about the advantages of arbitration in both financial and children work. As I said in my preface to the last edition, IFLA and their fellow arbitrators should be very grateful to Dennis Sheridan and Suzanne Kingston for this timely and useful guide to family arbitration under the IFLA Schemes.

Donald Cryan (Hon) LLD
Chairman of the Advisory Committee of IFLA
Formerly one of Her Majesty's Circuit Judges
A Bencher of the Honourable Society of the Inner Temple
London

Acknowledgements

Thanks are given to the following people for their assistance and contribution:

- Alexis Campbell QC
- Andrzej Bojarski
- Geoff Wilson
- Hannah Markham QC
- Sir Hugh Bennett
- James Ewins QC
- James Pirrie
- Jonathan Tecks
- Karen Doviston
- Nadia Beckett
- Rachael Kelsey

We also gratefully acknowledge the contributions of the following resources and organisations:

- FamilyArbitrator (www.familyarbitrator.com)
- Family Law Journal
- IFLA (www.ifla.org.uk)
- Resolution (www.resolution.org.uk)

Finally, a huge thanks to our respective assistants – Anita Kerley, Robyn Harsent and Nicola Rowlings – and to all our friends, family and colleagues who have supported us with this venture.

Dennis Sheridan and Suzanne Kingston
January 2022

Table of Abbreviations

AA	1996 Arbitration Act 1996
CA	1989 Children Act 1989
Cafcass	Children and Family Court Advisory and Support Service
Children Rules	Family Law Arbitration Children Scheme Arbitration Rules 2021
Children Scheme	Family Law Arbitration Children Scheme
Financial Rules	Family Law Arbitration Financial Scheme Arbitration Rules 2021
Financial Scheme	Family Law Arbitration Financial Scheme
FPR 2010	Family Procedure Rules 2010
IFLA	Institute of Family Law Arbitrators
ISW	Independent social worker(s)
ToLATA	Trusts of Land and Trustees Act 1996

Contents

Table of Cases

Table of Statutes

Table of Statutory Instruments

PART I

Family law arbitration in practice

CHAPTER 1

Introduction

1.1 BACKGROUND

The essence of family law arbitration is that it is a contractually binding agreement between parties to a dispute to accept the decision of an arbitrator to whom they have agreed to submit an issue or issues which they cannot resolve between themselves. An arbitrator is in effect a 'private judge' who is able, once appointed to undertake an arbitration, to make decisions in respect of family financial or property disputes or children disputes to which, as between themselves, the parties agree in advance to be bound. The 'award' (which is the document in which arbitrators set out their decisions in financial cases) and the 'determination' (which is the document in which arbitrators set out their decisions in relation to children disputes) may still be subject to final approval by a court. Accredited family law arbitrators operate in accordance with and subject to either the Family Law Arbitration Financial Scheme Arbitration Rules 2021 ('the Financial Scheme' and 'the Financial Rules') (see **Appendix 1.1**) or the Family Law Arbitration Children Scheme Arbitration Rules 2021 ('the Children Scheme' and 'the Children Rules') (see **Appendix 1.2**) and the Arbitration Act 1996 (AA 1996) (**Appendix 1.3**).

Both Schemes are administered by the Institute of Family Law Arbitrators (IFLA), a not-for-profit company. The Rules for both Schemes are very similar. They are produced in the same format and there are only some minor differences between them. The Children Rules concentrate on issues specific to children disputes (namely safeguarding and the voice of the child) but generally speaking the rule numberings are exactly the same and should be easily recognised. When the Financial Scheme first started it was the only Scheme and so the one application form was simply called Form ARB1. However, now there are two Schemes there are also two different forms. Form ARB1 is now known as Form ARB1FS (**Appendix 2.1**) and the application form for arbitration in a children case is known as Form ARB1CS (**Appendix 2.2**).

1.2 ARBITRATION AND THE APPLICABLE LAW

Finance and Children: The arbitrator will determine the substance of the dispute only in accordance with the law of England and Wales. The arbitrator may have regard to, and admit evidence of, the law of another country insofar as, and in the same way as, a judge exercising the jurisdiction of the High Court would do so.

Children: When determining any question relating to the upbringing of a child, the welfare of the child shall be the arbitrator's paramount consideration and in considering welfare the arbitrator shall have regard in particular to the welfare checklist set out in section 1(3) of the Children Act 1989 (CA 1989).

1.3 THE FINANCIAL SCHEME

1.3.1 Scope

The arbitrator deals with financial and property disputes arising from marriage, civil partnership or cohabitation and their respective breakdown, or arising from parenting or between those sharing parenting responsibilities, and also in respect of provision from the estate of a deceased person for his or her dependants. Article 2.2 of the Rules lists the statutes under which claims within the Scheme are most usually brought:

> 2.2…
>
> (a) the Married Women's Property Act 1882, s.17;
>
> (b) the Matrimonial Causes Act 1973, Part II;
>
> (c) the Inheritance (Provision for Family and Dependants) Act 1975;
>
> (d) the Matrimonial and Family Proceedings Act 1984, s.12 (financial relief after overseas divorce);
>
> (e) the Children Act 1989, Sched.1;
>
> (f) the Trusts of Land and Appointment of Trustees Act 1996; and
>
> (g) the Civil Partnership Act 2004 Sched.5, or Sched.7, Part 1, para.2 (financial relief after overseas dissolution).

The Scheme does not apply (see Article 2.3) to disputes directly concerning:

- the liberty of individuals;
- the status of individuals or of their relationship;
- the care or parenting of children;
- bankruptcy or insolvency; or
- any person or organisation which is not a party to the arbitration (unless they agree).

In addition, the Scheme does not cover:

- welfare benefits;
- jurisdictional stay cases; or
- issues over recognition of a foreign marriage or divorce.

1.4 THE CHILDREN SCHEME

1.4.1 Scope

The Children Scheme (Article 2.1) covers issues between parents (or other persons holding parental responsibility or with a sufficient interest in the child's welfare) which relate to the exercise of parental responsibility or the present or future welfare of the child concerned (including the child's upbringing, present or future living arrangements, contact and education) and extends but is not limited to matters which could be the subject of an application to the Family Court under section 8 of the CA 1989.

Disputes and issues *not* within the scope of the Children Scheme are set out in Article 2.2:

> 2.2…
>
> (a) any application under the inherent jurisdiction for the return of a child to England and Wales ('this jurisdiction') from a country which is not a signatory to the Hague Convention on the Civil Aspects of International Child Abduction of 25 October 1980 ('the 1980 Hague Convention');
>
> (b) any application for a child's summary return to this or another jurisdiction under the 1980 Hague Convention;
>
> (c) any application for permanent or temporary removal of a child from this jurisdiction except where the proposed relocation is to a jurisdiction or country which has ratified and acceded to the 1980 Hague Convention or the Hague Convention of 19 October 1996 on Jurisdiction, Applicable Law, Recognition, Enforcement and Co-Operation in Respect of Parental Responsibility and Measures for the Protection of Children ('the 1996 Hague Convention') and, for so long as the United Kingdom remains bound by the provisions of the Brussels IIA Regulation, to the jurisdiction of another member of the EU to which the Regulation also applies;
>
> (d) any application for the court 'to examine the question of custody of the child' under Art.11(7) of Council Regulation (EC) No 2201/2003 after an order of a foreign court on non-return to this jurisdiction made pursuant to Art.13 of the 1980 Hague Convention;
>
> (e) any application for cross-border access within the scope of Art.41 of the said Council Regulation which, if a judgment, would require a court to issue an Annex III Certificate;
>
> (f) any dispute relating to the authorisation of life-changing or life-threatening medical treatment or the progress of such treatment;
>
> (g) any case where a party lacks capacity under the Mental Capacity Act 2005;
>
> (h) any case where any person with parental responsibility for the child or who seeks to be a party to an arbitration under the Children Scheme

is a minor; and any case where any person with parental responsibility for the child is not a party to the arbitration; and

(i) any case where the child concerned has party status in existing proceedings relating to the same or similar issues, or should in the opinion of the arbitrator be separately represented in the arbitration.

1.4.2 Children Scheme

The Children Scheme, in principle, has the same advantages as set out in the case studies (see **Appendix 3**). Indeed, some may say that in children disputes the need to have a speedy resolution is even more pressing. It is for this reason that the Children Scheme has proven popular, particularly when considering discrete urgent issues (for example, arrangements for the summer or Christmas holidays).

Like financial arbitrations, children arbitrations offer a bespoke flexible process. It should be noted, however, that the Children Scheme has been very carefully drafted to deal with the important issues of safeguarding and listening to the voice of the child – see further at **2.6.1** and **2.6.2**.

1.5 ARBITRATION FORMS

It is imperative to ensure that the correct form is used for the commencement of an arbitration.

1.5.1 Financial Scheme (ARB1FS) 2021 edition

This form can be found at **Appendix 2.1** and on the IFLA website (ifla.org.uk). The form contains a box marked 'Important' which sets out the binding nature of arbitration. This box is reproduced below.

1.5.2 Children Scheme (ARB1CS) 2021 edition

This form (see **Appendix 2.2**) contains in addition to basic information and the box marked 'Important' as to the binding nature of arbitration, the need to complete a safeguarding questionnaire (see **Appendix 2.3**) and the obtaining of a basic disclosure check from the Disclosure and Barring Service or from Disclosure Scotland as well as any letters or reports from the Children and Family Court Advisory and Support Service (Cafcass) or any local authority children's services department or similar agency.

Arbitrators, if accredited to deal with both financial and children's issues, may if so nominated deal with both. The parties will need to complete both the financial scheme ARB1FS form and the children scheme form ARB1CS.

Important

Parties should be aware that:

- by signing ARB1FS or ARB1CS they are entering into a binding agreement to arbitrate (within the meaning of section 6 of the Arbitration Act 1996);
- after signing, neither party may avoid arbitration (unless they both agree to do so). Either party may rely on the arbitration agreement to seek a stay of court proceedings commenced by the other;
- arbitration is a process whose outcome is generally final.

The ability of a party to challenge an award or determination is discussed further at **2.14** and **3.3** below.

In addition to understanding the binding nature of arbitration, under the Children Scheme the parties must comply with the safeguarding procedures as set out in paragraph 8.3 of Form ARB1CS and Article 17 of the Children Rules. These requirements will be dealt with fully in **Chapter 2.**

CHAPTER 2

Procedure

2.1 PRE-COMMITMENT MEETING

It is envisaged that most arbitrations will start with a pre-commitment meeting – whether by face-to-face meeting, telephone call or Zoom/MS Teams or any other platform used so that the parties can meet the arbitrator and ensure that it is the right process for them. This process effectively enables the arbitrator to showcase how arbitration works and enables the parties to raise questions with the arbitrator before they are contractually bound.

It is imperative that the parties understand that any decision by the arbitrator is final and binding and the meeting gives an opportunity to both parties to check the extent of their commitment to the arbitration.

If the arbitrator offers a pre-commitment meeting, he/she may do so without a fee and without commitment. The arbitrator must be satisfied that all parties involved fully understand that an award at the conclusion of the process will, as between the parties, be binding.

It may be that the parties do not have legal representation and therefore will attend this meeting on their own. It is the role of the arbitrator to ensure that the parties fully understand the binding nature of arbitration and inform the parties that they should seek independent legal advice concerning the binding nature of arbitration.

The arbitrator may assist the parties by suggesting solicitors or barristers who may be able to provide independent legal advice – it may be that this is suggested by reference to the IFLA website so that those giving this advice are trained and accredited arbitrators.

Although a pre-commitment meeting is not an absolute requirement, many arbitrators will consider a pre-commitment discussion helpful to them and to the parties and legal representatives. The purpose of the pre-commitment discussion is to enable all parties to meet with the arbitrator, to confirm the issues that the parties wish the arbitrator to consider and, if possible, list the issues in order of importance. The discussion enables the parties and their legal representatives to learn how the arbitration is to proceed and to understand their obligations within the arbitration process.

The parties must be informed that, should one or other become dissatisfied with the way in which the arbitration is working and disengage from or demand the termination of the arbitration, the arbitrator remains in control, the arbitration remains operative, and, if and when an award is made, it will remain binding on both parties.

The list of issues before the arbitrator may change or be reformulated during or following the pre-commitment meetings as a result of the discussions and input of the arbitrator. It also enables the parties to agree the arbitrator's fees, the location of the arbitration proceedings and if possible, the timescale over which the matters will be dealt with.

2.2 SPECIFIC ISSUES FOR PRE-COMMITMENT MEETINGS FOR FINANCIAL MATTERS

The benefit of a pre-commitment discussion is that the parties will have a full understanding of the procedure that they are now entering into and will be fully aware of the binding nature of arbitration.

During this meeting the parties may wish to discuss the terms of the arbitrator's engagement and the conditions of their appointment, and to consider some very specific issues – for example, whether the arbitrator should incorporate the *Calderbank* principles and whether rights to appeal should be dismissed.

2.3 SPECIFIC ISSUES FOR PRE-COMMITMENT MEETINGS IN CHILDREN CASES

There are two very specific requirements that should be discussed in a pre-commitment meeting in a children case. Firstly, it is imperative that the parties and their representatives consider safeguarding both before and during the arbitration. This is dealt with in detail at **2.6.1**. In addition, the arbitrator will need to give early consideration as to whether an independent social worker (ISW) will be appointed to ascertain the wishes and feelings of the children. If an ISW is to be appointed, the arbitrator may suggest suitable potential ISWs, and it may be agreed at the pre-commitment meeting that a specific ISW will be approached to find out their availability and costs estimate. See also **2.6.2**.

2.4 SIGNING UP TO ARBITRATION

There are various ways in which an arbitrator may be appointed. These are set out in Article 4 of both the Children and Financial Rules. In short, these are:

- the parties may agree to nominate a particular arbitrator and they may approach a particular arbitrator directly to discuss this appointment;
- the parties may agree on a shortlist of arbitrators from the IFLA website and may ask IFLA to select one of the arbitrators on the shortlist without

reference to any criteria. The names of qualified family arbitrators can be found on the IFLA website – www.ifla.org.uk. The arbitrators' areas of expertise are denoted on the website by (F) for financial arbitration or (C) for children matters; arbitrators denoted with (F)(C) are trained in both. The website has been designed specifically to enable each arbitrator to set out a short profile so that an arbitrator may be selected from a particular locality or branch of the legal profession – perhaps a solicitor, barrister or a retired judge from one of a number of different levels of court. The list can also be searched to identify an arbitrator who has particular expertise or skills, including a foreign language or knowledge of religious or cultural customs; or

- IFLA will offer the appointment to a sole arbitrator from the website whom it considers appropriate having regard to the nature of the dispute; any preferences expressed by the parties as to the qualifications, area of experience, expertise or other attributes of the arbitrator; any preference expressed by the parties as to the geographical location of the arbitration; and any other relevant circumstances.

Sample letters for confirming the appointment of the chosen arbitrator (see **Appendices 2.4** and **2.5**) and corresponding with the parties regarding choosing an arbitrator (see **Appendix 2.6**) are included in this book.

It is important to emphasise that a matter being referred to arbitration must first be notified to IFLA (regardless of whether the name of the arbitrator is already agreed or the nomination is left to IFLA). The notification to IFLA is by way of either Form ARB1FS for financial matters (**Appendix 2.1**) or Form ARB1CS for children matters (**Appendix 2.2**).

2.5 FINANCIAL – FORM ARB1FS

Form ARB1FS requests details of the parties, and of their legal representatives (if any). Most importantly the main issues requiring arbitration must be set out. The form itself is not complex but it is important, as this document constitutes a binding agreement between the parties (as stated at **2.2**). Form ARB1FS records basic details concerning each party, each solicitor and barrister (if any); the issues that are in contention; and (if agreed) the name of the proposed arbitrator.

Each of the parties and their respective lawyers (if any) must sign Form ARB1FS. As in litigation there must be a lead party and generally the party who signs Form ARB1FS first will be referred to as the applicant. It must, however, be understood that there is no significance within an arbitration as to which party is designated applicant and which is the respondent, and that the arbitrator has the power to treat either as the applicant.

The completed and signed Form ARB1FS, after having been reviewed by the other party, must then be forwarded to IFLA; IFLA will then refer the case either to the chosen arbitrator or, if requested, to an arbitrator that it has nominated. The nominated arbitrator will then contact all parties to confirm that theirs is a suitable case on which the arbitrator can adjudicate.

2.6 CHILDREN – FORM ARB1CS

Form ARB1CS is almost the same as Form ARB1FS and is treated in the same way.

The main difference centres around the issue of safeguarding.

2.6.1 Safeguarding

The safeguarding requirements are set out in Article 17 of the Children Rules and paragraphs 7 and 8 of Form ARB1CS.

Article 17.1.1 of the Children Rules makes it clear that both parties have a duty prior to the commencement of the arbitration to provide accurate information regarding safeguarding in Form ARB1CS and in the safeguarding questionnaire (see **Appendix 2.3**) they are obliged to complete. In addition, the parties are obliged to obtain a basic disclosure check from the Disclosure and Barring Service or from Disclosure Scotland as appropriate and promptly send it to the arbitrator and to every other party. Also, if either party has a relevant letter or report prepared by Cafcass or any local authority children's services department or similar agency in relation to the welfare or safeguarding of any child who is the subject of the proposed arbitration, then that must be sent to the arbitrator and to every other party.

The precise information that the parties are to disclose is set out in Article 17.1.2. Such disclosure would generally include, but is not limited to, criminal convictions, cautions or involvement (concerning any child) with children's services.

If the arbitrator believes that there are safeguarding issues either prior to or during the arbitration then the arbitrator must consider whether the arbitration may safely continue (Article 17.2.1). If the arbitrator concludes that the dispute is no longer suitable for arbitration then he/she must inform the parties in writing of that decision and of the grounds, and will then terminate the proceedings (Articles 7.3 and 15.2(b)). Under Article 17.3.1, if the arbitrator becomes aware of any matters which lead them reasonably to apprehend that a child or any party has suffered or is likely to suffer significant harm by reason of the likely future behaviour of any party, then these concerns must be communicated to the relevant local authority or appropriate government agency as soon as possible. In those circumstances, there is no need for the arbitrator to inform the parties that they are going to contact the relevant local authority or appropriate government agency.

The arbitrator may also inform IFLA of a decision to decline an appointment or to terminate an arbitration on safeguarding or welfare grounds.

2.6.2 Voice of the child

It is clear from Article 8.3 of the Family Law Arbitration Children Scheme Arbitration Rules 2021 ('the Children Rules') that the arbitrator may not meet with the child who is the subject of the arbitration at any time, not even to communicate the decision made in arbitration. However, it is important that the arbitrator has a way of determining the wishes and feelings of the child – this will generally be facilitated by the instruction of an ISW, who will ascertain the wishes and feelings of the child and report to the arbitrator and the parties. Instruction of an ISW can either be proposed by the parties, subject to the confirmation and approval of the arbitrator (Article 8.2.3), or the arbitrator may of their own motion appoint an ISW (Article 8.2.4).

2.6.3 The 'no order' principle

Section 1(5) of the Children Act 1989 (CA 1989) makes it clear that the court should not make an order unless it is better for the child than not making an order. The arbitrator must apply this principle and therefore must consider whether an order is necessary. They should be set out in the determination and the reasoning for the decision.

2.6.4 Other principles the arbitrator must consider

When dealing with a children arbitration, the arbitrator will have section 1 of the CA 1989 firmly in mind – in other words, the child's welfare will be the paramount consideration. In order to do that, the arbitrator will pay particular attention to the welfare checklist as follows:

- the ascertainable wishes and feelings of the child concerned (considered in the light of his or her age and understanding);
- his or her physical, emotional and educational needs;
- the likely effect on him or her of any change in his or her circumstances;
- the child's age, sex, background and any other characteristics which the court considers relevant;
- any harm which he or she has suffered or is at risk of suffering;
- how capable each parent (and any other person in relation to whom the court considers the question to be relevant) is of meeting the child's needs; and
- the range of powers available to the court under the CA 1989 in the proceedings in question.

Another important point is for the tribunal to ensure that there are no unnecessary delays when considering the child's welfare. This is probably less of a problem in an arbitration than it would be in a court setting, since one of the main benefits of arbitration is that the pacing and speed can be adjusted to suit the case and the needs of the parties.

2.7 CONTACT WITH THE ARBITRATOR – FINANCIAL AND CHILDREN

We are now at the stage where the arbitrator has accepted their appointment.

There will probably have been a pre-commitment meeting where the arbitration will have been scoped out and now it is necessary to think about moving the arbitration forward with a potential directions appointment. In advance of that, the arbitrator may forward a checklist of matters for discussion at the first meeting. Proposed checklists are included at **Appendices 2.7** and **2.8**.

2.8 THE CONTRACT

Each arbitrator has their own form of letter of engagement. A typical example of a letter of engagement in a financial case is to be found at **Appendix 2.9**. The children letter of engagement will be very similar but will specifically mention issues such as safeguarding and the voice of the child. If there has been a pre-commitment discussion, the contents of the letter will have been discussed. If there has been no previous discussion, the letter of engagement will be submitted by the arbitrator to the legal representatives for them to discuss with their clients, ensuring that the clients fully understand the terms of the arbitration.

It is appropriate to confirm the appointment of an arbitrator with your client – suggested letters to this effect can be found at **Appendices 2.4** (financial) and **2.5** (children).

2.9 THE ARBITRATION PROCESS – FINANCIAL AND CHILDREN

Depending on the matter(s) to be resolved in arbitration, it may be appropriate for a hearing to take place to consider directions (directions hearing/ first meeting). The hearing will be set up by the arbitrator and will take place at a specific venue, time and date with the parties and their lawyers present. Since Covid-19 many of these interlocutory hearings are conducted by Zoom or MS Teams or other forms of video conferencing.

A number of arbitrators worked together during Covid-19 to prepare suggested guidance in relation to remote hearings and this can be found at **Appendix 4**.

The parties 'own' the process and the arbitrator will ordinarily be keen to follow the course suggested by the parties provided they are in agreement. If the parties are not in agreement, the arbitrator will give them the opportunity to make submissions (via their legal representatives if appropriate) and will then give directions which will be binding upon them. The arbitration is an informal process and the arbitrator will guide the parties through the process.

It is possible for these matters to be dealt with on paper – typically, in those circumstances, written submissions are made by both sides and the arbitrator then determines the appropriate directions.

Whether at a hearing or on paper, the arbitrator's directions are in many ways similar to those given in court and the following topics and provisions are set out by way of example:

- written statements of case;
- disclosure and production of documents as between the parties;
- the exchange of witness statements;
- the number and type of expert witnesses, exchange of their reports and any meetings they may have had (it is envisaged that in children arbitration cases, ISWs will be appointed to ascertain the wishes and feelings of the children);
- arrangements for any meeting or hearing and the procedures to be adopted; and
- time limits to be imposed on oral submissions, the examination of witnesses, and any other procedure for controlling the length of hearings.

Once the arbitrator has decided upon the directions, they will draft the directions order and will forward them to the parties within 7 to 14 days; alternatively, as is common, the arbitrator will hand down the directions immediately and provide printed copies to the parties.

2.10 DIRECTIONS

It should be noted here that a number of cases are resolved during the course of arbitration possibly because the arbitrator has provided a potential forum for discussion in relation to potential settlement. If an agreement is reached, the arbitration ends. The arbitrator may not be requested to provide a consent award or determination.

At Article 18 of the Children Rules and Article 16 of the Family Law Arbitration Financial Scheme Arbitration Rules 2021 ('the Financial Rules') it will be seen that the arbitrator may encourage the parties to consider using an alternative dispute resolution procedure other than arbitration such as mediation, negotiation or early neutral evaluation in relation to the whole dispute or a particular aspect of the dispute. If the parties do use alternative dispute resolution, then the arbitrator will facilitate its use and may if appropriate stay the arbitration for an appropriate period of time for alternative dispute resolution to take place.

The arbitrator may, with the agreement of all involved, recommend that a particular aspect of the case be referred to a specific expert, eg, an independent financial advisor or pensions expert. Again, this might be with a view to a settlement being reached in the arbitration process.

However, if there is no possibility of settlement the parties must comply with the directions and all disclosure and/or evidence must be submitted by the date set by the arbitrator in the directions order. The arbitrator will consider all of the information they have and, if satisfied that the final hearing can now take place, will proceed to that hearing.

One of the main benefits of arbitration is that it can be conducted at the speed and pace required by the parties. It is possible to deal with a full arbitration in a very short time frame by dealing with discrete points only rather than an entire case.

2.11 THE FINAL HEARING

If the case is to proceed by way of a full hearing it is the responsibility of the parties to find a venue which has at least one sufficiently sized room for the hearing to take place and two separate rooms where meetings can be held by the parties individually. The arbitration generally follows a similar pattern to what would happen in court; however, since the process is more flexible, the parties and their lawyers can provide their thoughts about how the hearing should be undertaken. The arbitrator will generally discuss how the room is going to be set up with the legal representatives and the usual approach is one of informality. There will be a bundle – probably electronic – and it must be properly formatted. This will be made available to the arbitrator. The preparation of the documents is normally dealt with by the applicant's solicitor. This however will be discussed in advance at a pre-trial review where the arbitrator will make sure that all of the arrangements for the final hearing are in place. There will be a witness template (probably agreed) and it will be the role of the arbitrator to ensure proper time management.

The arbitrator will want to make sure that refreshments are made available to the parties and the legal representatives throughout the final hearing and they will also need to have the necessary equipment to administer oaths if live evidence is to be heard. Further, the arbitrator will have canvassed with the parties whether and how a transcript of the hearing is going to be undertaken. This can be done in a number of ways – through a formal transcription service; a recording of the hearing being undertaken via a platform such as Zoom or a note taker being available in the hearing. The arbitrator will discuss these issues prior to the final hearing and ensure that that everything is in hand and the cost for transcription is factored in.

2.12 AWARD OR DETERMINATION

The final adjudication in a financial case is known as the award, whereas in a children case it is called a determination. At the conclusion of the hearing, the arbitrator will reserve their award or determination and advise the parties when it will be ready. It is common practice for the award or determination to be finalised well within 28 days and generally it will be forwarded to the parties to check that factual matters such as dates and times are correct. However, the arbitrator will require payment of their fees before releasing even a draft award.

It is important for the arbitrator to ensure that all relevant issues have been determined in the award or determination and that this document could serve as a standalone adjudication. At **Appendices 2.10** and **2.11** there are examples of drafting checklists which set out all of the main points to be contained in the document. Once the award or determination is finalised (ie signed and dated), it is sent out to the parties via email and post; the date on the arbitral award is the date from which any time for appeal will run.

2.13 ENFORCEMENT OF THE FINANCIAL AWARD

The arbitral award is intended to be final, subject to any right to challenge (see **2.14** and **3.3**).

Most parties will also obtain a court order from the Family Court to mirror and confirm the terms of the award. A draft letter to HM Courts and Tribunals Service can be found at **Appendix 2.12**. This will assist with enforcement, although in some instances an award can be enforced directly in the same way as a judgment or order of the court and to the same effect (section 66 of the Arbitration Act 1996 (AA 1996)). This may be the appropriate route for a Trusts of Land and Appointment of Trustees Act 1996 (ToLATA 1996) award but it is not appropriate in the case of a financial remedies award.

The draft consent order reflecting the decisions and directions contained in the arbitrator's award should be lodged at court for approval. It should follow the relevant paragraphs of the standard form for financial remedy orders. There will be a recital making it clear that settlement has been reached through the arbitration process and that the consent order reflects the terms of the arbitral award (see **Appendix 2.13**). On 23 November 2015, the then President of the Family Division (Sir James Munby) issued 'Arbitration in the Family Court – Practice Guidance' and this contains all of the relevant information regarding the lodging of the consent order (see **Appendix 1.4**). Further, Sir James Munby endorsed the use of a streamlined procedure in the High Court to fast track the review of draft consent orders which are the products of arbitral awards under the IFLA Scheme or something similar. The process was first used in *S* v *P* [2008] 2 FLR 2040 (see **Appendix 6.1**).

In order to use the streamlined procedure, the following documents must be lodged:

- a signed copy of the proposed order and the terms agreed;
- Forms A and D81;
- the arbitral award; and
- the agreement to arbitrate (Form ARB1FS).

The confidentiality of the award can be preserved by lodging it at court in a sealed envelope clearly marked with the name and number of the case and the words 'arbitration award – confidential'. The award will then remain on the court file, which should be placed in an envelope clearly marked as above and with the words 'not to be opened without the permission of the Judge of the Family Court'.

Although it is not possible for parties to give undertakings within arbitration, it is envisaged that these will be set out in a schedule of agreement attached to the award. These could then be made into full undertakings when the award is made into a court order.

2.14 CHALLENGING AN ARBITRAL AWARD

A great deal has happened since the last edition of this book in relation to challenging an arbitral award. There have been two recent seminal cases.

Haley v Haley [2020] EWCA Civ 1369 (**Appendix 6.4**)

In this case the Court of Appeal had to consider the interplay between the AA 1996 and the family law arena. Under the AA 1996 appeals are only permitted where there is lack of jurisdiction (section 67), where there has been a serious procedural irregularity (section 68) or where the arbitrator has erred in law (section 69). It was noted that there was a difference between the civil courts who strive for certainty and fairness as a concept which is used in the Family Court. It was determined that 'family cases are different from civil cases' and in the family context arbitration cannot oust the underlying jurisdiction of the court. The natural consequences of this analysis is that the Family Court must allow a review of an arbitral award where the award is 'wrong'. Consequently, the higher threshold that previously had been held to apply, ie requiring that the decision is 'obviously wrong' does not apply to family arbitrations under section 25 of the Matrimonial Causes Act 1973 (MCA 1973).

The 'wrong' test may be less restrictive but it is by no means pushing at an open door. Parties entering arbitration should continue to do so in full expectation of being bound by the eventual award made.

A v A [2021] EWHC 1889 (Fam) (**Appendix 6.5**)

Post *Haley*, there was some confusion amongst practitioners as to how exactly an application seeking to challenge or implement a financial remedy arbitral award was to be brought before the court. In the case of *A v A*, Mr Justice Mostyn provided welcome practical guidance.

Before any application to challenge or implement an award can be made, a Form A must be issued. For those cases where financial remedy proceedings were already issued but stayed to allow arbitration to take place, the stay will need to be lifted.

For those cases where a Form A needs to be issued, there is no need for the parties to attend a Mediation Information and Assessment Meeting (MIAM). The application itself should be made on Form D11 using the Part 18 Family Procedure Rules 2010 (FPR 2010) procedure.

Before embarking on such an application, it will be important to advise clients that, just as with appeals, costs will follow the event.

Key procedural points for those seeking to challenge an award are:

- the application should be filed within 21 dates of the final award;
- a skeleton argument (less than 20 pages), the award and a draft gatekeeping order will accompany the D11. A template gatekeeping order is provided at **Appendix 2.18**;
- any request for allocation to a High Court judge must be made in writing and submitted at the time of making the application;
- the respondent will have 14 days within which to file a skeleton argument and draft order in response;
- a circuit judge (or in the event of an allocation to a High Court judge – Mr Justice Mostyn (London/South Eastern Circuit) or the relevant Family Division Liaison Judge (elsewhere)) will triage the application on paper and decide whether or not to grant permission to appeal.

It should be highlighted that, at the time of writing, we await guidance on the extent to which *Haley v Haley* and *A v A* applies to the enforcement of or challenge to financial awards made in relation to ToLATA and other financial cases that are not a financial remedy (as defined at rule 2.3 of the FPR 2010).

2.15 ORDERS WITHIN ARBITRATION

The provisions relating to an arbitration claim most likely to be sought in the course of a financial arbitration are:

- stay pursuant to section 9 of the AA 1996;

- enforcement of peremptory orders of the arbitrator (section 42 of the AA 1996);
- securing the attendance of witnesses (section 43 of the AA 1996).

The following standard orders have been issued to meet each of these contingencies:

- stay pursuant to AA 1996, section 9 (see **Appendix 2.15**);
- enforcement of an arbitrator's peremptory order under AA 1996, section 42 (see **Appendix 2.16**); and
- order securing the attendance of witnesses under AA 1996, section 43 (see **Appendix 2.17**).

2.16 ENFORCEMENT OF THE CHILDREN DETERMINATION

The arbitrator must consider at the end of the proceedings whether following section 1(5) of the CA 1989 an order is necessary. It is envisaged that in most cases an order will be made and the way in which an order result from the court is the same in children matters as financial. The details of this are set out in the Practice Guidance from the President of the Family Division at **Appendix 1.4**.

It should be highlighted that, at the time of writing, we await guidance on the extent to which *Haley v Haley* and *A v A* apply to the enforcement of or challenge to children determinations.

CHAPTER 3

Guidance

3.1 THE ARBITRATOR

3.1.1 Responsibility of the arbitrator

Section 33 of the Arbitration Act 1996 (AA 1996) sets out in specific terms the general duty of a tribunal (in IFLA arbitrations this will be a single arbitrator).

> **General duty of the tribunal**
>
> 1. The tribunal shall:
>
>   (a) act fairly and impartially as between the parties, giving each party a reasonable opportunity of putting his case and dealing with that of his opponent, and
>
>   (b) adopt procedures suitable to the circumstances of the particular case, avoiding unnecessary delay or expense, so as to provide a fair means for the resolution of the matters falling to be determined.
>
> 2. The tribunal shall comply with that general duty in conducting the arbitral proceedings in its decisions on matters of procedure and evidence and in the exercise of all other powers conferred on it.

3.1.2 How to address the arbitrator

Most arbitrators will refer to the parties and their legal representatives by their title and surname and would expect to be addressed in the same way.

3.1.3 Does it matter where you sit?

No, but generally the client should be closer to the arbitrator than the legal representative.

3.1.4 Does it matter where the arbitration takes place?

No, although there should be three rooms available – one for the arbitrator and one for each of the parties to meet separately to hold individual discussions with their legal representatives. It is now very common for arbitrations to be dealt with online. Please refer to the suggested guidance for online arbitrations at **Appendix 4**.

3.1.5 Time

The time should be convenient to all parties and the arbitrator.

3.1.6 Contact with the arbitrator

Contact with the arbitrator should usually be by way of email or, in an emergency, by telephone, but all communication must be copied in to the other party. The parties (who are not the legal representatives) unless acting as litigant in person should not contact the arbitrator direct, unless authorised by both the arbitrator and all other parties involved.

3.2 BENEFITS OF ARBITRATION

- Immediate engagement with the other party, as early agreement has to be reached regarding the fact that the case will be dealt with by way of arbitration and regarding the appointment of the arbitrator.
- Direct and easy communication with the arbitrator once the nomination has been accepted. This saves time and is a positive experience for the parties.
- The parties together with legal representatives take an active part in the discussions as to location, date and time of the initial pre-commitment hearing. The parties are therefore involved from the outset in their matter rather than considering themselves 'outsiders'. The process is far more 'their own' than conventional litigation in which the court's procedures and requirements often leave litigants feeling disempowered. In particular, it should be noted that the whole concept of party autonomy is key in the arbitral process and parties are encouraged to participate and feel engaged throughout.
- A further benefit is that if it is necessary for hearings to take place in the evening and/or at a weekend, the arbitrator will, if possible, accommodate this.
- Takes place at a location suitable to all parties and representatives. This is a significant benefit; many courts are closing, meaning parties and representatives may live a long distance from the nominated court – sometimes this results in travel times that exceed an hour by car. Public transport to the court's location is often unobtainable or, if available, very expensive and time consuming.
- Continuity of the arbitrator (as decision-maker) throughout the matter. This leads to reassurance for all involved that the arbitrator will be fully aware of

all the issues that need to be decided upon and is not a decision-maker who merely picks the papers up immediately prior to the attendance of the parties before them at a hearing, as frequently happens in court.

- Arbitration, although a formal process, is less formal than the court process and takes place in a more informal setting. All attending at the various hearings before the arbitrator, including the arbitrator, will sit at the same table on the same level. It means all parties will feel able to communicate when necessary in the knowledge that all present will listen and be able to contribute within the hearing. The parties gain confidence that, when appropriate, they may directly contribute and that their comments will be heard and listened to by all others present, including the arbitrator. A further benefit of the somewhat less formal setting is that most arbitrators will have refreshments such as coffee, tea and water available.

- If during a hearing any individual present wants a short adjournment (a party may wish to have a few minutes away from the arbitration setting) the arbitrator will normally grant it, either immediately or when it is appropriate to take a break during the hearing. The arbitration process can be very sensitive to the needs of all attending.

- Early discussions will take place between the arbitrator, the parties and their legal representatives about how the arbitration will be recorded. There are various different methods which can be deployed, including recording the proceedings (video recording or just voice recording) or employing a minute taker. Sometimes it will be agreed that the parties' representatives will take notes and then prepare minutes of the directions hearing which will be circulated for all to consider and review.

- The speed at which the arbitration deals with the issues is determined by the arbitrator with the legal representatives and the parties. The potential costs savings through arbitration result from the comparatively speedy resolution achievable when contrasted with the delay inherent in court procedures. Concluding the matter expeditiously with a final and binding award means the parties can move on with their lives. Arbitration, by its ability to conclude matters speedily, removes the burden of outstanding and unsettled financial and children issues from the parties and enables them to continue their lives and their work (if employed) without the constant concern of court proceedings and endless involvement with lawyers (see the case studies at **Appendix 3**).

- The parties can discuss with the arbitrator how the arbitration procedures are to move forward and the timetable to be complied with.

- The general principle is that the arbitration and its outcome are confidential and remain so, and only the parties themselves can disclose what has happened at the arbitration if they are minded to do so. Any note or transcript of the proceedings is confidential and will be used solely for the purpose of the arbitration, its implementation and (if need be) in connection with any necessary application to the court, or the enforcement of the award.

- The arbitrator may at any point in the process agree that it would be appropriate for another dispute resolution procedure to be used, eg mediation or negotiation, in which case the arbitration will be adjourned until that has been attempted. Thus the arbitrator will do what they can to promote an amicable settlement of the issues separating the parties.
- The award of the arbitrator is final and binding upon the parties, and although there is provision for appeal the grounds for appeal are extremely limited. The parties can agree to waive their rights to appeal which provides even greater certainty and finality to the process.

3.3 HOW CAN AN ARBITRAL DECISION BE CHALLENGED?

In a commercial award, when the parties agree to arbitration they 'buy the right to get the wrong answer' – in other words, the grounds to correct or to challenge an award are very circumscribed. Similarly, when the parties sign the application form (ARB1FS or ARB1CS) they are agreeing to be bound by the adjudication of the arbitrator, and the grounds for challenging that arbitral decision are similar to the right to appeal a court order (see **2.14**).

3.3.1 Corrective jurisdiction

Under section 57(1) of the AA 1996, the parties are free to agree on the powers of the tribunal to correct an award or make an additional award. If they do not agree, then either party may, under s ection 57(3)–(4) of the Act, apply to the arbitrator within 28 days of the award to either:

> (3)…
>
> (a) correct an award so as to remove any clerical mistake or error arising from an accidental slip or omission or clarify or remove any ambiguity in the award, or
>
> (b) make an additional award in respect of any claim (including a claim for interest or costs) which was presented to the tribunal but was not dealt with in the award.

3.3.2 Appeal

In the case of *Haley v Haley* [2020] EWCA Civ 1369 (see **2.14** and **Appendix 6.5**) the Court of Appeal clarified that where one party opposes the making of an order in the terms of an arbitral award concluded under the Financial Scheme, the court should determine that challenge by reference to the appeals procedure under Part 30 of the Family Procedure Rules 2010 (FPR 2010). The test to be applied is that no reasonable arbitrator could have made such an order (the award is 'wrong').

It should be highlighted that, at the time of writing, we await guidance on the extent to which *Haley v Haley* and *A v A* apply to the enforcement of or challenge to financial awards made in relation to ToLATA and other financial cases that are not financial remedies (as defined at rule 2.3 of the FPR 2010) as well as to children determinations.

3.4 POINTS TO NOTE

3.4.1 Judicial encouragement

The recent case of *WL v HL* [2021] EWFC B10 confirms the Family Court's willingness to encourage dispute resolution solutions. In this case Mr Recorder Allen QC ordered an adjournment of the matter before him to enable the parties to engage in non-court dispute resolution pursuant to the Family Court's case management powers under Part 3 of the FPR 2010.

The case is set out at **Appendix 6.5**. The judge's decision is very interesting. The case stresses the importance of dispute resolution and that the parties must be aware that if they pursue their matter through the courts, the courts have the authority to adjourn proceedings, giving time to the parties to consider an appropriate dispute resolution procedure to resolve their case and engage with it.

3.4.2 Consent by both parties

Arbitration, like all other dispute resolution procedures, needs the consent of all parties before it can proceed. This is unlike court proceedings where one of the parties can (subject to the requirement for mediation first to be considered) make the decision to pursue litigation through the courts whether that is the wish of the other party or not.

3.4.3 Costs

The arbitrator will be paid a fee (often a fixed fee negotiated during the pre-commitment meeting) and expenses may be incurred for the use of a venue, recording equipment and the arbitrator's travel.

3.5 INTERNATIONAL ARBITRATION

It has been very interesting to speak to different practitioners around the world and to consider how arbitration is dealt with in their jurisdiction as well as England and Wales. As always, with the help of the fellows of the International Academy of Family Lawyers, we have been able to obtain information about arbitration and can now share with you our findings (**Appendix 5.5**).

3.6 CONCLUSION

The world has changed dramatically since the second edition of this book – Covid-19 has changed the world of work arguably forever. Now, practitioners and clients alike are used to engaging online and in the virtual world.

The court system is failing and becoming more challenging for family law clients. The delays are longer than ever and so it is no surprise that arbitration with all of the benefits highlighted at **3.2** has come to the rescue.

Now, more than ever before, arbitration in the family arena is becoming the 'go to' means of dispute resolution. We have a wealth of resources in this jurisdiction to help arbitration on its way. The judges have been immensely supportive and it is clear that with all of the judgements issued there is a real desire for family law arbitration to succeed. IFLA has guided family law arbitrators and we are extremely grateful to all of the committee and board members who have worked tirelessly to put family law arbitration on the map. The accredited arbitrators have worked collaboratively to market and raise the profile of family law arbitration under the auspices of the Forum of Family Arbitrators.

We hope that by the next edition of the book even more arbitration is being undertaken and that we will be reporting on the continued success of this relatively new form of dispute resolution in the family law world

APPENDIX 1

Legislation, Rules and Practice Guidance

Family Law Arbitration Financial Scheme Arbitration Rules 2021

(7th EDITION, EFFECTIVE 11 JANUARY 2021)

ARTICLE 1 – INTRODUCTORY

1.1 The Family Law Arbitration Financial Scheme ('the Financial Scheme') is a scheme under which financial or property disputes with a family background may be resolved by arbitration.

1.2 The Financial Scheme is administered and run by the Institute of Family Law Arbitrators Limited ('IFLA'), a company limited by guarantee whose members are the Chartered Institute of Arbitrators ('CIArb'), Resolution and the Family Law Bar Association ('FLBA').

1.3 Disputes referred to the Financial Scheme will be arbitrated in accordance with:

(a) the provisions of the Arbitration Act 1996 ('the Act'), both mandatory and non-mandatory;

(b) these Rules, to the extent that they exclude, replace or modify the non-mandatory provisions of the Act; and

(c) the agreement of the parties, to the extent that that excludes, replaces or modifies the non-mandatory provisions of the Act or these Rules; except that the parties may not agree to exclude, replace or modify Art.3 (Applicable Law).

1.4 The parties may not amend or modify these Rules or any procedure under them after the commencement of the arbitration unless the arbitrator agrees to such amendment or modification; and may not amend or modify Art.3 (Applicable Law) in any event.

1.5 Expressions used in these Rules which are also used in the Act have the same meaning as they do in the Act and any reference to a section number means the section of the Act so numbered, unless otherwise indicated.

ARTICLE 2 – SCOPE OF THE FINANCIAL SCHEME

2.1 The Financial Scheme covers financial and property disputes arising from:

(a) marriage and its breakdown (including financial provision on divorce, judicial separation or nullity);

(b) civil partnership and its breakdown;

(c) co-habitation and the ending of co-habitation;

(d) parenting or those sharing parental responsibility;

(e) provision for dependants from the estate of the deceased.

2.2 The Financial Scheme covers (but is not limited to) claims which would come within the following statutes:

(a) the Married Women's Property Act 1882, s.17;

(b) the Matrimonial Causes Act 1973, Part II;

(c) the Inheritance (Provision for Family and Dependants) Act 1975;

(d) the Matrimonial and Family Proceedings Act 1984, s.12 (financial relief after overseas divorce);

(e) the Children Act 1989, Sched. 1;

(f) the Trusts of Land and Appointment of Trustees Act 1996;

(g) the Civil Partnership Act 2004 Sched.5, or Sched.7, Part 1, para.2 (financial relief after overseas dissolution).

2.3 The Financial Scheme does not apply to disputes directly concerning:

(a) the liberty of individuals;

(b) the status either of individuals or of their relationship;

(c) the care or parenting of children;

(d) bankruptcy or insolvency;

(e) any person or organisation which is not a party to the arbitration.

ARTICLE 3 – APPLICABLE LAW

3. The arbitrator will decide the substance of the dispute only in accordance with the law of England and Wales. The arbitrator may have regard to, and admit evidence of, the law of another country insofar as, and in the same way as, a Judge exercising the jurisdiction of the High Court would do so.

ARTICLE 4 – STARTING THE ARBITRATION

4.1 The parties may refer a dispute to arbitration under the Financial Scheme by making an agreement to arbitrate in Form ARB1FS, signed by both parties or their legal representatives, and submitting it to IFLA.

4.2 IFLA has set up the IFLA Financial Panel of arbitrators ('the Financial Panel') comprising Members of the Chartered Institute of Arbitrators who are experienced family law professionals with particular expertise in financial matters and who have received specific training in the determination of family disputes relating to financial matters by means of arbitration.

4.3.1 The parties may agree to nominate a particular arbitrator from the Financial Panel; and may, if they are agreed, approach a particular arbitrator directly. Any arbitrator so nominated or directly approached must refer the nomination or approach to IFLA before accepting appointment in order to facilitate the completion of Form ARB1FS before the arbitration commences. IFLA will offer the appointment to the agreed arbitrator. If the appointment is not accepted by their first choice of arbitrator the parties may, if they agree, make a second or subsequent choice. Otherwise, it will be offered to another member of the Financial Panel chosen by IFLA in accordance with paragraph 4.3.3 below.

4.3.2 Alternatively, the parties may agree on a shortlist of arbitrators from the Financial Panel any one of whom would be acceptable to them, and may ask IFLA to select one of the arbitrators on the shortlist without reference to any criteria. In this case, IFLA will offer the appointment to one of the shortlisted arbitrators chosen at random. If the appointment is not accepted by the first choice of arbitrator, IFLA will offer the appointment to a second or subsequent shortlisted arbitrator, similarly chosen at random. If none of the shortlisted arbitrators accepts the appointment, IFLA will inform the parties and invite them to submit further agreed names.

4.3.3 In all other cases (including if so requested by the parties) IFLA will offer the appointment to a sole arbitrator from the Financial Panel whom it considers appropriate having regard to the nature of the dispute; any preferences expressed by the parties as to the qualifications, areas of experience, expertise or other attributes of the arbitrator; any preference expressed by the parties as to the geographical location of the arbitration; and any other relevant circumstances.

4.4 If, after considering Form ARB1FS and any representations from the parties, either IFLA or the arbitrator considers that the dispute is not suitable for arbitration under the Financial Scheme, then the parties will be so advised and their reference of the matter to the Financial Scheme will be treated as withdrawn.

4.5 The arbitration will be regarded as commenced when the arbitrator communicates to the parties his or her acceptance of the appointment.

4.6 Except as provided in Art.4.7, a party to an arbitration under the Financial Scheme may be represented in the proceedings by a lawyer or other person chosen by that party; or, if he is acting in person, may receive the advice and assistance of a McKenzie Friend.

4.7 If at any time the arbitrator forms the view that the participation of a non-lawyer representative or the assistance given by a McKenzie Friend unreasonably impedes or is likely to impede the conduct of the arbitral proceedings or the administration of justice, he may direct that the relevant party should not continue to be so represented or assisted, as the case may be, and will state his reasons in writing.

ARTICLE 5 – ARBITRATOR'S APPOINTMENT

5.1 Before accepting the appointment or as soon as the relevant facts are known, the arbitrator will disclose to the parties any actual or potential conflict of interest or any matter that might give rise to justifiable doubts as to his or her impartiality.

5.2 In the event of such disclosure, the parties, or either of them (as appropriate), may waive any objection to the arbitrator continuing to act, in which case the arbitrator may commence or continue with the arbitration. If an objection is maintained, the arbitrator will decide whether to continue to act, subject to any agreement by the parties to revoke his or her authority or intervention by the court.

5.3 An arbitrator may not accept appointment in any dispute in relation to which he or she has acted in a different capacity; and after accepting appointment, the arbitrator may not concurrently or subsequently act in relation to the same dispute in a different capacity.

5.4 If the arbitrator ceases to hold office through revocation of his or her authority, removal by the court, resignation or death, or is otherwise unable, or refuses, to act, and either party or the existing arbitrator so requests, IFLA may appoint a replacement arbitrator from the Financial Panel.

5.5 The replacement arbitrator may determine whether and if so to what extent the previous proceedings should stand.

ARTICLE 6 – COMMUNICATIONS BETWEEN PARTIES, THE ARBITRATOR AND IFLA

6.1 Any communication between the arbitrator and either party will be copied to the other party.

6.2 Unless agreed by the parties, the arbitrator will designate one party as the lead party. For the purposes of the Act, the lead party will equate to a claimant, but will be formally referred to in the arbitration as the 'Applicant'. The other party will equate to a respondent, and will be formally referred to in the arbitration as the 'Respondent'.

6.3 The arbitrator will not discuss any aspect of the dispute or of the arbitration with either party or their legal representatives in the absence of the other party or their legal representatives, unless such communication is solely for the purpose of making administrative arrangements.

6.4 Neither IFLA, the CIArb, Resolution nor the FLBA will be required to enter into any correspondence concerning the arbitration or its outcome.

ARTICLE 7 – POWERS OF THE ARBITRATOR

7.1 The arbitrator will have all the powers given to an arbitrator by the Act including those contained in section 35 (consolidation of proceedings and concurrent hearings); and section 39 (provisional orders), but limited as provided by Art.7.2.

7.2 In relation to substantive relief of an interim or final character, the arbitrator will have the power to make orders or awards to the same extent and in the same or similar form as would a Judge exercising the jurisdiction of the

High Court. (For the avoidance of doubt, the arbitrator's power does not extend to interim injunctions; committal; or jurisdiction over non-parties without their agreement.)

7.3 The arbitrator will have the power to award interest in accordance with section 49 (interest) whether or not it is specifically claimed.

7.4 If the arbitrator considers that the dispute is not suitable for arbitration under the Financial Scheme the arbitrator will have the power to terminate the proceedings.

7.5 The parties may agree that a third party or parties be joined to the arbitration provided that the third party or parties agree in writing: (a) to be so joined; (b) to abide by the Financial Scheme Rules; and (c) to be bound by any award made by the arbitrator. In such a case, the arbitrator may join the third party or parties to the arbitration on such terms as may be agreed by all relevant parties, or as may be directed by the arbitrator.

ARTICLE 8 – POWERS OF THE ARBITRATOR CONCERNING PROCEDURE

8.1 The arbitrator will decide all procedural and evidential matters (including, but not limited to, those referred to in section 34(2)), subject to the right of the parties to agree any matter (if necessary, with the concurrence of the arbitrator (see Art.1.4)).

8.2 In accordance with section 37 (power to appoint experts), the arbitrator may appoint experts to report on specific issues or prepare valuations.

8.3 The arbitrator may limit the number of expert witnesses to be called by any party or may direct that no expert be called on any issue or issues or that expert evidence may be called only with the permission of the arbitrator.

8.4 Further, and/or in particular, the arbitrator will have the power to:

(a) direct a party to produce information, documents or other materials in a specified manner and/or within a specified time;

(b) give directions in relation to any property, documents or materials which are the subject of the proceedings or as to which any question arises in the proceedings, and which are owned by or are in the possession or control of a party to the proceedings for their inspection, photographing, valuation, preservation, custody or detention by the tribunal, an expert or a party.

8.5 If, without showing sufficient cause, a party fails to comply with its obligations under section 40 (general duty of parties) or with these Rules, or is in default as set out in section 41(4) (failure to attend a hearing or make submissions), then, after giving that party due notice, the arbitrator may continue the proceedings in the absence of that party or without any written evidence or submissions on their behalf and may make an award on the basis of the evidence before him or her.

8.6 The parties agree that if one of them fails to comply with a peremptory order made by the arbitrator and another party wishes to apply to the court for an order requiring compliance under s.42 (enforcement of peremptory orders of tribunal), the powers of the court under that section are available.

ARTICLE 9 – FORM OF PROCEDURE

9.1 The parties are free to agree as to the form of procedure (if necessary, with the concurrence of the arbitrator (see Art.1.4)) and, in particular, to adopt a documents-only procedure or some other simplified or expedited procedure.

9.2 If there is no such agreement, the arbitrator will have the widest possible discretion to adopt procedures suitable to the circumstances of the particular case in accordance with section 33 (general duty of the tribunal).

ARTICLE 10 – GENERAL PROCEDURE

10.1 Generally, on commencement of the arbitration, the arbitrator will invite the parties to make submissions setting out briefly their respective views as to the nature of the dispute, the issues, what form of procedure should be adopted, the timetable and any other relevant matters.

10.2 If appropriate, the arbitrator may convene a preliminary meeting, telephone conference or other suitable forum for exchange of views.

10.3 Within a reasonable time of ascertaining the parties' views, the arbitrator will give directions and set a timetable for the procedural steps in the arbitration, including (but not limited to) the following:

(a) written statements of case;

(b) disclosure and production of documents as between the parties;

(c) the exchange of witness statements;

(d) the number and type of expert witnesses, exchange of their reports and meetings between them;

(e) arrangements for any meeting or hearing and the procedures to be adopted at these events;

(f) time limits to be imposed on oral submissions or the examination of witnesses, or any other procedure for controlling the length of hearings.

10.4 The arbitrator may at any time direct any of the following to be delivered in writing:

(a) submissions on behalf of any party;

(b) questions to be put to any witness;

(c) answers by any witness to specific questions.

ARTICLE 11 – APPLICATIONS FOR DIRECTIONS AS TO PROCEDURAL OR EVIDENTIAL MATTERS

11.1 The arbitrator may direct a time limit for making or responding to applications for directions as to procedural or evidential matters.

11.2 Any application by a party for directions as to procedural or evidential matters will be accompanied by such evidence and/or submissions as the applicant may consider appropriate or as the arbitrator may direct.

11.3 A party responding to such an application will, if feasible, have a reasonable opportunity to consider and agree the order or directions proposed.

11.4 Any agreement will be communicated to the arbitrator promptly and will be subject to the arbitrator's concurrence, if necessary (see Art.1.4).

11.5 Unless the arbitrator convenes a meeting, telephone conference or other forum for exchange of views, any response to the application will be followed by an opportunity for the party applying to comment on that response; and the arbitrator will give directions within a reasonable time after receiving the applicant's comments.

ARTICLE 12 – ALTERNATIVE PROCEDURE

12.1 In any case where it is appropriate, the parties may agree or the arbitrator may decide to adopt the procedure set out in this Article.

12.2 The parties may at any stage agree (with the concurrence of the arbitrator) or the arbitrator may direct any variation or addition to the following steps and/or timetable. In particular, the arbitrator may at any stage allow time for the parties to consider their positions and pursue negotiations with a view to arriving at an amicable settlement (see, also, Arts. 17.1 and 17.2).

12.3 Within 56 days of the arbitrator communicating to the parties his or her acceptance of the appointment, each party will complete and send to the arbitrator and to the other party a sworn statement as to their financial situation (in the form of the 'Form E' or 'Form E1' Financial Statement in accordance with the Family Procedure Rules 2010, as appropriate) together with such further evidence or information as the arbitrator may direct.

12.4 Within 28 days of receipt of the other party's financial statement, each party may send to the arbitrator and to the other party a questionnaire raising questions and/or requesting information and/or documents.

12.5 Within 14 days of receipt of a questionnaire, a party may send to the arbitrator and to the other party reasoned objections to answering any of the questions or meeting any of the requests, together with a submission as to whether a preliminary meeting is required.

12.6 Within 14 days of receipt of objections or, if there is a preliminary meeting, within a reasonable time after that meeting, the arbitrator will direct in respect of each party:

(a) which questions are to be answered and which requests are to be met, together with the time within which these things are to be done;

(b) which property is to be valued, who is to undertake the valuation, how they are to be appointed and the time within which the valuation is to be carried out; and

(c) any other steps for providing information, dealing with enquiries or clarifying issues as may be appropriate.

12.7 Within a reasonable time of receipt from both parties of replies to questionnaires, valuations and any other information as may have been required, the arbitrator may convene a further meeting to review progress, address outstanding issues and consider what further directions are necessary.

12.8 The arbitrator will give detailed directions for all further procedural steps in the arbitration including (but not limited to) the following:

(a) the drawing up of lists of issues and schedules of assets;

(b) written submissions;

(c) arrangements for any meeting or hearing and the procedures to be adopted at these events;

(d) time limits to be imposed on oral submissions or the examination of witnesses, or any other procedure for controlling the length of hearings.

ARTICLE 13 – AWARDS

13.1 The arbitrator will deliver an award within a reasonable time after the conclusion of the proceedings or the relevant part of the proceedings.

13.2 Any award will be in writing, will state the seat of the arbitration, will be dated and signed by the arbitrator, and (unless the parties agree otherwise or the award is by consent) will contain sufficient reasons to show why the arbitrator has reached the decisions it contains.

13.3 Once an award has been made, it will be final and binding on the parties, subject to any of the following:

(a) any challenge to the award by any available arbitral process of appeal or review or in accordance with the provisions of Part 1 of the Act;

(b) insofar as the subject matter of the award requires it to be embodied in a court order (see Art.13.4), any changes which the court making that order may require, or the refusal by the court, where it has jurisdiction to do so, to embody the award or any part of it in a court order;

(c) insofar as the award provides for continuing payments to be made by one party to another, or to a child or children, a subsequent award or court order reviewing and varying or revoking the provision for continuing payments, and which supersedes an existing award;

(d) insofar as the award provides for continuing payments to be made by one party to or for the benefit of a child or children, a subsequent assessment by the Child Maintenance Service (or its successor) in relation to the same child or children.

13.4 If and so far as the subject matter of the award makes it necessary, the parties will apply to an appropriate court for an order in the same or similar terms as the award or the relevant part of the award and will take all reasonably necessary steps to see that such an order is made. In this context, 'an appropriate court' means a court which has jurisdiction to make a substantive order in the same or similar terms as the award, whether on primary application or on transfer from another division of the court. The court may have a discretion as to whether, and in what terms, to make an order.

13.5 The arbitrator may refuse to deliver an award to the parties except upon full payment of his or her fees or expenses. Subject to this entitlement, the arbitrator will send a copy of the award to each party or its legal representatives.

ARTICLE 14 – COSTS

14.1 In this Article any reference to costs is a reference to the costs of the arbitration as defined in section 59 (costs of the arbitration) including the fees and expenses of IFLA, unless otherwise indicated.

14.2 The arbitrator may require the parties to pay his or her fees and expenses accrued during the course of the arbitration at such interim stages as may be agreed with the parties, and in the absence of agreement, at reasonable intervals.

14.3 The arbitrator may order either party to provide security for the arbitrator's fees and expenses and the fees and expenses of IFLA.

14.4 Unless otherwise agreed by the parties, the arbitrator will make an award allocating costs as between the parties in accordance with the following general principle:

(a) the parties will bear the arbitrator's fees and expenses and the fees and expenses of IFLA in equal shares;

(b) there will be no order or award requiring one party to pay the legal or other costs of another party.

This principle is subject to the arbitrator's overriding discretion set out in Art.14.5.

14.5 Where it is appropriate to do so because of the conduct of a party in relation to the arbitration (whether before or during it), the arbitrator may at any stage order that party:

(a) to bear a larger than equal share, and up to the full amount, of the arbitrator's fees and expenses and the fees and expenses of IFLA;

(b) to pay the legal or other costs of another party;

and may make an award accordingly.

14.6 In deciding whether, and if so, how to exercise the discretion set out in Art.14.5, the arbitrator will have regard to the following:

(a) any failure by a party to comply with these Rules or any order or directions which the arbitrator considers relevant;

(b) any open offer to settle made by a party;

(c) whether it was reasonable for a party to raise, pursue or contest a particular allegation or issue;

(d) the manner in which a party has pursued or responded to a claim or a particular allegation or issue;

(e) any other aspect of a party's conduct in relation to the arbitration which the arbitrator considers relevant; and

(f) the financial effect on the parties of any costs order or award.

14.7 Unless the parties agree otherwise, no offer to settle which is not an open offer to settle shall be admissible at any stage of the arbitration.

14.8 These rules as to costs will not apply to applications made to the court where costs fall to be determined by the court.

ARTICLE 15 – CONCLUSION OF THE ARBITRATION

15.1 The agreement to arbitrate will be discharged (and any current arbitration will terminate) if:

(a) a party to the arbitration agreement dies; or

(b) a party to the arbitration agreement lacks, or loses, capacity (within the meaning of the Mental Capacity Act 2005); except that:

(i) if the party is represented by an attorney who has the power so to act, the attorney may, in his or her discretion, continue with the arbitration or terminate it;

(ii) if a Deputy is appointed by the Court of Protection in relation to that party and has the power so to act, the Deputy may, in his or her discretion, continue with the arbitration or terminate it.

15.2 The arbitration will be terminated:

(a) If the arbitrator considers that the dispute is not suitable for arbitration under the Financial Scheme and terminates the proceedings;

(b) If and insofar as a court entertains concurrent legal proceedings and declines to stay them in favour of arbitration;

(c) If the parties settle the dispute and, in accordance with section 51 (settlement), the arbitrator terminates the proceedings;

(d) If the parties agree in writing to discontinue the arbitration and notify the arbitrator accordingly;

(e) On the arbitrator making a final award dealing with all the issues, subject to any entitlement of the parties to challenge the award by any available arbitral process of appeal or review or in accordance with the provisions of Part 1 of the Act.

ARTICLE 16 – CONFIDENTIALITY

16.1 The general principle is that the arbitration and its outcome are confidential, except insofar as disclosure may be necessary to challenge, implement, enforce or vary an award (see Art.13.3(c)), in relation to applications to the court or as may be compelled by law.

16.2 All documents, statements, information and other materials disclosed by a party will be held by any other party and their legal representatives in confidence and used solely for the purpose of the arbitration, unless otherwise agreed by the disclosing party or compelled by law.

16.3 Any transcript of the proceedings will be provided to all parties and to the arbitrator. It will similarly be confidential and used solely for the purpose of the arbitration, implementation or enforcement of any award or applications to the court, unless otherwise agreed by the parties or compelled by law.

16.4 The arbitrator will not be called as a witness by any party either to testify or to produce any documents or materials received or generated during the course of the proceedings in relation to any aspect of the arbitration, unless with the agreement of the arbitrator or compelled by law.

ARTICLE 17 – GENERAL

17.1 At relevant stages of the arbitration, the arbitrator may encourage the parties to consider using an alternative dispute resolution procedure other than arbitration, such as mediation, negotiation or early neutral evaluation, in relation to the dispute or a particular aspect of the dispute.

17.2 If the parties agree to use an alternative dispute resolution procedure such as mediation, negotiation or early neutral evaluation, then the arbitrator will facilitate its use and may, if appropriate, stay the arbitration or a particular aspect of the arbitration for an appropriate period of time for that purpose.

17.3.1 In the event that the dispute is settled (following a mediation or otherwise), the parties will inform the arbitrator promptly and section 51 (settlement) will apply. Fees and expenses accrued due to the arbitrator by that stage will remain payable.

17.3.2 In the event that an arbitrator under the Financial Scheme is at the same time conducting a parallel financial arbitration under the IFLA Children Scheme which involves one or more of the same parties, then in the event of any conflict between the two Scheme Rules, the arbitrator shall have sole discretion to decide which will prevail. For the avoidance of doubt, subject to the discretion of the arbitrator, all evidence adduced and all reports and documents disclosed in each arbitration shall stand as evidence in the other.

17.4 The parties will inform the arbitrator promptly of any proposed application to the court and will provide him or her with copies of all documentation intended to be used in any such application.

17.5 IFLA, the CIArb, Resolution, the FLBA, their employees and agents will not be liable:

(a) for anything done or omitted in the actual or purported appointment or nomination of an arbitrator, unless the act or omission is shown to have been in bad faith;

(b) by reason of having appointed or nominated an arbitrator, for anything done or omitted by the arbitrator (or his employees or agents) in the discharge or purported discharge of his functions as an arbitrator;

(c) for any consequences if, for whatever reason, the arbitral process does not result in an award or, where necessary, a court order embodying an award by which the matters to be determined are resolved.

Family Law Arbitration Children Scheme Arbitration Rules 2021

(5th EDITION, EFFECTIVE 11 JANUARY 2021)

> **Safety and welfare of children**
>
> **The safety and welfare of children is of the utmost importance to the Family Law Arbitration Children Scheme. Measures providing for safeguarding appear at Article 17 (below) and in the Form ARB1CS and Safeguarding Questionnaire which has to be completed by the parties. These steps are intended to ensure that matters accepted for arbitration are suitable for that process, and that the child(ren) concerned will be safe from harm.**

CONTENTS:

ARTICLE 1 – INTRODUCTORY

1.1 The Family Law Arbitration Children Scheme ('the Children Scheme') is a scheme under which disputes concerning the exercise of parental responsibility and other private law issues about the welfare of children may be resolved by the determination of an arbitrator.

1.2 The Children Scheme is administered and run by the Institute of Family Law Arbitrators Limited ('IFLA'), a company limited by guarantee whose members are the Chartered Institute of Arbitrators ('CIArb'), Resolution and the Family Law Bar Association ('FLBA').

1.3 Disputes referred to the Children Scheme will be determined by arbitration in accordance with:

(a) the provisions of the Arbitration Act 1996 ('the Act') both mandatory and non-mandatory;

(b) these Rules, to the extent that they exclude, replace or modify the non-mandatory provisions of the Act; and

(c) the agreement of the parties, to the extent that that excludes, replaces or modifies the non-mandatory provisions of the Act or these Rules; except that the parties may not agree to exclude, replace or modify Art.3 (Applicable Law).

1.4 The parties may not amend or modify these Rules or any procedure under them after the commencement of the arbitration unless the arbitrator agrees to such amendment or modification; and may in any event neither amend nor modify Art.3 (Applicable Law) nor agree to exclude the right of any party to appeal to the court on a question of law (section 69).

1.5 Expressions used in these Rules which are also used in the Act have the same meaning as they do in the Act, except that in these Rules 'determine' and 'determination' have an equivalent meaning to 'award' in the Act; and any reference to a section number means the section of the Act so numbered, unless otherwise indicated.

ARTICLE 2 – SCOPE OF THE CHILDREN SCHEME

2.1 Save as provided by Art.2.2 below, the Children Scheme covers issues between parents (or other persons holding parental responsibility or with a sufficient interest in the child's welfare) which relate to the exercise of parental responsibility or the present or future welfare of the child concerned (including the child's upbringing, present or future living arrangements, contact and education) and extends but is not limited to matters which could be the subject of an application to the Family Court under section 8 of the Children Act 1989.

2.2 The following disputes and issues are not within the scope of the Children Scheme:-

(a) any application under the inherent jurisdiction for the return of a child to England and Wales ('this jurisdiction') from a country which is not a signatory to the Hague Convention on the Civil Aspects of International Child Abduction of 25 October 1980 ('the 1980 Hague Convention');

(b) any application for a child's summary return to this or another jurisdiction under the 1980 Hague Convention;

(c) any application for permanent or temporary removal of a child from this jurisdiction except where the proposed relocation is to a jurisdiction or country which has ratified and acceded to the 1980 Hague Convention or the Hague Convention of 19 October 1996 on Jurisdiction, Applicable Law, Recognition, Enforcement and Co-Operation in Respect of Parental Responsibility and Measures for the Protection of Children ('the 1996 Hague Convention') and, for so long as the United Kingdom remains bound by the provisions of the Brussels HA Regulation, to the jurisdiction of another member of the EU to which the Regulation also applies;

(d) any application for the court 'to examine the question of custody of the child' under Art.11(7) of Council Regulation (EC) No 2201/2003 after an order of a foreign court on non-return to this jurisdiction made pursuant to Art.13 of the 1980 Hague Convention;

(e) any application for cross-border access within the scope of Art.41 of the said Council Regulation which, if a judgment, would require a court to issue an Annex III Certificate;

(f) any dispute relating to the authorisation of life-changing or life-threatening medical treatment or the progress of such treatment;

(g) any case where a party lacks capacity under the Mental Capacity Act 2005;

(h) any case where any person with parental responsibility for the child or who seeks to be a party to an arbitration under the Children Scheme is a minor; and any case where any person with parental responsibility for the child is not a party to the arbitration;

(i) any case where the child concerned has party status in existing proceedings relating to the same or similar issues, or should in the opinion of the arbitrator be separately represented in the arbitration.

ARTICLE 3 – APPLICABLE LAW

3.1 The arbitrator will determine the substance of the dispute only in accordance with the law of England and Wales. The arbitrator may have regard to, and admit evidence of, the law of another country insofar as, and in the same way as, a Judge exercising the jurisdiction of the High Court would do so.

3.2 When determining any question relating to the upbringing of a child, the welfare of the child shall be the arbitrator's paramount consideration and in considering welfare the arbitrator shall have regard in particular to the welfare checklist set out in section 1(3) of the Children Act 1989.

ARTICLE 4 – STARTING THE ARBITRATION

4.1.1 The parties may refer a dispute to arbitration under the Children Scheme by making an agreement to arbitrate in Form ARB1CS, signed by both parties or their legal representatives, and submitting it to IFLA.

4.1.2 Form ARB1CS and the Safeguarding Questionnaire shall be in the form of Annex 1 to these Rules.

4.2 IFLA has established the IFLA Children Panel of arbitrators ('the Children Panel') comprising Members of the Chartered Institute of Arbitrators who are experienced family law professionals with particular expertise in children matters and who have received specific training in the determination of family disputes relating to children by means of arbitration.

4.3.1 The parties may agree to nominate a particular arbitrator from the Children Panel; and may, if they are agreed, approach a particular arbitrator directly. Any arbitrator so nominated or directly approached must refer the nomination or approach to IFLA before accepting appointment in order to facilitate the completion of Form ARB1CS and the Safeguarding Questionnaires before the arbitration commences. IFLA will offer the appointment to the agreed arbitrator. If the appointment is not accepted by their first choice of arbitrator the parties may, if they agree, make a second or subsequent choice. Otherwise, it will be offered to another member of the Children Panel chosen by IFLA in accordance with paragraph 4.3.3 below.

4.3.2 Alternatively, the parties may agree on a shortlist of arbitrators from the Children Panel any one of whom would be acceptable to them, and may ask IFLA to select one of the arbitrators on the shortlist without reference to any criteria. In this case, IFLA will offer the appointment to one of the shortlisted arbitrators chosen at random. If the appointment is not accepted by the first choice of arbitrator, IFLA will offer the appointment to a second or subsequent shortlisted arbitrator, similarly chosen at random. If none of the shortlisted arbitrators accepts the appointment, IFLA will inform the parties and invite them to submit further agreed names.

4.3.3 In all other cases (including if so requested by the parties) IFLA will offer the appointment to a sole arbitrator from the Children Panel whom it considers appropriate having regard to the nature of the dispute; any preferences expressed by the parties as to the qualifications, areas of experience, expertise or other attributes of the arbitrator; any preference expressed by the parties as to the geographical location of the arbitration; and any other relevant circumstances.

4.4 If, after considering Form ARB1CS, the Safeguarding Questionnaires and any representations from the parties, either IFLA or the arbitrator considers that the dispute is not suitable for arbitration under the Children Scheme, the parties will be so advised and their reference of the matter to the Children Scheme will be treated as withdrawn.

4.5 The arbitration will be regarded as commenced when the arbitrator communicates to the parties his or her acceptance of the appointment. The arbitrator may not accept the appointment or start the arbitration until he or she has received and considered all the relevant safeguarding information and documentation which the parties are required to provide (including, in all cases, Safeguarding Questionnaires together with Basic Disclosures and/or CAFCASS reports and/or Schedule 2 letters, as applicable: see Art.17.1.1).

4.6 Except as provided in Art.4.7, a party to an arbitration under the Children Scheme may be represented in the proceedings by a lawyer or other person chosen by that party; or, if a party is acting in person, may receive the advice and assistance of a McKenzie Friend.

4.7 If at any time the arbitrator forms the view that the participation of a non-lawyer representative or the assistance given by a McKenzie Friend unreasonably impedes or is likely to impede the conduct of the arbitral proceedings or the administration of justice, the arbitrator may direct that the relevant party should not continue to be so represented or assisted, as the case may be, and will state the reasons in writing.

ARTICLE 5 – ARBITRATOR'S APPOINTMENT

5.1 Before accepting the appointment or as soon as the relevant facts are known, the arbitrator will disclose to the parties any actual or potential conflict of interest or any matter that might give rise to justifiable doubts as to his or her impartiality.

5.2 In the event of such disclosure, the parties or either of them (as appropriate) may waive any objection to the arbitrator continuing to act, in which case the arbitrator may commence or continue with the arbitration. If an objection is maintained, the arbitrator will decide whether to continue to act, subject to any agreement by the parties to revoke his or her authority or intervention by the court.

5.3 An arbitrator may not accept appointment in any dispute in relation to which he or she has acted in a different capacity; and after accepting appointment, the arbitrator may not concurrently or subsequently act in relation to the same dispute in a different capacity.

5.4 If the arbitrator ceases to hold office through revocation of his or her authority, removal by the court, resignation or death, or is otherwise unable, or refuses, to act, and either party or the existing arbitrator so requests, IFLA may appoint a replacement arbitrator from the Children Panel.

5.5 The replacement arbitrator may determine whether and if so to what extent previous proceedings shall stand.

ARTICLE 6 – COMMUNICATIONS BETWEEN THE PARTIES, THE ARBITRATOR AND IFLA

6.1 Any communication between the arbitrator and either party will be copied to the other party.

6.2 Unless agreed by the parties, the arbitrator will designate one party as the lead party. For the purposes of the Act, the lead party will equate to a claimant, but will be formally referred to in the arbitration as the 'Applicant'. The other party will equate to a respondent, and will be formally referred to in the arbitration as the 'Respondent'.

6.3 The arbitrator will not discuss any aspect of the dispute or of the arbitration with either party or their legal representatives in the absence of the other party or then-legal representatives, unless such communication is solely for the purpose of making administrative arrangements.

6.4 Neither IFLA, the CIArb, Resolution nor the FLBA will be required to enter into any correspondence concerning the arbitration or its outcome.

ARTICLE 7 – POWERS OF THE ARBITRATOR

7.1 The arbitrator will have all the powers given to an arbitrator by the Act including those contained in section 35 (consolidation of proceedings and concurrent hearings); and section 39 (provisional orders), but limited as provided by Art.7.2.

7.2 In relation to substantive relief of an interim or final character, the arbitrator will have the power to make orders or determinations to the same extent and in the same or similar form as would a Judge exercising the jurisdiction of the High Court. (For the avoidance of doubt, the arbitrator's power does not extend to interim injunctions; committal; or jurisdiction over non-parties without their agreement).

7.3 If the arbitrator at any stage prior to determination of the issues considers that the dispute is no longer suitable for arbitration under the Children Scheme on welfare or other grounds the arbitrator will have the power to terminate the proceedings (see Arts.15.2(b) and 17.2).

7.4 The parties may agree that a third party or parties be joined to the arbitration provided that the third party or parties agree in writing: (a) to be so joined; (b) to abide by the Children Scheme Rules; and (c) to be bound by any determination made by the arbitrator. In such a case, the arbitrator may join the third party or parties to the arbitration on such terms as may be agreed by all relevant parties, or as may be directed by the arbitrator.

ARTICLE 8 – POWERS OF THE ARBITRATOR CONCERNING PROCEDURE

8.1 The arbitrator will decide all procedural and evidential matters (including, but not limited to, those referred to in section 34(2)), subject to the right of the parties to agree any matter (if necessary, with the concurrence of the arbitrator (see Art.1.4)).

8.2.1 In accordance with section 37 (power to appoint experts), the arbitrator may appoint experts to report on specific issues.

8.2.2 The arbitrator may limit the number of expert witnesses to be called by any party or may direct that no expert is to be called on any issue or issues or that expert evidence may be called only with the permission of the arbitrator.

8.2.3 Where the parties propose the instruction as an expert of an independent social worker to ascertain the wishes and feelings of a child or otherwise to advise on welfare issues and to report, such instruction will be subject to the confirmation and approval of the arbitrator who will decide the identity of the independent social worker if the parties cannot agree.

8.2.4 The arbitrator may of his or her own motion appoint as an expert an independent social worker of appropriate expertise and standing to ascertain the wishes and feelings of a child or otherwise to advise on welfare issues and to report if the arbitrator considers that such evidence will assist in determining the issues. Such an appointment may be made irrespective of whether or not the parties agree.

8.3 The arbitrator may not meet with the child concerned at any stage of the proceedings including any meeting with the child to discuss or explain the determination or its implementation.

8.4 Further and/or in particular, the arbitrator will have the power to:

(a) direct a party to produce information, documents or other materials in a specified manner and/or within a specified time;

(b) give directions in relation to any documents or other materials as to which any question arises in the proceedings, and which are owned by or are in the possession or control of a party to the proceedings for their inspection, photographing, valuation, preservation, custody or detention by the tribunal, an expert or a party.

8.5 If, without showing sufficient cause, a party fails to comply with his or her obligations under section 40 (general duty of parties) or with these Rules, or is in default as set out in section 41(4) (failure to attend a hearing or make submissions), then, after giving that party due notice, the arbitrator may continue the proceedings in the absence of that party or without any written evidence or submissions on their behalf and may make a determination on the basis of the evidence before the arbitrator.

8.6 The parties agree that if one of them fails to comply with a peremptory order made by the arbitrator and another party wishes to apply to the court for an order requiring compliance under section 42 (enforcement of peremptory orders of tribunal), the powers of the court under that section are available.

ARTICLE 9 – FORM OF PROCEDURE

9.1 The parties are free to agree as to the form of procedure (if necessary, with the concurrence of the arbitrator (see Art.1.4)) and, in particular, to adopt a documents-only procedure or some other simplified or expedited procedure.

9.2 If there is no such agreement, the arbitrator will have the widest possible discretion to adopt procedures suitable to the circumstances of the particular case in accordance with section 33 (general duty of the tribunal).

ARTICLE 10 – GENERAL PROCEDURE

10.1 Generally, on commencement of the arbitration, the arbitrator will invite the parties to make submissions setting out briefly their respective views as to the nature of the dispute, the issues, the outcome they seek, what form of procedure should be adopted, the timetable and any other relevant matters.

10.2 If appropriate, the arbitrator may convene a preliminary meeting, telephone conference or other suitable forum for the exchange of a summary of each party's position on the matters set out in Art.10.1.

10.3 Within a reasonable time of ascertaining the parties' views but in any event not more than 14 days, the arbitrator will give such directions as appear appropriate and set a timetable for the procedural steps in the arbitration, including (but not limited to) the following:

(a) written statements of case;

(b) disclosure and production of documents as between the parties;

(c) the exchange of witness statements;

(d) the number and type of expert witnesses, exchange of their reports and meetings between them;

(e) arrangements for any meeting or hearing and the procedures to be adopted at these events;

(f) time limits to be imposed on oral submissions or the examination of witnesses, or any other procedure for controlling the length of hearings.

10.4 The arbitrator may at any time direct any of the following to be delivered in writing:

(a) submissions on behalf of any party;

(b) questions to be put to any witness;

(c) answers by any witness to specific questions.

ARTICLE 11 – APPLICATIONS FOR DIRECTIONS AS TO PROCEDURAL OR EVIDENTIAL MATTERS

11.1 The arbitrator may direct a time limit for making or responding to applications for directions as to procedural or evidential matters.

11.2 Any application by a party for directions as to procedural or evidential matters will be accompanied by such evidence and/or submissions as the applicant may consider appropriate or as the arbitrator may direct.

11.3 A party responding to such an application will have a reasonable opportunity to consider and agree the order or directions proposed.

11.4 Any agreement shall be communicated to the arbitrator promptly and will be subject to the arbitrator's concurrence if necessary (see Art. 1.4).

11.5 Unless the arbitrator convenes a meeting, telephone conference or other forum for exchange of views, any response to the application will be followed by an opportunity for the party applying to comment on that response; and the arbitrator shall give directions within a reasonable time after receiving the applicant's comments.

ARTICLE 12 – ALTERNATIVE PROCEDURE

12.1 In any case where it is appropriate, the parties may agree or the arbitrator may decide to adopt the procedure set out in this Article.

12.2 The parties may at any stage agree (with the concurrence of the arbitrator) or the arbitrator may direct any variation or addition to the following steps and/or timetable. In particular, the arbitrator may at any stage allow time for the parties to consider their positions and pursue negotiations with a view to arriving at an amicable settlement (see, also, Arts.18.1 and 18.2).

12.3 Within 14 days of the arbitrator communicating to the parties his or her acceptance of the appointment, each party will complete and send to the other party a sworn statement setting out their case, a brief outline of the facts upon which they rely and the outcome that they seek, together with such further evidence or information as the arbitrator may direct.

12.4 Within 14 days of receipt of the other party's statement, each party may send to the arbitrator and to the other party a questionnaire raising questions and/or requesting information and/or documents.

12.5 Within 7 days of receipt of a questionnaire, a party may send to the arbitrator and to the other party reasoned objections to answering any of the questions together with a submission as to whether a preliminary meeting is required.

12.6 In the absence of any such objection, the party in receipt of the questionnaire shall within 14 days provide succinct answers and/or documents.

12.7 In the event of such objection, the arbitrator will consider and decide in writing whether and to what extent the request should be answered together with a time limit or, alternatively, convene a meeting between the parties face-to-face or in such other form as he or she may decide to be the most appropriate having regard to convenience and costs and may require short written submissions in support of each party's position.

12.8. 14 days after exchange of statements or, in the event that questionnaires have been served and allowed, within a reasonable time of receipt from both parties of the responses thereto, the arbitrator may convene a further meeting to review progress, address outstanding issues and consider what further directions are necessary, if he or she deems it appropriate having regard to costs and the avoidance of delay.

12.9 If he or she considers it appropriate having regard to the scope of the dispute between the parties, the arbitrator will give detailed directions for all further procedural steps in the arbitration including (but not limited to) the following:

(a) the drawing up of a list of issues and/or a schedule of points of agreement or disagreement;

(b) written submissions;

(c) arrangements for any meeting or hearing and the procedures to be adopted at these events;

(d) time limits to be imposed on oral submissions or the examination of witnesses, or any other procedure for controlling the length of hearings.

ARTICLE 13 – THE ARBITRATOR'S DETERMINATION

13.1 The arbitrator will deliver a determination within a reasonable time after the conclusion of the proceedings or the relevant part of the proceedings.

13.2 Any determination will be in writing, will state the seat of the arbitration, will be dated and signed by the arbitrator, and will contain sufficient reasons to show why the arbitrator has reached the decisions it contains.

13.3 Once a determination has been made, it will be final and binding on the parties, subject only to any of the following:

(a) any challenge to the determination by any available arbitral process of appeal or review or in accordance with the provisions of Part 1 of the Act;

(b) insofar as the subject matter of the determination requires it to be embodied in a court order (see Art.13.4), any changes which the court making that order may require, or the refusal by the court, where it has jurisdiction to do so, to embody the determination or any part of it in a court order;

(c) any subsequent determination superseding the determination; or any changes to the determination or subsequent order superseding the determination which the Family Court considers ought to be made in the exercise of its statutory and/or inherent jurisdiction whether under the Children Act 1989 or otherwise.

13.4 If and so far as the subject matter of the determination makes it necessary, the parties will apply to an appropriate court for an order in the same or similar terms as the determination or the relevant part of the determination or to assist or enable its implementation and will take all reasonably necessary steps to see that such an order is made. In this context, 'an appropriate court' means the Family Court or such other court in England and Wales which has jurisdiction to make a substantive order in the same or similar terms as the determination. The court has a discretion as to whether, and in what terms, to make an order.

13.5 Where the subject matter of the dispute includes an issue as to the permanent relocation of any child to any of the jurisdictions identified in Art.2.2(c), the arbitrator, after liaising with the parties to the arbitration, shall identify in the determination the steps necessary to give full effect to the terms of the relocation in the proposed jurisdiction including, in particular, contact with the party remaining in the jurisdiction. Such steps may include (following the appointment of an independent social worker to assist in ascertaining the wishes and feelings of the child concerned) recording the wishes and feelings of the child concerned by an appropriate finding in the determination. If a determination is made concerning a proposed relocation to which the Brussels IIA Regulation applies, the arbitrator shall attach to the determination a certificate in the form of and complying with Annexe III to the Regulation.

13.6 Where the terms of the determination require any party to give an undertaking, the determination shall not take effect unless and until a suitable form of undertaking has been lodged with and accepted by an appropriate court.

13.7 The arbitrator may refuse to deliver the determination to the parties except upon full payment of his or her fees or expenses. Subject to this entitlement, the arbitrator will send a copy of the determination to each party or their legal representatives.

ARTICLE 14 – COSTS

14.1 In this Article any reference to costs is a reference to the costs of the arbitration as defined in section 59 (costs of the arbitration) including the fees and expenses of IFLA and the fees of any expert, unless otherwise stated.

14.2 The arbitrator may require the parties to pay his or her fees and expenses accrued during the course of the arbitration at such interim stages as may be agreed with the parties or, in the absence of agreement, at reasonable intervals.

14.3 The arbitrator may order either party to provide security for the arbitrator's fees and expenses and the fees and expenses of IFLA.

14.4 Unless otherwise agreed by the parties, the arbitrator will make a determination allocating costs as between the parties in accordance with the following general principles:

(a) the parties will bear the arbitrator's fees and expenses, the costs of any expert and the fees and expenses of IFLA in equal shares;

(b) there will be no order or determination requiring one party to pay the legal or other costs of another party.

These principles are subject to the arbitrator's overriding discretion set out in Arts.14.5 and 14.6.

14.5 Where it is appropriate to do so because of the conduct of a party in relation to the arbitration (whether before or during it), the arbitrator may at any stage order that party:

(a) to bear a larger than equal share, and up to the full amount, of the arbitrator's fees and expenses and the fees and expenses of IFLA;

(b) to pay the legal or other costs of another party;

and may make a determination accordingly.

14.6 In deciding whether, and if so, how to exercise the discretion set out in Art.14.5, the arbitrator will have regard to the following:

(a) the principles applied by the courts in relation to cases concerning child welfare;

(b) any failure by a party to comply with these Rules or any order or directions which the arbitrator considers relevant;

(c) any open offer to settle made by a party;

(d) whether it was reasonable for a party to raise, pursue or contest a particular allegation or issue;

(e) the manner in which a party has pursued or responded to a claim or a particular allegation or issue;

(f) any other aspect of a party's conduct in relation to the arbitration which the arbitrator considers relevant;

(g) the financial effect on the parties of any costs order or determination.

14.7 Unless the parties agree otherwise, no offer to settle which is not an open offer to settle shall be admissible at any stage of the arbitration.

14.8 These rules as to costs will not apply to applications made to the court where costs fall to be determined by the court.

ARTICLE 15 – CONCLUSION OF THE ARBITRATION

15.1 The agreement to arbitrate will be discharged (and any current arbitration will terminate) if:

(a) a party to the arbitration agreement dies; or

(b) a party to the arbitration agreement lacks, or loses, capacity (within the meaning of the Mental Capacity Act 2005).

15.2 The arbitration will be terminated:

(a) if the arbitrator considers that the dispute is not suitable for arbitration under the Children Scheme and terminates the proceedings;

(b) if the arbitrator at any time after the commencement of the arbitration considers that the dispute is no longer suitable for arbitration under the Children Scheme on welfare or other grounds (see Arts.7.3 and 17.2);

(c) if and insofar as a court entertains concurrent legal proceedings and declines to stay them in favour of arbitration;

(d) if the parties settle the dispute and, in accordance with section 51 (settlement), the arbitrator terminates the proceedings (however, the parties may not request the arbitrator to record the settlement in the form of an agreed determination);

(e) if the parties agree in writing to discontinue the arbitration and notify the arbitrator accordingly;

(f) on the arbitrator making a final determination dealing with all the issues, subject to any entitlement of the parties to challenge the determination by any available arbitral process of appeal or review or in accordance with the provisions of Part 1 of the Act.

ARTICLE 16 – CONFIDENTIALITY

16.1 The general principle is that the arbitration and its outcome are confidential, except insofar as disclosure may be necessary:

(a) to challenge, implement, enforce or vary a determination, or in relation to applications to the court;

(b) in the performance under Art.17 of an arbitrator's duty to convey information relating to the welfare of the child to any appropriate local authority or government agency, or in the exercise of an arbitrator's obligation to inform IFLA of a decision to decline an appointment or to terminate an arbitration; or

(c) as may otherwise be compelled by law.

16.2.1 All documents, statements, information and other materials disclosed by a party to the arbitration will be held by any other party and their legal representatives in confidence and used solely for the purpose of the arbitration unless otherwise agreed by the disclosing party; or if required to be disclosed to any appropriate protection/safeguarding authority; or as may otherwise be compelled by law; or as may be provided for by a direction given by the arbitrator under Art.16.2.2 below.

16.2.2 Upon application by a party to the arbitration, the arbitrator may direct that any document, statement, information or other material disclosed in the arbitration by any party may be disclosed to any person mentioned in Art.16.2.3 below (the person and purpose of disclosure being identified in the direction), upon that person agreeing in writing to confine their use of the disclosure to the terms of the direction.

16.2.3 The arbitrator may permit disclosure under Art.16.2.2 above to a professional acting in furtherance of the protection of children; or to any other person to whom disclosure is necessary, for one or more of the following purposes:

(a) to enable that person to provide expert or other evidence for the purposes of the arbitration or related legal proceedings;

(b) to enable a party to the arbitration, by confidential discussion, to obtain support, advice (whether legal or other professional) or assistance in the conduct of the arbitration or related legal proceedings;

(c) to enable a party to the arbitration to make and pursue a complaint against a person or body concerned in the arbitration;

(d) to make and pursue a complaint regarding the law, policy or procedure relating to arbitration as it concerns children.

16.3 Any transcript of the proceedings will be provided to all parties and to the arbitrator. It will similarly be confidential and used solely for the purpose of the arbitration, implementation or enforcement of any determination or applications to the court unless otherwise agreed by the parties, or if it forms part of any necessary disclosure to any appropriate protection/ safeguarding authority, or as may otherwise be compelled by law, or as directed by the arbitrator under Art.16.2.2 above.

16.4 The arbitrator will not be called as a witness by any party either to testify or to produce any documents or materials received or generated during the course of the proceedings in relation to any aspect of the arbitration unless with the agreement of the arbitrator, or in connection with any necessary disclosure to any appropriate protection/safeguarding authority, or as may otherwise be compelled by law.

ARTICLE 17 – DISCLOSURE OF ISSUES RELATING TO SAFEGUARDING AND WELFARE

17.1.1 Prior to the commencement of the arbitration (see Art.4.5) each party shall have a duty:

(a) to provide accurate information regarding safeguarding and protection from harm in their Form ARB1CS and Safeguarding Questionnaire;

(b) to obtain a Basic Disclosure from the Disclosure and Barring Service or from Disclosure Scotland, as appropriate, and promptly send it to the arbitrator and to every other party; or alternatively, to provide an up to date CAFCASS report or Schedule 2 letter prepared in current proceedings concerning the safeguarding and welfare of the child(ren), if applicable;

(c) to send to the arbitrator and to every other party any other relevant letter or report prepared by CAFCASS or any local authority children's services department or similar agency in relation to the welfare or safeguarding of any child who is the subject of the proposed arbitration.

17.1.2 Prior to the commencement of the arbitration and at every stage of the process each party shall have a continuing duty to disclose fully and completely to the arbitrator and to every other party any fact, matter or document in their knowledge, possession or control which is or appears to be relevant to the physical or emotional safety of any other party or to the safeguarding or welfare of any child the subject of the proceedings, or to a decision by the arbitrator under Art.17.2.1. Such disclosure shall include (but not be limited to) any criminal conviction, caution or involvement (concerning any child) with children's services in respect of any party or any person with whom the child is likely to have contact.

17.2.1 If at any time prior to or during the arbitration but prior to communication of the determination to the parties the arbitrator (whether as a result of information received or by reason of behaviour on the part of either party) forms the view that there are reasonable grounds to believe that there may be a risk to the physical or emotional safety of any party or to the safeguarding or welfare of any child, it is the arbitrator's duty to consider whether the arbitration may safely continue.

17.2.2 If in such a case the arbitrator concludes that the dispute is no longer suitable for arbitration under the Children Scheme then he or she must inform the parties in writing of that decision and of its grounds, and will terminate the proceedings (see Arts.7.3 and 15.2(b)). The arbitrator must also inform IFLA of a decision to decline an appointment or to terminate an arbitration on safeguarding or welfare grounds.

17.3.1 If at any time during the arbitration but prior to communication of the determination to the parties the arbitrator becomes aware of any matters which lead him or her reasonably to apprehend that a child or any party has suffered or is likely to suffer significant harm by reason of the actual or likely future behaviour of any party, it is the arbitrator's duty to communicate his or her concerns as soon as possible to the relevant local authority or appropriate government agency.

17.3.2 In such a case the arbitrator shall be entitled, if he or she considers it appropriate, to communicate such concerns to the relevant local authority or appropriate government agency without prior intimation to any party of an intention so to do.

ARTICLE 18 – GENERAL

18.1 At relevant stages of the arbitration, the arbitrator may encourage the parties to consider using an alternative dispute resolution procedure other than arbitration, such as mediation, negotiation or early neutral evaluation, in relation to the dispute or a particular aspect of the dispute.

18.2 If the parties agree to use an alternative dispute resolution procedure such as mediation, negotiation or early neutral evaluation, then the arbitrator will facilitate its use and may, if appropriate, stay the arbitration or a particular aspect of the arbitration for an appropriate period of time for that purpose.

18.3 In the event that the dispute is settled (following a mediation or otherwise), the parties will inform the arbitrator promptly and section 51 (settlement) will apply (however, the parties may not request the arbitrator to record the settlement in the form of an agreed determination). Fees and expenses accrued due to the arbitrator by that stage will remain payable.

18.4 In the event that an arbitrator under the Children Scheme is at the same time conducting a parallel financial arbitration under the IFLA Financial Scheme which involves one or more of the same parties, then in the event of any conflict between the two Scheme Rules, the arbitrator shall have sole discretion to decide which will prevail. For the avoidance of doubt, subject to the discretion of the arbitrator, all evidence adduced and all reports and documents disclosed in each arbitration shall stand as evidence in the other.

18.5 The parties will inform the arbitrator promptly of any proposed application to the court and will provide him or her with copies of all documentation intended to be used in any such application.

18.6 IFLA, the CIArb, Resolution and the FLBA, their employees and agents will not be liable:

(a) for anything done or omitted in the actual or purported appointment or nomination of an arbitrator, unless the act or omission is shown to have been in bad faith;

(b) by reason of having appointed or nominated an arbitrator, for anything done or omitted by the arbitrator (or his employees or agents) in the discharge or purported discharge of his functions as an arbitrator;

(c) for any consequences if, for whatever reason, the arbitral process does not result in a determination or, where necessary, a court order embodying a determination by which the matters to be determined are resolved.

Arbitration in the Family Court –Practice Guidance issued on 23 November 2015

ARBITRATION IN THE FAMILY COURT

PRACTICE GUIDANCE

issued on 23 November 2015 by

SIR JAMES MUNBY, PRESIDENT OF THE FAMILY DIVISION

1. This Guidance concerns the interface between the Family Court and Arbitrations conducted in accordance with the provisions of the Arbitration Act 1996 (AA96) where the parties to a post-relationship breakdown financial dispute have agreed to submit issues for decision by an arbitrator whose award is to be binding upon them.

2. It is a fundamental requirement of this Guidance that the arbitrator will decide the substance of the dispute only in accordance with the law of England and Wales. This Guidance does not apply to, or sanction, any arbitral process based on a different system of law nor, in particular, one where there is reason to believe that, whatever system of law is purportedly being applied, there may have been gender-based discrimination.

3. To avoid unnecessary complication this Guidance is directed towards what may well be the most common form of arbitration with which the Family Court will become concerned, where the issues between the parties involve relief or an award by way of one or more of the financial remedies listed in rule 2.3 of the Family Procedure Rules 2010 (FPR).

4. In order to be effective, elements of some arbitral awards (by comprehensive dismissal of claims to create a clean break, or so as to bind the provider to a pension split, for example) will require their terms to be reflected in a Family Court order. If enforcement of the award becomes necessary, doing so via Family Court processes will be available only if orders reflecting the award are obtained. (Paragraph 30 below describes an alternative route which may be available via section 66 of AA96 in the county court or in the Family Division of the High Court.)

5. But it should be borne in mind that not every award need be brought before the Family Court for a financial order to be made, and that it may be more appropriate for some to be brought (if necessary) before a court which does not exercise family jurisdiction. Thus, for instance, where an arbitrator has decided upon the title to or possession of property under the Married Women's Property Act 1882, or has determined the respective beneficial interests of the disputants in a property or fund, the parties may simply choose to operate in accordance with the award and thus have no need

for a court order to reflect it. Or a Trustees of Land and Appointment of Trustees Act 1996 ("TOLATA") award might more appropriately be made the subject of an order in the County Court if it simply declares the interests of the parties and does not involve any financial remedy element. It should be noted, however, that (pending any statutory changes to facilitate the Family Court hearing them) only the High Court and county court have jurisdiction to determine applications made under TOLATA or the Inheritance (Provision for Family and Dependants) Act 1975.

6. Taking the most common example of an arbitration where the agreed issues are what periodical payments, lump sum and adjustment of property awards should be received by a claimant spouse, it is important first to establish whether or not financial remedy proceedings have already been instituted and a Form A issued.

A: Where there are subsisting proceedings seeking the same relief as is in issue in the arbitration

Stay of proceedings:

7. The court should be invited to stay the financial remedy proceedings pending delivery of the award. The arbitration agreement (in the case of an IFLA Scheme arbitration, the Form ARB1) will in most instances only recently have been signed by both parties, and thus contested applications for a stay will likely be rare. CPR rule 62.3(2) provides that such an application "must be made by application notice to the court dealing with those proceedings".

8. The Family Court has an obligation under FPR 3.3(l)(b) "where the parties agree, to enable non-court dispute resolution to take place." Section 9(4) of AA96 requires that the court "shall grant a stay unless satisfied that the arbitration agreement is null and void, inoperative, or incapable of being performed" and makes it clear that a stay application should be made to the court where the subsisting proceedings are pending. By paragraph 6.2 of Form ARB1 the parties will have agreed that they "will apply for or consent to a stay of any existing court proceedings, as necessary."

9. In such circumstances where the application to stay is by consent or unopposed it should be dealt with on paper and (absent any unusual circumstances indicating a need) without listing or hearing.

10. Parties seeking such a stay should (in person or through their solicitors, who need not for this purpose be on the court record in the financial remedy proceedings) lodge in the place where the proceedings have been commenced, and within those proceedings, clear evidence of their agreement (or lack of opposition) to the stay order, together with a copy of their signed arbitration agreement (such as the IFLA Form ARB1). One of the standard orders approved for use in conjunction with arbitrations provides for a stay, and a copy completed with the details of the case, and signed by both parties or their representatives to signify approval, should be lodged with the other documents. The file will then be placed before a judge

for approval, or for queries to be raised and dealt with by correspondence, and/or (if necessary) a hearing listed. The suite of arbitration-specific standard orders are Annexed to this Guidance: see *below*.

Applying for an order to reflect the award: by consent

11. The terms of the proposed consent order will be drafted to reflect the decisions and directions contained in the award. Insofar as financial remedy orders are involved, their form should follow the relevant paragraphs of the standard orders, which contain recitals apt for an arbitration award case. Together with a signed copy of the proposed order in the terms agreed, the parties, in order to take advantage of this accelerated procedure, should at the same time lodge their Forms A and D81, a copy of the arbitrator's award and (unless already on the court file) their Form ARB1. There is no reason in principle why unopposed applications for a consent order should not be dealt with on paper by a District Judge, although the court will always retain the ability to raise questions in correspondence or to call for a hearing.

12. Attention is drawn to my observations in *S v S (Financial Remedies: Arbitral Award)* [2014] EWHC 7 (Fam), [2014] 1 FLR 1257, about the attitude likely to be adopted by the court in such cases: "where the parties are putting the matter before the court by consent, … it can only be in the rarest of cases that it will be appropriate for the judge to do other than approve the order."

13. Draft orders submitted which invite the court to make orders it has no jurisdiction to make (or which are otherwise in unacceptable form) will, like any other defective consent order submitted, be returned for reconsideration. There is of course no objection to recitals which express the parties' agreement to provisions which fall outside the scope of the available statutory relief. Nor indeed is there anything to prevent parties agreeing to change the terms of an award if they are agreed upon a revised formulation. In that event, though, it would be sensible for the covering correspondence to make it clear which provisions of the award have been overtaken by what subsequent arrangement arrived at by the parties.

14. Parties anxious to preserve the privacy and to maintain the confidentiality of the award should lodge that document in a sealed envelope, clearly marked with the name and number of the case and the words **"Arbitration Award: Confidential".** The award will remain on the court file but should be placed in an envelope clearly marked as above, plus **"not to be opened without the permission of a judge of the Family Court."** The request for the award to be sealed once the order has been approved should be made prominently in the covering letter.

Applying for an order to reflect the award: opposed

15. The party seeking to have the award reflected in a court order will need to proceed adopting what at para [25] of *S* v *S* was described as the "notice to show cause" procedure. An alternative formulation of the Arbitration recital for such a situation is contained in each standard order.

16. Similar documentation should be submitted with the application, except of course that the order proposed is likely to have been unilaterally drafted on behalf of the party seeking to obtain the order. An application of this sort will ordinarily be listed for a hearing before a judge of Circuit Judge or High Court Judge level.

17. Attention is drawn to my observations in *S v S* concerning the attitude likely to be adopted by the court in opposed cases:

> "The court will no doubt adopt an appropriately robust approach, both to the procedure it adopts in dealing with such a challenge and to the test it applies in deciding the outcome. ... The parties will almost invariably forfeit the right to anything other than a most abbreviated hearing; only in highly exceptional circumstances is the court likely to permit anything more than a very abbreviated hearing."

18. Applications for consent orders are specifically placed outside the scope of the MIAMs requirement by Practice Direction 3A, para 13(2). So, by virtue of the same provision, are proceedings "for enforcement of any order made in proceedings for a financial remedy or of any agreement made in or in contemplation of proceedings for a financial remedy." Parties who have agreed to arbitrate but have become engaged in any post-arbitral award dispute, as for instance a contested "show cause" application, should not be required to deviate into a MIAM.

B: Arbitration claims

19. An "arbitration claim" is a term of art, and its scope for the purposes of its application to arbitrations conducted under AA96 is defined by CPR rule 62.2(1) in these terms:

[*In relation to AA96*] 'arbitration claim' means –

(a) any application to the court under the 1996 Act;

(b) a claim to determine –

(i) whether there is a valid arbitration agreement;

(ii) whether an arbitration tribunal is properly constituted; or

what matters have been submitted to arbitration in accordance with an arbitration agreement;

(c) a claim to declare that an award by an arbitral tribunal is not binding on a party; and

(d) any other application affecting –

(i) arbitration proceedings (whether started or not); or

(ii) an arbitration agreement.

20. The court where "arbitration claims" as so defined are to be commenced is governed by CPR PD62 para 2 and the High Court and County Courts (Allocation of Arbitration Proceedings) Order 1996 (S.I. 1996/3215) as amended (the 1996 Order), which do not currently cater for such claims to be launched in the Family Court. Pending changes made to CPR PD62 and/

or the 1996 Order, an applicant for an "arbitration claim" should issue the requisite Form (see *below)* in the Commercial Court and should at the time of issue seek transfer to the Family Division. Para [6] of the 1996 Order does not as yet permit the transfer of any such application to the Family Court – the transfer must therefore be to the Family Division of the High Court.

21. The Form N8 initiating such a claim should be prominently marked **"Family business: direction sought for transfer to the Family Division of the High Court"** and should detail (where there are subsisting Family Court proceedings, albeit stayed) the case title and number.

22. Attention is drawn to sections 42 (enforcement of peremptory orders of the arbitrator) and 43 (securing the attendance of witnesses) of AA96 which are the provisions in relation to which an "arbitration claim" is most likely to be sought in the course of an ongoing post-separation financial arbitration. Attention is also drawn to the provisions of section 44 (court powers exercisable in support of arbitral proceedings). Standard Orders have been issued to meet each of these contingencies: see Annex A, *below.*

23. As these are all within the CPR definition of "arbitration claims," pending changes to para [2] of CPR PD62 such applications should (as described *above)* be issued in the Commercial Court and bear prominently upon them a request for speedy transfer to the Family Division (or, in the case of, for instance, a TOLATA claim which does not also invoke the family court jurisdiction, to the relevant county court).

24. In relation to applications under sections 42 and 43 the standard orders are self-explanatory. Such applications should be heard by a judge of High Court level.

C: Arbitrations conducted when there are no subsisting proceedings seeking relevant relief

Stay of proceedings:

25. An application to stay legal proceedings under section 9 of AA96 is in effect excluded from the definition of and procedural requirements for "arbitration claims" by CPR rule 62.3(2), which provides that such an application "must be made by application notice to the court dealing with those proceedings".

26. In the case of an IFLA Scheme arbitration the parties will have agreed (by paragraph 6.2 of their Form ARB1) that they "will not commence court proceedings … in relation to the same subject matter". If however such proceedings are thereafter initiated then it is open to either party to apply for a stay pursuant to section 9 of AA96 in the court where the proceedings have been commenced, and within those proceedings. If a stay remains opposed an early hearing will obviously be required to determine the application.

Applying for an order to reflect the award: by consent

27. The principles discussed in Part A apply, but if the relief awarded and sought to be reflected in an order includes one or more financial remedies

only capable of being made on or after pronouncement of a decree, then it will be necessary for "status proceedings" seeking divorce, judicial separation, nullity or (in the case of civil partners) dissolution to have been instituted, the relevant financial remedies applied for, and the stage in the proceedings reached when it will be appropriate for the court to make an order. In the case of divorce proceedings that would normally predicate a decree nisi having been pronounced, but see *JP* v *NP* [2014] EWHC 1101 (Fam), [2015] 1 FLR 659.

Applying for an order to reflect the award: opposed

28. The section of Part A describing the "show cause" procedure applies, and again it would be necessary to have the necessary status proceedings in being for financial remedy orders to be made.

29. Where the aid of the Court is needed in support of a family financial arbitration in relation to which status proceedings have not yet been commenced, then the route suggested in paragraph 20 *et seq. above* must be followed, and transfer from the Commercial Court sought. It will however be necessary for the FPR Part 18 procedure to be adopted in order to bring the arbitration claim (for instance, under section 42 or section 43 of AA96) before the Family Division.

D: Enforcement

30. Section 3 of CPR Part 62 (rules 62.17 and 62.18) make provision for the direct enforcement of awards. In some situations it may be possible to pray section 66 of AA96 in aid to enforce an award. Para 4 of the 1996 Order authorises the commencement in any county court of section 66 proceedings under which awards can, with the court's permission, be enforced in the same way as a judgment or order of the court to the same effect. This may prove effective in the case of a TOLATA award but is not appropriate in the case of a financial remedy award.

E: Challenging the Award under sections 67 to 71 of the Arbitration Act

31. Some very specific bases for challenging arbitrations are contained in these sections of AA96. They are hedged about with preconditions and limitations, and the commercial experi•ence in arbitration is that they are relatively rarely successful. In relation to an arbitration dealing with family financial issues, however, it would ordinarily be appropriate for a High Court Judge of the Family Division to hear them, and thus it is to be expected that applications commenced pursuant to these provisions will by the same route be transferred to that court.

F: Arbitration-specific standard court orders

32. This suite now consists of three orders for use in conjunction with arbitrations. They are reproduced in their approved form within Annex A to this Guidance and comprise orders to:

- Stay pursuant to Arbitration Act 1996 section 9 and/or under the court's case management powers

XX

I understand the undertaking that I have given and that if I break any of my promises to the court I may be sent to prison, or fined, or my assets may be seized, for contempt of court.

....

YY

Definitions

2. IFLA is the Institute of Family Law Arbitrators.

3. Form ARB1 is the arbitration agreement signed by the parties of which a copy has been lodged with the court.

4. The arbitration is an arbitration which is to be conducted in accordance with the rules of the IFLA arbitration scheme.

Recitals

5. *(In the case of an order made without notice)*

   (a) This order was made at a hearing without notice to the respondent. The reason why the order was made without notice to the respondent was [*set out*]

   (b) The Judge read the following affidavits/witness statements [*set out*] and heard oral testimony from [*name*].

6. *(In the case of an order made following the giving of short informal notice)*

   This order was made at a hearing without full notice having been given to the respondent. The reason why the order was made without full notice having been given to the respondent was [*set out*].

7. The applicant/respondent has applied to this court for financial remedies.

8. The court must by rules 3.2 and 3.3 of the Family Procedure Rules 2010 at every stage in proceedings consider whether alternative dispute resolution is appropriate and, if so, whether to adjourn those proceedings so to enable alternative dispute resolution to take place; and has power pursuant to its general powers of management under rule 4.1 to stay the whole or any part of proceedings either generally or until a specified date or event.

...

Agreements

9. By their Form ARB1 the parties have agreed to refer to arbitration the issues described in it which include some or all of the financial remedies for which applications are pending in this court.

10. …

Undertakings to the court

11. …

12. …

IT IS ORDERED (BY CONSENT) THAT:

13. The pending application(*s*) for financial remedies is/*are* stayed pending receipt of the award in the arbitration (or until the parties may reach agreement in respect of the arbitration issues).

14. Upon receipt of the award (or upon reaching agreement) either party may in a form agreed with the other seek an order of this court to give effect to the award (or their agreement).

15. [*or if the parties cannot reach agreement upon the form of an order to give effect to the award*] Failing agreement between the parties as to the form of an order to give effect to the award either party may apply for the other to show why an order should not be made in the terms of the draft proposed.

16. Any application under either of the preceding 2 paragraphs shall be lodged together with a copy of the award, Form(s) D81 and with a draft of the order which the court is requested to make.

17. [*Provision for the costs of the stay application*]

Dated

Enforcement of an arbitrator's peremptory order under Arbitration Act 1996 s42

In the Family Court Sitting at [Place] No:

The Arbitration Act 1996 section 42

The Marriage/Civil Partnership/Relationship/Family of XX and YY

After hearing [*name the advocate(s) who appeared*]

After consideration of the documents lodged by the parties

(In the case of an order made without notice)

After reading the statements and hearing the witnesses specified in the recitals below

ORDER MADE BY [NAME OF JUDGE] ON [DATE] SITTING IN OPEN COURT/PRIVATE

The parties

1. The applicant is XX

   The respondent is YY

   The second respondent is ZZ

   Specify if any party acts by a litigation friend

[Where undertakings have been given]

Notice pursuant to PD 37A para 2.1

You XX, and you YY, may be held to be in contempt of court and imprisoned or fined, or your assets may be seized, if you break the promises that you have given to the court.

Statement pursuant to PD 37A para 2.2

I understand the undertaking that I have given and that if I break any of my promises to the court I may be sent to prison, or fined, or my assets may be seized, for contempt of court.

....

XX

I understand the undertaking that I have given and that if I break any of my promises to the court I may be sent to prison, or fined, or my assets may be seized, for contempt of court.

....

YY

Definitions

2. IFLA is the Institute of Family Law Arbitrators.
3. Form ARB1 is the arbitration agreement signed by the parties of which a copy has been lodged with the court.
4. The arbitration is an arbitration which is to be conducted in accordance with the rules of the IFLA arbitration scheme.

5. The arbitrator is [*name*].

6. The arbitrator's order is a peremptory order made on [*date*] pursuant to section 41(5) of the Arbitration Act 1996 which required the respondent to comply with its terms [by [*date*]] *or* [without prescribing a date for compliance].

Recitals

7. *(In the case of an order made without notice)*

   (a) This order was made at a hearing without notice to the respondent. The reason why the order was made without notice to the respondent was [*set out*]

   (b) The Judge read the following affidavits/witness statements *[set out]* and heard oral testimony from *[name]*

8. *(In the case of an order made following the giving of short informal notice)*

   This order was made at a hearing without full notice having been given to the respondent. The reason why the order was made without full notice having been given to the respondent was *[set out]*

9. *(In the case of an application commenced elsewhere than in the Family Court)*

   This application was transferred to this court from the *[specify]* Division/ Court by order *of [name of judge]* on *[date].*

10. The arbitration has commenced and is continuing.

11. The parties have by their Form ARB1 and their acceptance of the IFLA arbitration scheme rules agreed that the powers of the court under section 42 of the Arbitration Act 1996 (enforcement of peremptory orders of tribunal) are available, so that if one of them fails to comply with a peremptory order made by the arbitrator then another party may apply to the court for an order requiring compliance.

12. The arbitrator's order is (so far as relevant to this application) in the following terms:

    [*set out in the words of the arbitrator's order*]

13. This application is for an order under section 42 of the Arbitration Act 1996 for the enforcement of the arbitrator's order and is made:

    [by the applicant.] (*or*)

    [by the arbitrator, upon notice to the parties.]

14. This court is satisfied that:

    (a) the applicant has exhausted all available arbitral process in respect of the respondent's failure to comply with that/*those* provision(*s*) of the peremptory order; and

(b) the respondent has failed to comply with that/*those* provision(*s*) of the peremptory order [within the time prescribed by the order] *or* [within a reasonable time, no time for compliance having been prescribed].

Agreements

15. …

Undertakings to the court

16. …

IT IS ORDERED (BY CONSENT):

17. The respondent shall comply with the peremptory order by no later than [*date*].

[*or*]

18. [*Other orders*]

19. *[If applied for]* Permission to appeal against this decision is granted/ *refused.*

20. *[Provision for costs]*

Dated

Order securing the attendance of witnesses under Arbitration Act 1996 s43

In the Family Court Sitting at [Place] No:

The Arbitration Act 1996 section 43

The Marriage/Civil Partnership/Relationship/Family of XX and YY

After hearing [*name the advocate(s) who appeared*]

After consideration of the documents lodged by the parties

(In the case of an order made without notice)

After reading the statements and hearing the witnesses specified in the recitals below

ORDER MADE BY [NAME OF JUDGE] ON [DATE] SITTING IN OPEN COURT/PRIVATE

The parties

1. The applicant is XX

   The respondent is YY

   The second respondent is ZZ

   Specify if any party acts by a litigation friend

[Where undertakings have been given]

Notice pursuant to PD 37A para 2.1

You XX, and you YY, may be held to be in contempt of court and imprisoned or fined, or your assets may be seized, if you break the promises that you have given to the court.

Statement pursuant to PD 37A para 2.2

I understand the undertaking that I have given and that if I break any of my promises to the court I may be sent to prison, or fined, or my assets may be seized, for contempt of court.

....

XX

I understand the undertaking that I have given and that if I break any of my promises to the court I may be sent to prison, or fined, or my assets may be seized, for contempt of court.

....

YY

Definitions

2. IFLA is the Institute of Family Law Arbitrators.

3. Form ARB1 is the arbitration agreement signed by the parties of which a copy has been lodged with the court.

4. The arbitration is an arbitration which is to be conducted in accordance with the rules of the IFLA arbitration scheme.

5. The arbitrator is [*name*].

6. The *witness/witnesses is/are [name(s)]*

Recitals

7. *(In the case of an order made without notice)*

   (a) This order was made at a hearing without notice to the respondent. The reason why the order was made without notice to the respondent was *[set out]*

   (b) The Judge read the following affidavits/witness statements *[set out]* and heard oral testimony from *[name]*

8. *(In the case of an order made following the giving of short informal notice)*

   This order was made at a hearing without full notice having been given to the respondent. The reason why the order was made without full notice having been given to the respondent was *[set out]*

9. *(In the case of an application commenced elsewhere than in the Family Court)*

   This application was transferred to this court from the *[specify]* Division/ Court by order *of [name of judge]* on *[date].*

10. The arbitration has commenced and is being conducted in England and Wales and the witness/*witnesses* are in the United Kingdom.

11. This application is for an order pursuant to section 43 of the Arbitration Act 1996 to secure the attendance before the arbitrator of the witness/*witnesses* in order:

    [to give oral testimony] *(and/or)*

    [to produce documents or other material evidence which the *witness/witnesses* can be compelled to produce in legal proceedings, namely [*specify*].]

12. This application is made:

    [by the applicant with the permission of the tribunal.] *(or)*

    [with the agreement of the other party/*parties* to the arbitration.]

Agreements

13. …

Undertakings to the court

14. …

IT IS ORDERED (BY CONSENT):

15. *[Insert the form of order or notice appropriate to secure the attendance of a witness in order to give oral testimony and/or to produce documents or other material evidence.]*

16. *[Other orders]*

17. *[Provision for costs]*

Dated

ANNEX B

Recitals for use where "omnibus" orders to reflect an arbitral award are sought for either Financial Remedy or Children Act Schedule 1 Final Orders

For the Financial Remedy Final Order Omnibus:

...

Arbitration award recital 19.

a. The documents lodged in relation to this application include the parties' arbitration agreement (Form ARB1), their Form(s) D81, a copy of the arbitrator's award, and a draft of the order which the court is requested to make.

b. By their Form ARB1 the parties agreed to refer to arbitration the issues described in it which include some or all of the financial remedies for which applications are pending in this court. The issues were referred to [insert arbitrator] under the IFLA scheme, who made an arbitral award on [insert date].

c. ***Either:***

[The parties have invited the court to make an order in agreed terms which reflects the arbitrator's award.] ***or:***

[There has been no agreement between the parties as to the form of an order to give effect to the arbitrator's award. The [applicant]/[respondent] has applied for the other party to show why an order should not be made in the terms of the draft proposed; and the court having considered the representations made by each party has directed that an order be made in the terms of this order.]

For the Children Act Schedule 1 Final Order Omnibus:

...

Arbitration award recital 18.

a. The documents lodged in relation to this application include the parties' arbitration agreement (Form ARB1), their Form(s) D81, a copy of the arbitrator's award, and a draft of the order which the court is requested to make.

b. By their Form ARB1 the parties agreed to refer to arbitration the issues described in it which encompass the application under Schedule 1 to the Children Act 1989 now pending in this court. The issues were referred to [insert arbitrator] under the IFLA scheme, who made an arbitral award on [insert date].

c. ***Either:***

[The parties have invited the court to make an order in agreed terms which reflects the arbitrator's award.] ***or:***

[There has been no agreement between the parties as to the form of an order to give effect to the arbitrator's award. The [applicant]/[respondent] has applied for the other party to show why an order should not be made in the terms of the draft proposed; and the court having considered the representations made by each party has directed that an order be made in the terms of this order.

APPENDIX 2

Forms, Precedents and Standard Orders

ARB1FS 2021

FAMILY LAW ARBITRATION FINANCIAL SCHEME

FORM ARB1FS –7TH EDITION (EFFECTIVE 11 JANUARY 2021)

APPLICATION FOR FAMILY ARBITRATION, FINANCIAL SCHEME

1. We, the parties to this application, whose details are set out below, apply to the Institute of Family Law Arbitrators Limited for the nomination and appointment of a sole arbitrator from the Family Arbitration Financial Panel ('the Financial Panel') to resolve the dispute referred to at paragraph 2 below by arbitration in accordance with the Arbitration Act 1996 ('the Act') and the Rules of the Family Law Arbitration Financial Scheme ('the Financial Scheme'):

Applicant's name	
Address	
Telephone	
Mobile	
Email	
Fax	
Represented by*	
Address	
Telephone	
Mobile	
Email	
Fax	

Respondent's name	
Address	
Telephone	
Mobile	
Email	
Fax	
Represented by*	
Address	
Telephone	
Mobile	
Email	
Fax	

*Delete as applicable.

Add, if necessary, the names of other parties on a separate sheet.

2. The dispute concerns the following issue(s):

(Set these out on a separate sheet if preferred, but as concisely as possible.)

....

....

....

Please complete EITHER paragraph **3(a)** OR **3(b)** OR paragraph **4** below:

3(a) We wish to nominate the following member of the Financial Panel for appointment in this matter:

(This paragraph applies if the parties agree that they would like the matter to be referred to a particular arbitrator and / or have approached a particular arbitrator directly. The appointment will be offered to the nominated arbitrator. If the appointment is not accepted by their first choice of arbitrator the parties may, if they agree, make a second or subsequent choice. Otherwise, it will be offered to another suitable member of the Financial Panel in accordance with paragraph 4 below.)

....

3(b) We wish the Institute of Family Law Arbitrators Limited to select one of the members of the Financial Panel from the agreed shortlist below for appointment in this matter:

(This paragraph applies if the parties have agreed on a shortlist of arbitrators from the Financial Panel any one of whom would be acceptable to them, and wishes IFLA to select one of the arbitrators on the shortlist without reference to any criteria. In this case, IFLA will offer the appointment to one of the shortlisted arbitrators chosen at random. If the appointment is not accepted by the first choice of arbitrator, IFLA will offer the appointment to a second or subsequent shortlisted arbitrator, similarly chosen at random. If none of the shortlisted arbitrators accepts the appointment, IFLA will inform the parties and invite them to submit further agreed names.)

....

....

....

4. We wish the Institute of Family Law Arbitrators Limited to nominate a member of the Financial Panel for appointment in this matter.

(This paragraph applies if the parties have not identified a particular arbitrator to whom they wish the matter to be referred. Please set out below the nature of the dispute (insofar as it is not apparent from paragraph 2 above). Please also set out below any preferences as to the arbitrator's qualifications, areas of experience, expertise and / or any other attributes; or as to the geographical location of the arbitration; and any other relevant circumstances.)

....

....

....

5. If court proceedings are current, please identify the nature of the proceedings, in which court they are taking place and what stage they have reached. (Please attach copies of any relevant documents and court orders.)

....

....

....

6. We confirm the following:

6.1 We have been advised about and understand the nature and implications of this agreement to arbitrate;

6.2 Once the arbitration has started, we will not commence court proceedings or continue existing court proceedings in relation to the same subject matter (and will apply for or consent to a stay of any existing court proceedings, as necessary), unless it is appropriate to make an application to the court arising out of or in connection with the arbitration, or some relief is required that would not be available in the arbitration;

6.3 We have read the current edition of the Rules of the Financial Scheme ('the Rules') and will abide by them. In particular, we understand our obligation to comply with the decisions, directions and orders of the arbitrator and, when required, to make full and complete disclosure relating to our financial circumstances;

6.4 We understand and agree that any award of the arbitrator appointed to determine this dispute will be final and binding on us, subject to any of the following:

(a) any challenge to the award by any available arbitral process of appeal or review or in accordance with the provisions of Part 1 of the Act;

(b) insofar as the subject matter of the award requires it to be embodied in a court order (see 6.5 below), any changes which the court making that order may require, or the refusal by the court, where it has jurisdiction to do so, to embody the award or any part of it in a court order;

(c) insofar as the award provides for continuing payments to be made by one party to another, or to a child or children, a subsequent award or court order reviewing and varying or revoking the provision for continuing payments, and which supersedes an existing award;

(d) insofar as the award provides for continuing payments to be made by one party to or for the benefit of a child or children, a subsequent assessment by the Child Maintenance Service (or its successor) in relation to the same child or children.

6.5 If and so far as the subject matter of the award makes it necessary, we will apply to an appropriate court for an order in the same or similar terms as the award or the relevant part of the award. We will take all reasonably necessary steps to see that such an order is made. (In this context, 'an appropriate court' means a court which has jurisdiction to make a substantive order in the same or similar terms as the award, whether on primary application or on transfer from another division of the court.) However, we understand that the court may have a discretion as to whether, and in what terms, to make an order;

6.6 We understand and agree that although the Rules provide for each party, generally, to bear an equal share of the arbitrator's fees and expenses (see Art. 14.4(a)), if any party fails to pay their share, then the arbitrator may initially require payment of the full amount from any other party, leaving it to them to recover from the defaulting party;

6.7 We agree to the arbitration of this dispute in accordance with the Rules of the Financial Scheme.

IMPORTANT

Parties should be aware that:

- **By signing this form they are entering into a binding agreement to arbitrate (within the meaning of s.6 of the Arbitration Act 1996).**
- **After signing, neither party may avoid arbitration (unless they both agree to do so). Either party may rely on the arbitration agreement to seek a stay of court proceedings commenced by the other.**
- **Arbitration is a process whose outcome is generally final.**

Signed..

(Applicant *or* Applicant's legal representative, for and on behalf of Applicant)

Dated..

Signed..

(Respondent *or* Respondent's legal representative, for and on behalf of Respondent)

Dated..

Please send your completed form, preferably by email, to info@ifla.org.uk, or it can be sent by post to IFLA, 91-95 Southwark Bridge Road, London SE1 0AX.

Note that by submitting this Form, the parties consent to the processing by IFLA (and/or by Resolution, on IFLA's behalf) of the information and personal data provided in it and in associated documentation for the purposes of this Financial Scheme arbitration. This includes retaining and storing the information and personal data for as long as is necessary in connection with this agreement. It may also be retained for research, training and statistical purposes in connection with family arbitration, but on the understanding that if so used, any information or details about individuals will have been removed so that they cannot be personally identified.

ARB1CS 2021

FAMILY LAW ARBITRATION CHILDREN SCHEME

FORM ARB1CS – 5TH EDITION (EFFECTIVE 11 JANUARY 2021)

APPLICATION FOR FAMILY ARBITRATION, CHILDREN SCHEME

1. We, the parties to this application, whose details are set out below, apply to the Institute of Family Law Arbitrators Limited for the nomination and appointment of a sole arbitrator from the IFLA Children Panel ('the Children Panel') to resolve the dispute referred to at paragraph 3 below by arbitration in accordance with the Arbitration Act 1996 ('the Act') and the Rules of the Family Law Arbitration Children Scheme ('the Children Scheme'). We confirm that all the persons who have parental responsibility for the child(ren) concerned are parties to this arbitration.

Applicant's name	
Address	
Telephone	
Mobile	
Email	
Fax	
Represented by*	
Address	
Telephone	
Mobile	
Email	
Fax	

Respondent's name	
Address	
Telephone	
Mobile	
Email	
Fax	
Represented by*	
Address	
Telephone	
Mobile	
Email	
Fax	

*Delete as applicable.

Add, if necessary, the names of other parties on a separate sheet.

2. The child(ren) concerned is/are:

Please insert names and dates of birth and relationship of each child to the parties and whether (as regards each party) they have parental responsibility. Please also state the current location of each child.

....

....

3. The dispute concerns the following issue(s):

(Set these out on a separate sheet if preferred, but as concisely as possible.)

....

....

....

Please complete EITHER paragraph **4(a)** OR **4(b)** OR paragraph **5** below:

4(a) We wish to nominate the following member of the Children Panel for appointment in this matter:

(This paragraph applies if the parties agree that they would like the matter to be referred to a particular arbitrator and / or have approached a particular arbitrator directly. The appointment will be offered to the nominated arbitrator. If the appointment is not accepted by their first choice of arbitrator the parties may, if they agree, make a second or subsequent choice. Otherwise, it will be offered to another suitable member of the Children Panel in accordance with paragraph 5 below.)

....

4(b) We wish the Institute of Family Law Arbitrators Limited to select one of the members of the Children Panel from the agreed shortlist below for appointment in this matter:

(This paragraph applies if the parties have agreed on a shortlist of arbitrators from the Children Panel any one of whom would be acceptable to them, and wishes IFLA to select one of the arbitrators on the shortlist without reference to any criteria. In this case, IFLA will offer the appointment to one of the shortlisted arbitrators chosen at random. If the appointment is not accepted by the first choice of arbitrator, IFLA will offer the appointment to a second or subsequent shortlisted arbitrator, similarly chosen at random. If none of the shortlisted arbitrators accepts the appointment, IFLA will inform the parties and invite them to submit further agreed names.)

....

....

....

5. We wish the Institute of Family Law Arbitrators Limited to nominate a member of the Children Panel for appointment in this matter.

(This paragraph applies if the parties have not identified a particular arbitrator to whom they wish the matter to be referred. Please set out below the nature of the dispute (insofar as it is not apparent from paragraph 3 above). Please also set out below any preferences as to the arbitrator's qualifications, areas of experience, expertise and / or any other attributes; or as to the geographical location of the arbitration; and any other relevant circumstances.)

....

....

....

6. If any court proceedings are current in relation to the child(ren), or your marriage or relationship, please identify the nature of the proceedings, in which court they are taking place and what stage they have reached. (Please attach copies of any relevant documents and court orders.)

....

....

7. Please carefully read paragraphs 8.3(a)-(d) below and provide with this Form (or in respect of the Basic Disclosure, upon receipt):

- **a Safeguarding Questionnaire (as attached to this Form) completed and signed by each party, together with any relevant documentation;**
- **a Basic Disclosure from the Disclosure and Barring Service or from Disclosure Scotland, as appropriate, in relation to each party; or alternatively, an up to date CAFCASS report or Schedule 2 letter prepared in current proceedings concerning the safeguarding and welfare of the child(ren), if applicable;**
- **any other relevant letter or report prepared by CAFCASS or any local authority children's services department or similar agency in relation to the safeguarding or welfare of the child(ren) concerned (if there is one).**

8. We confirm the following:

8.1 We have been advised about and understand the nature and implications of this agreement to arbitrate;

8.2 Once the arbitration has started, we will not commence court proceedings or continue existing court proceedings in relation to the same subject matter (and will apply for or consent to a stay of any existing court proceedings, as necessary), unless it is appropriate to make an application to the court arising out of or in connection with the arbitration, or some relief is required that would not be available in the arbitration;

8.3 We have read the current edition of the Rules of the Children Scheme ('the Rules') and will abide by them. In particular, we understand our obligations:

(a) to provide accurate information regarding safeguarding in this Form and in the attached Safeguarding Questionnaire;

(b) before the arbitration starts, to obtain a Basic Disclosure from the Disclosure and Barring Service or from Disclosure Scotland, as appropriate, and promptly send it to the arbitrator and to every other party; or alternatively, to provide an up to date CAFCASS report or Schedule 2 letter prepared in current proceedings concerning the safeguarding and welfare of the child(ren), if applicable;

(c) to send to the arbitrator and to every other party any other relevant letter or report prepared by CAFCASS or any local authority children's services department or similar agency in relation to the welfare or safeguarding of the child(ren) concerned.

(d) before the arbitration starts and at every stage of the process (as a continuing duty) to disclose fully and completely to the arbitrator and to every other party any fact, matter or

document in our knowledge, possession or control which is or appears to be relevant to the physical or emotional safety of any party or to the safeguarding or welfare of any child the subject of the proceedings, or to a decision by the arbitrator whether to terminate the arbitration under Art.17.2.1. Such disclosure shall include (but not be limited to) any criminal conviction, caution or involvement (concerning any child) with children's services in respect of any party or any person with whom the child is likely to have contact;

(e) **at all stages of the process, to comply with the decisions, directions and orders of the arbitrator;**

8.4 We understand and agree that any determination of the arbitrator appointed to determine this dispute will be final and binding on us, subject to any of the following:

(a) any challenge to the determination by any available arbitral process of appeal or review or in accordance with the provisions of Part 1 of the Act;

(b) insofar as the subject matter of the determination requires it to be embodied in a court order (see 8.5 below), any changes which the court making that order may require, or the refusal by the court, where it has jurisdiction to do so, to embody the determination or any part of it in a court order;

(c) any subsequent determination superseding the determination; or any changes to the determination or subsequent order superseding the determination which the Family Court considers ought to be made in the exercise of its statutory and/or inherent jurisdiction whether under the Children Act, 1989 or otherwise.

8.5 If and so far as the subject matter of the determination makes it necessary, we will apply to an appropriate court for an order in the same or similar terms as the determination or the relevant part of the determination. We will take all reasonably necessary steps to see that such an order is made. (In this context, 'an appropriate court' means a court which has jurisdiction to make a substantive order in the same or similar terms as the determination.) However, we understand that the court has a discretion as to whether, and in what terms, to make an order;

8.6 We understand and agree that although the Rules provide for each party, generally, to bear an equal share of the arbitrator's fees and expenses (see Art. 14.4(a)), if any party fails to pay their share, then the arbitrator may initially require payment of the full amount from any other party, leaving it to them to recover from the defaulting party;

8.7 We agree to the arbitration of this dispute in accordance with the Rules of the Children Scheme.

IMPORTANT

Parties should be aware that:

- **By signing this form they are entering into a binding agreement to arbitrate (within the meaning of s.6 of the Arbitration Act 1996).**
- **After signing, neither party may avoid arbitration (unless they both agree to do so). Either party may rely on the arbitration agreement to seek a stay of court proceedings commenced by the other.**
- **Arbitration is a process whose outcome is generally final.**

Signed...

(Applicant *or* Applicant's legal representative, for and on behalf of Applicant)

Dated...

Signed...

(Respondent *or* Respondent's legal representative, for and on behalf of Respondent)

Dated...

Please send your completed form, preferably by email, to info@ifla.org.uk, or it can be sent by post to IFLA, 91-95 Southwark Bridge Road, London SE1 0AX.

Note that by submitting this Form, the parties consent to the processing by IFLA (and/or by Resolution, on IFLA's behalf) of the information and personal data provided in it and in associated documentation for the purposes of this Children Scheme arbitration. This includes retaining and storing the information and personal data for as long as is necessary in connection with this agreement. It may also be retained for research, training and statistical purposes in connection with family arbitration, but on the understanding that if so used, any information or details about individuals will have been removed so that they cannot be personally identified.

ARB1CS 2021 Safeguarding Questionnaire

FAMILY LAW ARBITRATION CHILDREN SCHEME

FORM ARB1CS SAFEGUARDING QUESTIONNAIRE

Each party should complete and individually sign a copy of this Safeguarding Questionnaire. (Please make further copies as necessary.)

Name ....

Applicant / Respondent / Other Party ....

1. Have there been any court proceedings in relation to the child(ren), or your marriage or relationship, other than as mentioned in paragraph 6 of Form ARB1CS?

   Yes / No

   (If 'Yes', please identify the nature of the proceedings, in which court they took place and the outcome. Please attach copies of any relevant documents and court orders.)

   ....

   ....

2. Has a child protection plan been put in place by a local authority in relation to the child(ren), or have a local authority's children's services been involved in any way?

   Yes / No, or not to my knowledge

   (If 'Yes', please provide details and say whether the local authority's involvement is continuing.)

   ....

   ....

3. Have you, or any person with whom the child(ren) is/are likely to have contact ever been convicted of an offence concerning a child, or ever been cautioned or investigated in that connection?

   Yes / No

   (If 'Yes', please provide full details.)

   ....

   ....

4. Do you have any concerns that the child(ren) has/have experienced, or is/are at risk of experiencing, harm of any the following kinds from any person with whom the child(ren) is/are likely to have contact?

    - Any form of domestic violence Yes / No
    - Child abduction Yes / No
    - Child abuse Yes / No
    - Drugs, alcohol or substance abuse Yes / No
    - Other safety or welfare concerns Yes / No

    (If 'Yes' to any of the above, please provide full details of your concerns.)

    ....

    ....

I confirm that:

(a) the information I have provided in response to this Safeguarding Questionnaire is true and complete to the best of my knowledge and belief;

AND

(b) I have applied to the Disclosure and Barring Service or Disclosure Scotland for a Basic Disclosure and, upon receipt, will promptly send it to the arbitrator and to every other party;

OR

I attach an up to date CAFCASS report or Schedule 2 letter prepared in current proceedings concerning the safeguarding and welfare of the child(ren). (Please delete whichever is inapplicable.)

Signed ....

Dated ....

Suggested letter solicitor to client confirming appointment of Arbitrator – Financial

Dear [CLIENT]

<u>Family Law Arbitration- Finance</u>

I thank you for confirming your agreement to pursuing the finance dispute issues with [xxx] through the Arbitration procedure.

I have spoken with your [xxx] solicitors and we have recommended xxx xxx to be the nominated Arbitrator OR will have the Arbitrator nominated by one of the following options:

a) We each provide three nominations and if possible to agree one of those nominated

b) to forward to the Institute of Family Law Arbitrators (IFLA) three nominations for them to nominate one of those three

c) request the IFLA to nominate

When the Arbitrator has been appointed they will provide their Terms of Engagement.

At this point all parties will need to decide whether they would wish for a pre-engagement meeting for which generally there will be no fee and where at the meeting we will get to know the Arbitrator, agree procedure, review their Terms of Engagement and the form ARB1FS.

By way of clarification the ARB1FS is a document which constitutes a binding agreement between all parties. It sets out the issues in dispute. It is important I emphasise that by signing the ARB1FS you will be entering into a binding agreement to Arbitrate and once signed neither you nor [xxx] may avoid Arbitration. The Arbitrator's award is final and binding and there are very limited basis for raising a challenge or appeal.

Alternatively, if everybody agrees there is no need for a pre-engagement meeting, arrangements will be made for you to sign the Arbitrator's Terms of Engagement and the ARB1FS. Once the two documents are signed by all parties including the Arbitrator, the Arbitration commences and directions follow as to how the matter is to proceed.

I must advise my preference is generally to arrange a pre-engagement meeting as it gives you the opportunity to discuss face to face with the Arbitrator how your case is to move forward and its practicalities.

Following the pre-engagement meeting the Arbitrator will arrange for a copy of the minutes of that meeting to be forwarded to all present for signature. This is very helpful as it gives the opportunity to reflect upon the discussions that took place and their acceptance.

If you however decide there is no necessity for a pre-engagement meeting I will ask you to sign a Letter of Disclaimer confirming you have understood.

I will write as soon as I have details of the nominated Arbitrator.

Kind regards.

Yours sincerely,

For and on behalf of
(Solicitor)

Suggested letter solicitor to client confirming appointment of Arbitrator – Children

Dear [CLIENT]

Family Law Arbitration- Children

I thank you for confirming your agreement to pursuing the children dispute issues with [xxx] through the Arbitration procedure.

I have spoken with your [xxx] solicitors and we have recommended xxx xxx to be the nominated Arbitrator OR will have the Arbitrator nominated by one of the following options:

a) We each provide three nominations and if possible to agree one of those nominated

b) to forward to the Institute of Family Law Arbitrators (IFLA) three nominations for them to nominate one of those three

c) request the IFLA to nominate

When the Arbitrator has been appointed they will provide their Terms of Engagement.

At this point all parties will need to decide whether they would wish to undertake a pre-engagement meeting which will generally be free and will be an opportunity for the parties to get to know the Arbitrator, agree procedure, review their Terms of Engagement and the form ARB1CS.

By way of clarification, the ARB1CS is a document which constitutes a binding agreement between all parties. It sets out the issues in dispute. You need to be aware that by signing the Form ARB1CS you will be entering into a binding agreement to Arbitrate and once signed neither you nor [xxx] may avoid Arbitration. The Arbitrator's award is final and binding and there are very limited basis for raising a challenge or appeal.

Alternatively, if you would prefer and if everybody agrees there is no need for a pre-engagement meeting. In that instance, you will both sign the Arbitrator's

Terms of Engagement and the ARB1CS and the Arbitration will then commence by way of a preliminary meeting.

Kind regards.

Yours sincerely,

For and on behalf of
(Solicitor)

Suggested letter from solicitor to client regarding choosing an arbitrator

Dear [CLIENT]

Arbitrators are experienced family justice professionals with extensive experience working in family disputes. The Institute of Family Law Arbitrators (IFLA) train family arbitrators to meet high professional standards and a panel of qualified arbitrators is maintained by IFLA

One of the key benefits of arbitration is that you can choose an arbitrator best suited to the particular circumstances of your case. You can find an arbitrator through the IFLA website (http://ifla.org.uk/) and, provided we have agreement with [NAME OF OTHER PARTY], in the Form ARB1FS OR Form ARB1CS we can nominate that a specific arbitrator be appointed to deal with your case. Alternatively, we can ask IFLA to choose an arbitrator from their panel instead or from an agreed short list prepared by you and [NAME OF OTHER PARTY]. Many clients wish to nominate a specific arbitrator and it is not unusual to name a preferred arbitrator within the Form ARB1FS OR Form ARB1CS.

Your choice of arbitrator can take into account where you and [NAME OF OTHER PARTY] live and/or are based, the extent and complexity of the issues and the professional background of the arbitrator (for example whether they are a solicitor, barrister or retired judge) as well as their experience and any specialisms they offer. There is no "one size fits all" approach to appointing an arbitrator.

If we are able to decide on a named arbitrator with [NAME OF OTHER PARTY], IFLA will offer the appointment to them. However, if they are unable or unwilling to accept the appointment, you will have the option of nominating someone else.

I would be grateful if you could contact me so we can discuss the choice of arbitrator and complete the Form ARB1FS OR FormARB1CS.

Kind regards.

Yours sincerely,

For and on behalf of
(Solicitor)

Checklist of matters for discussion at an IFLA Family Arbitration First Meeting/Directions Hearing – Long form

CHECKLIST OF MATTERS FOR DISCUSSION AT AN IFLA FAMILY ARBITRATION FIRST MEETING/DIRECTIONS HEARING

1. **The arbitrator may use this checklist during the first meeting / directions appointment, it will assist him focus on the key issues if each party is able to complete this checklist electronically prior to the meeting.**
2. **The party shown as applicant on Form ARB1 should complete the checklist first and then email it to the respondent for completion and return to the arbitrator (copying it also to the applicant)**
3. **Lengthy responses are not required. Please note that at the outset of the arbitration some of these questions will not yet be capable of being answered. Please feel free to say so.**
4. **You are not formally bound by the indications given in this document. The arbitrator will listen to the parties representations and determine directions in due course.**
5. **Both parties are encouraged to discuss this document with their legal advisors before it is completed and again once both parties have competed it.**

PART I: PRELIMINARY MATTERS

Ref	Issue	Applicant's response	Respondent's response	Arbitrator's notes
1	Confirm that you have completed the pre-engagement questionnaire.			
2	Your preferred mode of address (Mr, Mrs, Miss, Ms, etc.) and how would you like to address arbitrator? Formal or informal?			
3	Which party should be designated as the lead party in the arbitration?			

Ref	Issue	Applicant's response	Respondent's response	Arbitrator's notes
3	If the arbitrator has made any disclosures of interest or conflict to you do you waive any objection to those disclosures of interest made by the arbitrator or do you wish him to stand down?			
4	Do you wish the arbitrator to have the authority to record any agreements reached at the preliminary and subsequent meetings on your behalf?			

PART II: PROCEDURAL AND INTERIM MATTERS

Ref	Issue	Applicant's position	Respondent's position	Arbitrator's notes
5	Save for the Form ARB1, have you agreed anything in writing which affects the procedure for the arbitration?			
6	Any there any particular points in the Rules which you wish to suggest might be amended or qualified for the purposes of this arbitration (save for Art 3)?			
7	Do the issues suggest that any other person, company or trust should be invited to join the arbitration?			
8	Are you content with the costs rule at Article 14, or do you wish a different presumption to apply?			
9	Do you want ***Calderbank*** principles to apply?			
10	Should the other party provide security for fees and expenses?			
11	Do you consider that there are any aspects of the dispute (or indeed the whole arbitration) that may be appropriate for a cap on recoverable costs?			
12	What procedure should be adopted for the arbitration, i.e. Art 10 or Art 12 or some adaptation?			

Ref	Issue	Applicant's position	Respondent's position	Arbitrator's notes
13	If Art 10 is to be followed, are written statements of claim and defence to be prepared? If so, in what sequence and by when? What form should they take: e.g. pleadings, or statements with evidence exhibited?			
14	Is there or is there likely to be any application for provisional relief under s. 39 of the Arbitration Act 1996 as restricted by Art 7.2 of the Rules (as the arbitrator's power does not extend to interim injunctions; committal; or jurisdiction over non-parties without their agreement). If so, indicate the nature of the provisional relief likely to be sought.			
15	[If the parties to the arbitration are married] has decree nisi been ordered and, if not, has a date been set?			
16	Are there any preliminary issues or discrete findings of fact which would be more appropriately, conveniently or economically determined prior to a final hearing?			
17	Should there be disclosure/ discovery of documents, and if so, to what extent and by when?			
18	Should there be an oral final (or interim) hearing or is this arbitration suitable for written submissions only?			
19	Any other points of concern or procedural/case management issues that need to be raised at first meeting?			

PART III: EVIDENCE AND EXPERTS

Ref	Issue	Applicant's position	Respondent's position	Arbitrator's notes
21	Are strict rules of evidence to be applied or a more flexible approach adopted?			

Ref	Issue	Applicant's position	Respondent's position	Arbitrator's notes
22	When and how (exchanged simultaneously or sequentially) should witness statements be supplied?			
23	Are expert witnesses to be appointed? If so, what are the terms of reference and what type of declaration (e.g. CPR Part 35 or FPR Part 25) is to be used?			
24	Should the arbitrator appoint an expert to assist him as an assessor (e.g. an accountant)?			
25	Is the arbitrator to receive evidence on oath? If yes, do you have a preference as to swearing (and upon what holy book) or affirming?			
26	How is evidence to be received? E.g. examination-in-chief limited to written statements only or are further questions to be permitted? Is there to be any time limit on cross-examination?			
27	May witnesses be in the hearing room when not giving evidence?			

PART IV: CONTESTED INTERIM AND FINAL HEARINGS

Ref	Issue	Applicant's position	Respondent's position	Arbitrator's notes
28	Where do you wish any oral hearing to take place?			
29	Do you wish to undertake the costs of professional transcription of the final hearing, or any part of it?			
30	Please indicate your estimate of the length of hearing, to include final submissions (unless these are to be delivered in writing subsequently).			
31	How many witnesses do you wish to call? At this stage are you able to state what issue they go to? The parties will need to agree a witness template once this information has been provided.			

Ref	Issue	Applicant's position	Respondent's position	Arbitrator's notes
32	Need for skeleton arguments and/or written openings and/or chronologies and/or statement of issues? What do you suggest?			
33	Bundle format – PD27A?			
34	Do you wish to suggest draft directions? If so, these should be typed on a separate sheet and appended to this document.			
49	Do you wish expressly to exclude the right of appeal on a point of law (an option available under s. 69(1) of the 1996 Act)?			
50	Do you wish to agree to dispense with reasons for the award? (Note that to do so is treated as an agreement to exclude the court's jurisdiction to appeal on a point of law: see s. 69(1): it is strongly urged that the parties should require a reasoned award, so that any court will know the basis upon which the award has been reached.)			
35	Do you (upon payment of the balance then outstanding of the arbitrator's fees and any expenses jointly between the parties) wish to be provided with the award in draft so that you have an opportunity to suggest any factual corrections and any areas you maintain should have been covered in the reasons as then stated? [This provision does not afford the opportunity for further substantive argument upon points which have been determined.]			
36	Who has completed this document and on what date?			
37	If completed by a representative, please confirm your authority to do so on behalf of the party.			

Checklist of matters for discussion at an IFLA Family Arbitration First Meeting/Directions Hearing – Short form

FAMILYARBITRATOR – IFLA FINANCIAL ARBITRATION CHECKLIST

- All parties and proposed arbitrator content with wording in ARB1FS? Has it been signed by/on behalf of all parties?
- All parties and proposed arbitrator signed arbitration agreement?
- Any safeguarding concerns? If so, how will they be managed?
- Any reasonable adjustments required?
- Do any existing court proceedings need to be stayed?
- If parties married, is there a decree nisi or if civil partners is there a conditional order?
- Will a case management appointment be required prior to the substantive arbitration?
- Do any disclosures made by the arbitrator (if relevant) impinge on impartiality? Are they waived or not?
- What procedure is to be adopted? Art 10 or Art 12 of IFLA financial rules (or some adaptation)?
- Do the default IFLA financial rules apply or require any bespoke refinement for hearing (e.g. costs)?
- How should disclosure and receipt of evidence be managed?
- What venue or remote platform?
- If remote platform, who will set up and manage the session?
- Length of hearing estimate and number of witnesses?
- Bundle format PD27A (augmented by Remote Access Family Court Guide (v5) para 20) or Chancery Guide chapter 21, applied in full or some bespoke arrangement?
- Which party to arrange recording of the hearing?
- How is the oath or affirmation to be administered? (Remote Access Family Court Guide (v5) para 5.11 useful for remote hearings)
- Do parties wish to expressly exclude the right of appeal on a point of law? (s.69(1) Arbitration Act 1996)

Suggested letter of engagement for arbitrator to send to the parties – Financial

ARBITRATION – TERMS OF ENGAGEMENT

This letter sets out the terms of engagement upon which [FIRM] will provide my services as family arbitrator under the Institute of Family Law Arbitrators (IFLA) Family Arbitration Scheme. I am a [DETAILS]. Reference to "party" or "parties" is to one or both of you respectively.

If the parties wish to appoint me as arbitrator, please read the terms below carefully and sign where indicated on the final page. Receipt of a copy counter-signed by me will constitute formal acceptance of the appointment for the purposes of rule 4.5 of the IFLA Arbitration Rules (IFLA Rules) and the commencement of the arbitration.

1 **Conduct of the arbitration**

1.1 During the course of the arbitration [FIRM] will make me available to assist the parties on reasonable notice and having regard to my other professional commitments.

1.2 Unless exceptional circumstances arise, I will make my award available to the parties promptly and in any event within 28 days of the conclusion of any final hearing.

2 **Neutrality**

2.1 It is critically important that my neutrality is not put at risk or perceived by either party as being prejudiced. All communications between me or [FIRM] and the parties or their representatives must be transparent and always be copied to all parties.

2.2 No legal advice will be given to the parties. The parties acknowledge that it is open to them to take independent legal advice in respect of all matters pertaining to the arbitration.

2.3 We have carried out conflict checks and I can confirm that I am able to accept the appointment. However, there may be circumstances where I would be unable to continue with the appointment. This might happen where:

- 2.3.1 a conflict of interest, or a significant risk of the same, arises between [FIRM] (or an existing [FIRM] client) and any of the parties;
- 2.3.2 by continuing with the appointment I would be professionally embarrassed.

3 **Confidentiality**

3.1 Arbitration proceedings are confidential and [FIRM] is used to dealing with cases confidentially and to taking effective steps to preserve that confidentiality.

3.2 We will keep confidential all information provided to us in connection with the arbitration unless:

- 3.2.1 we are required or permitted to disclose it by law, or by any regulatory or fiscal authorities, in which case (and to the extent that we are permitted to do so) we will endeavour to give the parties as much advance notice as possible of any such required disclosure;
- 3.2.2 we are authorised in writing by all parties to the arbitration to disclose it;
- 3.2.3 the information is in or comes into the public domain without any breach of confidentiality by us.

3.3 We may disclose confidential information provided to us in connection with the arbitration to:

- 3.3.1 our auditors, external assessors or other advisers; or
- 3.3.2 our insurers for the purposes of our professional indemnity insurance renewal or in order to assist us to comply with the terms of our professional indemnity insurance cover.

3.4 If at any time a third party requests access to documents held by us or asks to interview us in connection with the work undertaken, we may be required as a matter of law to comply with this request. Any fees, disbursements and expenses incurred in dealing with any such request, including the fees, disbursements and expenses involved in identifying relevant documents, attending interviews or making or defending any application in connection with the validity of the request, will be charged in accordance with the provisions above relating to fees, disbursements and expenses.

3.5 We shall be permitted to make and retain copies of the arbitration papers and of any written material produced by the parties, subject to our duty of confidentiality.

3.6 On occasion we will use external agencies to undertake typing, printing, photocopying and other business support services. Before doing so we ensure that appropriate safeguards are in place to protect confidentiality.

4 **Data protection and our use of your information**

4.1 The way in which we use your personal data is regulated by data protection legislation in addition to our professional duty of confidentiality. Our up-to-date privacy notice is available [DETAILS]. We may amend our privacy notice periodically to ensure that it is operating effectively and complies with relevant laws and regulations. Where you provide any personal data to us (including that of third parties involved in the matter), you are responsible for ensuring that disclosure by you or on your behalf to us for the use by us in the provision of our services complies with the requirements of data protection legislation. You have the sole responsibility for the accuracy quality and legality of the personal data you provide to us.

5 **Booking and diary arrangements**

5.1 Arrangements for hearings should be either made directly with me or a member of my office.

6 **Meeting your needs**

6.1 As a firm, we are committed to catering to the specific needs of our clients. If there are adjustments we can put in place to support you during this matter, please let me know.

Below are some examples of common adjustments we can make, though this is by no means an exhaustive list and you will be best placed to tell us what you need:

- For letters and emails – large font or adjustments to text/paper colour.
- For meetings in our offices – hearing loops, accessible parking and meeting rooms.
- For remote meetings – subtitles and/or transcripts, changes to backgrounds.
- For phone calls – avoiding non-urgent calls during rest periods or work/care responsibilities.
- For all communications – translations or BSL remote interpreter support.

Some clients also find they have a preferred method of communication with us (eg, hard copy letters, emails, or phone calls). If you find one method works best for you, please bring this to our attention at any time.

7 **Fees**

7.1 I normally charge for my work on a daily rate for final hearings and an hourly basis for other hearings (whether by telephone or personal attendance), reading and preparation and writing the award.

7.2 My hourly rate is [£[ ] + VAT.]

7.3 My daily rate is [£[ ]+VAT], which unless otherwise agreed in advance by me and the parties will be charged for any hearing that is scheduled to last for three hours or more, whether or not it does so.

7.4 When a hearing date has been fixed I enter it into my diary, together with the appropriate number of additional days for award-writing. If those dates are cancelled, we reserve the right to charge a cancellation fee of the following percentage of the fees that would have been payable had the hearing proceeded:

- 7.4.1 if cancelled with one week's notice or more, 25% of the estimated hearing time;
- 7.4.2 if cancelled with less than one week's notice, 50% of the estimated hearing time.

7.5 In many cases I will be able to agree a fixed fee for all or part of the work involved. For example, I may agree a fixed fee for a hearing to include anticipated preparation for that hearing and the writing of the award. The work to be covered by any fixed fee will be set out clearly in writing by me. Where a fixed fee is not agreed, I will provide an estimate of anticipated cost based on the information provided in the ARB1 and in the initial scoping discussions.

8 **Disbursements and expenses**

8.1 As well as the fees for the time I spend on the arbitration, disbursements and expenses may also be charged. Disbursements are items which we pass on with no extra charge and may include travel, accommodation, venue and recording charges and courier fees. Expenses are items we do make an additional charge for and may include photocopying charges, special bank transaction costs and any communication costs such as video-link or international phone charges.

8.2 Chargeable disbursements and expenses are payable on receipt of [FIRM'S] invoice.

9 **Value Added Tax**

9.1 Where appropriate, Value Added Tax is added to the above fees, disbursements and expenses at the rate prevailing when the work/disbursement is billed.

10 **Joint and several liability for fees**

10.1 Each of the parties to the arbitration is jointly and severally liable to [FIRM] for the whole of our fees, disbursements and expenses in connection with this arbitration.

10.2 I shall be entitled, at any time, to direct the provision within a reasonable time of reasonable security for our fees, disbursements and expenses.

11 **Billing and the time when fees are payable**

11.1 We reserve the right to bill fees, disbursements and expenses from time to time during the course of the arbitration. Billing will be in arrears, but will not be more frequent than monthly.

11.2 Unless otherwise agreed, payment is to be made either:

- 11.2.1 In the case of a fixed fee being agreed, within 7 days of the fee being agreed; or
- 11.2.2 Where there is no fixed fee agreed, as a pre-condition to delivery of the award;

We reserve the right to ask for a payment on account.

11.3 Cancellation fees are payable within 10 days after the first of the cancelled days.

11.4 [FIRM] does not accept any payment in cash. If this policy is avoided by depositing cash directly with our bank, we may decide to charge for any additional checks we decide are necessary to prove the source of the funds.

11.5 All bills must be paid in sterling. If bills are not paid in sterling and we incur currency conversion charges or other bank charges, or we suffer exchange-rate losses, we reserve the right to charge additional sums to cover such items.

11.6 Where we receive money from you which is to be applied on your behalf (including payments on account), it will (unless agreed otherwise with you) be held in our general client account which is subject to the strict provisions of the Solicitors' Accounts Rules ("SAR") which can be found at www.sra.org.uk. Subject always to the SAR we are not responsible for any loss arising from the insolvency of any bank where funds are held. If we make a claim under the Financial Services Compensation Scheme (FSCS) in respect of money which we hold for you, you agree that we may give certain information about you to the FSCS to help them identify amounts to which you are entitled in our client account.

11.7 As required by the SAR, money held by us will be taken in payment or part payment of our invoices within 14 days of the date of the invoice, unless that money is held for any other purpose. You agree that we can retain monies against unbilled and unpaid disbursements.

11.8 We are required to account to you for interest on any balance(s) we hold on your behalf, when it is fair and reasonable to do so in all the circumstances in order to achieve a fair outcome. A full version of our policy is available on request or from [DETAILS].

11.9 If you have any problems with a bill please see the guidance in paragraph 19 ("Complaints handling") below. In addition, you have a right to object to a bill by applying to the court for an assessment of the bill under Part III of the Solicitors Act 1974. If you apply to the court, the Legal Ombudsman (see paragraph 19 below for details) may decide not to deal with a complaint about the bill.

12 <u>Failure to comply with the payment provisions</u>

12.1 Failure to pay billed fees in full by the date agreed gives rise to a right on our part to cease further work on the arbitration, or to decline to deliver the award as provided in rule 13.5 of the IFLA Rules. These rights are in addition to any other right that I or [FIRM] may have under these terms, the terms of the IFLA Rules and/or the general law.

12.2 If a bill (or part of a bill) remains unpaid beyond the time for payment set out above, we reserve the right to charge interest at the rate applicable to judgment debts until payment is made.

12.3 If a third party agrees to be responsible for payment of some or all of our fees, disbursements and expenses on your behalf, and payment is not made in accordance with these terms, you will be responsible for paying to us any outstanding amount.

13 Resignation

13.1 I reserve the right to terminate the arbitration by resignation in writing at any point in any of the following circumstances

- 13.1.1 if a conflict of interest arises;
- 13.1.2 if I would be professionally embarrassed if I continued to act
- 13.1.3 if any other circumstances arise that result in me determining that I am unable to discharge my duties as an arbitrator

13.2 In the event that I exercise that right to resign, our fees, disbursements and expenses shall be due in full up to the date of resignation, and upon such resignation I shall not be liable to the parties in any way.

14 Anti-money laundering

14.1 To comply with the law, we need to get evidence of the parties' identities as soon as possible. Where the parties are represented by solicitors we will obtain confirmation from the parties' representatives that they have undertaken the necessary checks and that we may rely on those checks. If the parties are unrepresented we will need to obtain the appropriate evidence and will let you know what forms of evidence (if any) we need from you.

14.2 In order to comply with its statutory obligations, the firm operates an anti-money laundering reporting procedure. If the firm knows or suspects that you (or any other party) are involved in money laundering or hold the proceeds of crime, the firm may be required by law to make a report to the National Crime Agency (NCA) and if notification is made, the firm is prohibited from advising the suspected party that it is doing so. These requirements override the firm's duty of confidentiality to you.

14.3 Proceeds of crime are assets or income which have been acquired through some illegal activity, for example drug-trafficking, non-payment of tax or fraudulently obtaining benefits. If a report is made to NCA, the firm must stop work on the matter until it is authorised by NCA to proceed.

14.4 Any fees, disbursements and expenses incurred in complying with the above will be charged to the parties. There may be circumstances in which the firm considers that it is obliged to make a report to NCA which it later turns out was not required by law. By instructing the firm you agree that such reports can be made. The firm cannot accept responsibility or liability for any loss, damage or expense (whether direct, consequential or otherwise) arising from any delay or otherwise as a result of making any reports to NCA and ensuring compliance with its statutory obligations.

15 **Limitation of liability**

15.1 Subject always to any claim of immunity from suit, the liability of [FIRM] for any claim in contract, tort, negligence, for breach of statutory duty or otherwise, for any loss or damage, costs, expenses or any contractual or statutory interest howsoever caused arising out of or in connection with the services provided shall, in relation to each matter, be limited to the sum of £[X].

15.2 [FIRM] alone will provide the services and this agreement is solely with [FIRM]. The parties to the arbitration agree that they will not bring any claim whether in contract, tort, negligence, for breach of statutory duty or otherwise against any service company owned or controlled by or on behalf of [FIRM] or any of the members of [FIRM] or against any member of, consultant to, or employee or agent of [FIRM] or of any service company owned or controlled by or on behalf of [FIRM] or any of the members of [FIRM]. Those service companies, members, consultants, employees and agents assume no personal liability for the provision of services and shall be entitled to rely on these terms insofar as they limit or exclude their liability.

15.3 We shall not be liable for any indirect loss or damage or any loss of profit, income, anticipated savings, production or accruals arising in any circumstances whatsoever, whether in contract, tort, negligence, for breach of statutory duty or otherwise, and howsoever caused.

15.4 Nothing in these terms shall exclude or restrict our liability for death or personal injury resulting from our negligence or for fraudulent misrepresentation or in any other circumstances where liability may not be so limited or excluded under any applicable law or regulation.

16 **Electronic communication**

16.1 Unless otherwise directed by the parties, I may correspond by means of electronic mail, the parties agreeing:

- 16.1.1 to accept the risks of using electronic mail, including but not limited to the risks of viruses, interception and unauthorised access;
- 16.1.2 to use commercially reasonable procedures to maintain security of electronic mail;
- 16.1.3 to check for commonly known viruses in information sent and received electronically;
- 16.1.4 that [FIRM] and I shall not be responsible for any loss or damage arising from the unauthorised interception, re-direction, copying or reading of emails including any attachments;
- 16.1.5 that [FIRM] and I shall not be responsible for the effect on any hardware or software (or any loss or damage arising from such effect) of any emails or attachment which may be transmitted by us (except where this is caused by our negligence or wilful default).

17 **Data protection**

17.1 [FIRM] is a data controller for the purposes of the Data Protection Act 1998 and is bound by that Act (amongst other considerations) to take appropriate technical and organisational measures against unauthorised processing of personal data and against accidental loss or destruction of, or damage to, personal data.

17.2 We are entitled to process (which includes obtaining, consulting, holding, using and disclosing) personal data of the parties to conduct the arbitration, to produce management data, to prevent crime, to comply with regulatory requirements and as permitted or required by law.

17.3 The parties each have a right of access and a right of correction in respect of their personal data which I and [FIRM] hold about them, in accordance with data protection legislation.

18 **Intellectual property rights**

18.1 We retain full and exclusive ownership of all copyright and all other intellectual property rights in my awards and directions, including all documents, reports, or other materials (in any form including, without limitation, in electronic form) ("work product") we create, develop or generate in the course of providing the services. We now grant the parties and their representatives a non-exclusive, non-transferable, non-sublicensable licence to use the work product for the particular arbitration and the particular purpose for which it is prepared. If the parties or their representatives wish to use copies of the work product for purposes other than those for which it is prepared, this will require express written permission.

19 **Complaints**

19.1 We have a complaints procedure, a copy of which is available on request (or at [DETAILS)]). We will endeavour to deal with any complaint as soon as practicable. If we are unable to resolve your complaint to your satisfaction within eight weeks of receiving full details of your complaint, you may have the right to refer the issue to the Legal Ombudsman at PO Box 6806, Wolverhampton, WV1 9WJ or by email to enquiries@legalombudsman.org.uk. Normally, you will need to bring a complaint to the Legal Ombudsman within six months of receiving a final written response from us about your complaint or within six years of the act or omission about which you are complaining occurring (or if outside of this period, within three years of when you should reasonably have been aware of it). The act or omission, or when you should reasonably have known there was cause for complaint, must have been after 5 October 2010. Please note that the Legal Ombudsman may consider complaints from prospective clients in certain circumstances but may decline to deal with complaints from certain types of clients. For further information you should contact the Legal Ombudsman on 0300 555 0333 or go to www.legalombudsman.org.uk.

20 **Waiver**

20.1 Except where expressly stated, nothing done or omitted to be done by me, [FIRM] or the parties constitutes a waiver of my or that party's rights under these terms of engagement.

21 **Severability**

21.1 If any provision of these terms of engagement is found by any court of competent jurisdiction to be illegal, invalid or otherwise unenforceable then that provision shall, to the extent necessary, be severed and shall be ineffective but without affecting the other provisions of these terms of engagement which will remain in full force and effect.

22 **Exclusion of rights of third parties**

22.1 Subject to 15.2 above, no third party shall have any right under the Contracts (Rights of Third Parties) Act 1999 to enforce any of the terms in this letter.

23 **Entire agreement**

23.1 The provisions of these terms of engagement may be varied if, but only if, expressly agreed by the parties and/or their representatives and by [FIRM] in writing (including by exchange of emails).

23.2 Subject to paragraph 23.1 these terms of engagement, incorporating these provisions, comprises the entire agreement between the parties to the exclusion of all other terms and conditions and prior or collateral agreements, negotiations, notices of intention and representations and the parties agree that they have not been induced to enter into the agreement on the basis of any representation.

24 **Governing law, jurisdiction and dispute resolution**

24.1 These terms of engagement are governed by and will be construed in accordance with the law of England and Wales.

24.2 Unless any alternative dispute resolution procedure is agreed between the parties, the parties agree to submit to the exclusive jurisdiction of the courts of England and Wales in respect of any dispute which arises out of or under these terms of engagement.

25 **Status disclosure and definitions**

25.1 [FIRM] provides legal services in England & Wales, is authorised and regulated by the Solicitors Regulation Authority (number [X]) and is subject to the SRA Code of Conduct 2011, which can be viewed at www.sra.org.uk/solicitors/handbook/code. [FIRM] maintains professional indemnity insurance in accordance with the rules of the Solicitors Regulation Authority. Details of the insurer and the territorial coverage of the policy are available for inspection at our offices.

25.2 In this letter references to "we", "us", "our", "firm" and "[FIRM]" mean or refer to [FIRM] (a limited liability partnership registered in England and Wales with registered number [X] and VAT number [X] whose registered office is at [ADDRESS] and any successor practice and any service company owned or controlled by or on behalf of [FIRM] or any of its members and, as the context requires, all members of, consultants to and employees and agents of, [FIRM] and of any service company owned or controlled by or on behalf of [FIRM] or any of its members.

26 **Payment Methods**

Payment of monies on account can be made using one of the following methods:

1 By cheque, made payable to [FIRM].

2 By BACS payment to the account set out below, using the reference at the top of this letter:

[DETAILS]

3 Over the telephone, by credit or debit card. Please call [NUMBER] to make the payment, quoting the reference at the top of this letter and informing the operator that you wish to pay for a fixed fee initial consultation.

Conclusion

Please do not hesitate to call me if you have any queries about the contents of this letter and/or the terms of engagement. Before I can assist you further, I should be grateful if you would print, sign and date a copy of both this letter and the Agreement to Commence Work and return them to me as soon as possible by scan and email, post or fax.

Please do not hesitate to contact me if you have any queries about the terms of engagement set out above.

NOTICE OF THE RIGHT TO CANCEL

The Consumer Contracts (Information, Cancellation and Additional Charges) Regulations 2013 give you the right to cancel your agreement with the firm, without giving any reason, at any time during the 14 days immediately following the day that you return the copy of this letter duly signed (which is the day when the contract between us is concluded).

If you wish to exercise the right to cancel, please let me know of your decision to cancel this contract by a clear statement (eg, a letter sent to me by post, fax or email). My contact details are at the top of this letter. You can use the attached form, headed “Cancellation form”, if you wish but you do not have to do so. To meet the cancellation deadline, it is sufficient for you to send your communication concerning your exercise of the right to cancel before the cancellation period has expired.

If you would like me to commence work before the end of the cancellation period, please complete the attached form, headed "Agreement to commence work", when signing and returning the copy of this letter of engagement, or later if appropriate. This may mean you lose the right to cancel.

You will be required to pay for the services provided to you, with your written agreement, before the end of the cancellation period.

Please note that up until the point at which the arbitration formally starts (from which point neither party to the arbitration can withdraw from the process without the consent of the other (you have the right to instruct me to stop work at any time) whether during or after the cancellation period).

Yours sincerely

[ ]

[DETAILS] and Family Arbitrator

for [FIRM]

I confirm acceptance of the terms of engagement set out above and that I wish to appoint [ ] as family arbitrator in accordance with the above terms of engagement.

Signed by [client 1] ....

(print name)

....

(signed)

Dated

I confirm acceptance of the terms of engagement set out above and that I wish to appoint [ ] as family arbitrator in accordance with the above terms of engagement.

Signed by [client 2] ....

(print name)

....

(signed)

....

Dated

SIGNATURE OF ARBITRATOR

Signed by [ ]..

Family Arbitrator (print name)

....

(signed)

....

Dated

CANCELLATION FORM

If you wish to cancel the contract it is preferable if you do so in writing and deliver personally or send (which may be by electronic mail) this to the person named below. You may use this form if you wish to do so, but you do not have to.

(Complete and return this form ONLY IF YOU WISH TO CANCEL THE CONTRACT.)

To: [ ]

[insert office address]

I hereby give notice that I cancel my contract with [FIRM] for legal services, as detailed in the letter of engagement dated [DATE].

Signed: ....

Name and address: ....

....

....

Date: ....

Signed: ....

Name and address: ....

....

....

....

Date: ....

AGREEMENT TO COMMENCE WORK

To: [ ]

[FIRM]

[insert office address]

I agree to the commencement of the performance of the contract for legal services, as detailed in the letter of engagement (a copy of which is attached to this notice), before the cancellation period has expired and I will pay the fees, as set out in the letter of engagement. I acknowledge that this means the right to cancel may be lost.

Signed: ....

Name and address: ....

....

....

Date: ....

Signed: ....

Name and address: ....

....

....

Date: ....

Final Award Checklist – Financial

Set out below are some suggested headings and a format for a Final Award in a Financial case. It is not necessary to follow this exact format but it would be helpful to make sure that all of the matters set out below have been considered somewhere in the Award.

GENERAL INTRODUCTION

- Formalities
- Headings
- Reference to the Arbitration Act 1996
- Reference to the IFLA Scheme (Financial)
- Reference to parties' names
- Heading of the document in tramlines

GENERAL BACKGROUND

- Identifying
  - Parties/relationship
  - Dispute/issues – what is it that the parties are asking the arbitrator to decide?
  - Arbitration agreement – Form ARB1FS – when was it signed?
  - Appointment of arbitrator
  - Acceptance by arbitrator of appointment
  - Procedure adopted – oral hearings, telephone hearings, when and briefly what was decided
  - Place and date of hearing
  - Representation – Solicitors/Counsel
- Summary of the background in narrative form

GENERAL ANALYSIS

- Identifying common ground between the parties
- Identifying issues and points that will need to be decided by the arbitrator
- Evaluating the evidence/arguments – consideration of all that the arbitrator heard during the Final Hearing

- Knowledge of law and application – statutes/cases referred to and consideration by the arbitrator as to their relevance and arbitrator's view on the law. Remember to consider the Section 25 checklist if appropriate and any specific cases referred to in the arbitration.
- Conclusion on issues – what does the arbitrator think should happen bearing in mind all of the considerations above?

AWARD

- Heading/dated/signed
- Orders – financial
- Costs – will the normal rules of arbitration apply or will there be a change in relation to the costs position?
- Arbitrator's fees shared/reimbursement to one of the parties
- Schedule of Agreement (if any)

TO CONSIDER

- In a financial case it is a good idea to include the asset schedule and the net effect schedule and to cross check that all of the assets listed in the asset schedule have been dealt with in the Award

Final Determination Checklist – Children

FINAL AWARD CHECKLIST

General Introduction

- Formalities
- Headings
- Arbitration Act 1996
- IFLA Scheme (Children or Financial)
- Identifying:
  - Parties/relationship
  - Dispute/issues
  - Arbitration Agreement
  - Appointment
  - Acceptance
  - Procedure adopted
  - Place and date of hearing
  - Representation/Solicitors/Counsel
- Summary of background

General analysis

- Identifying common ground
- Identifying issues
- Evaluating evidence/arguments
- Knowledge of law and application
- Conclusion on issues

Award/Determination

- Heading/dated/signed
- Orders – financial or children
- Costs – order?

- Arbitrators fees shared/reimbursement
- Schedule of Agreement (if any)

To consider

- Financial Award – include asset schedule and net effect schedule
- Children determination – note re safeguarding, the voice of the child and the no order principle

Suggested letter to the Family Court enclosing a consent order incorporating the terms of an arbitral award

Dear Court

Request for approval of a consent order pursuant to [LEGISLATION] following an arbitration conducted under the IFLA Family Law Arbitration Scheme

We represent [CLIENT]. [OTHER PARTY'S SOLICITORS] represent [OTHER PARTY].

[CLIENT] and [OTHER PARTY] have used the IFLA Family Law Arbitration Scheme to resolve the issues between them. We are pleased to confirm that the arbitrator has issued their [AWARD] [DETERMINATION]. The parties wish to have this decision converted into a consent order.

Please find enclosed:

1. The [AWARD] [DETERMINATION] dated [DATE].
2. A signed consent order as agreed between the parties and which reflects the terms of the [AWARD] [DETERMINATION].
3. [FORM ARB1FS] [FORMARB1CS]
4. [FORM A and FORM D81]

Please take the court fee of £[X] from PBA account [NUMBER].

Thank you for your assistance.

ANNEX B

Recitals for use where "omnibus" orders to reflect an arbitral award are sought for either Financial Remedy or Children Act Schedule 1 Final Orders

For the Financial Remedy Final Order Omnibus:

…

Arbitration award recital 19.

a. The documents lodged in relation to this application include the parties' arbitration agreement (Form ARB1), their Form(s) D81, a copy of the arbitrator's award, and a draft of the order which the court is requested to make.

b. By their Form ARB1 the parties agreed to refer to arbitration the issues described in it which include some or all of the financial remedies for which applications are pending in this court. The issues were referred to [insert arbitrator] under the IFLA scheme, who made an arbitral award on [insert date].

c. ***Either:***

[The parties have invited the court to make an order in agreed terms which reflects the arbitrator's award.] ***or:***

[There has been no agreement between the parties as to the form of an order to give effect to the arbitrator's award. The [applicant]/[respondent] has applied for the other party to show why an order should not be made in the terms of the draft proposed; and the court having considered the representations made by each party has directed that an order be made in the terms of this order.]

For the Children Act Schedule 1 Final Order Omnibus:

…

Arbitration award recital 18.

a. The documents lodged in relation to this application include the parties' arbitration agreement (Form ARB1), their Form(s) D81, a copy of the arbitrator's award, and a draft of the order which the court is requested to make.

b. By their Form ARB1 the parties agreed to refer to arbitration the issues described in it which encompass the application under Schedule 1 to the Children Act 1989 now pending in this court. The issues were referred to [insert arbitrator] under the IFLA scheme, who made an arbitral award on [insert date].

c. ***Either:***

[The parties have invited the court to make an order in agreed terms which reflects the arbitrator's award.] ***or:***

[There has been no agreement between the parties as to the form of an order to give effect to the arbitrator's award. The [applicant]/[respondent] has applied for the other party to show why an order should not be made in the terms of the draft proposed; and the court having considered the representations made by each party has directed that an order be made in the terms of this order.

Order to stay or adjourn proceedings for arbitration under the Court's case management powers

Order 6.1: Stay or Adjourn Proceedings for Arbitration under the Court's Case Management Powers

In the Family Court sitting at [*Court name*]

No: [*Case number*]

The Family Procedure Rules 2010 rules 2.3 and 3.3

The [Marriage] / [Relationship] / [Family] of [*applicant name*] and [*respondent name*]

(Adapt As Necessary)

After hearing [*name the advocates(s) who appeared*]

After consideration of the documents lodged by the parties

(In the case of an order made without notice) After reading the statements and hearing the witness(es) specified in the Recitals below

ORDER MADE BY [*NAME OF JUDGE*] ON [*DATE*] SITTING IN [OPEN COURT] / [PRIVATE]

THE PARTIES

1. The applicant is [*applicant name*]

   The respondent is [*respondent name*]

   [The second respondent is [*name*]]

   (Specify if any party acts by a litigation friend)

DEFINITIONS

2. IFLA is the Institute of Family Law Arbitrators.

3. Form ARB1FS is the arbitration agreement signed by the parties of which a copy has been lodged with the court.

4. The arbitration is an arbitration which is to be conducted in accordance with the rules of the IFLA arbitration scheme.

RECITALS

5. **(In the case of an order made without notice)**

   a. This order was made at a hearing without notice to the respondent. The reason why the order was made without notice to the respondent was [*set out*].

   b. The Judge read the following affidavits/witness statements [*set out*] and heard oral testimony from [*name*].

6. **(In the case of an order made following the giving of short informal notice)**

   This order was made at a hearing without full notice having been given to the respondent. The reason why the order was made without full notice having been given to the respondent was [*set out*].

7. The [applicant] / [respondent] has applied to this court for financial remedies.

8. The court must by rules 3.2 and 3.3 of the Family Procedure Rules 2010 at every stage in proceedings consider whether alternative dispute resolution is appropriate and, if so, whether to adjourn those proceedings so to enable alternative dispute resolution to take place; and has power pursuant to its general powers of management under rule 4.1 to stay the whole or any part of proceedings either generally or until a specified date or event.

AGREEMENTS

9. By their Form ARB1FS the parties have agreed to refer to arbitration the issues described in it which include some or all of the financial remedies for which applications are pending in this court.

UNDERTAKINGS TO THE COURT

10. [*Set out*]

IT IS ORDERED (BY CONSENT) THAT:

11. The pending application[s] for financial remedies [is] / [are] [stayed] / [adjourned] pending receipt of the award in the arbitration (or until the

parties may reach agreement in respect of the arbitration issues) [or until [*specify date or event*]] or further order meanwhile.

12. Upon receipt of the award (or upon reaching agreement) either party may in a form agreed with the other seek an order of this court to give effect to the award (or their agreement).
13. **(Or if the parties cannot reach agreement upon the form of an order to give effect to the award)** Failing agreement between the parties as to the form of an order to give effect to the award either party may apply for the other to show why an order should not be made in the terms of the draft proposed.
14. Any application under either of the preceding 2 paragraphs shall be lodged together with a copy of the award, Form(s) D81 and with a draft of the order which the court is requested to make.
15. **(Provision for the costs of the stay application)**

Dated [*date*]

(Where undertakings have been given)

Notice

You [*applicant name*, and you [*respondent name*], may be sent to prison for contempt of court if you break the promises that have been given to the court

Statement of understanding

I understand the undertakings that I have given, and that if I break any of my promises to the court I may be sent to prison for contempt of court

____

[*applicant name*]

I understand the undertakings that I have given, and that if I break any of my promises to the court I may be sent to prison for contempt of court

____

[*respondent name*]

Order to stay proceedings pursuant to section 9 Arbitration Act 1996 or the Court's case management powers

ANNEX A

Stay pursuant to Arbitration Act 1996 section 9 and/or under the court's case management powers

In the Family Court Sitting at [Place] No:

The Family Procedure Rules 2010 rules 3.2 and 3.3

The Marriage/Civil Partnership/Relationship/Family of XX and YY

After hearing [*name the advocate(s) who appeared*]

After consideration of the documents lodged by the parties

(In the case of an order made without notice) After reading the statements and hearing the witnesses specified in the Recitals below

ORDER MADE BY [NAME OF JUDGE] ON [DATE] SITTING IN OPEN COURT/PRIVATE

The parties

1. The applicant is XX

   The respondent is YY

   The second respondent is ZZ

   Specify if any party acts by a litigation friend

[*Where undertakings have been given*]

Notice pursuant to PD 37A para 2.1

You XX, and you YY, may be held to be in contempt of court and imprisoned or fined, or your assets may be seized, if you break the promises that you have given to the court.

Statement pursuant to PD 37A para 2.2

I understand the undertaking that I have given and that if I break any of my promises to the court I may be sent to prison, or fined, or my assets may be seized, for contempt of court.

....

XX

I understand the undertaking that I have given and that if I break any of my promises to the court I may be sent to prison, or fined, or my assets may be seized, for contempt of court.

....

YY

Definitions

2. IFLA is the Institute of Family Law Arbitrators.

3. Form ARB1 is the arbitration agreement signed by the parties of which a copy has been lodged with the court.

4. The arbitration is an arbitration which is to be conducted in accordance with the rules of the IFLA arbitration scheme.

Recitals

5. *(In the case of an order made without notice)*

   (a) This order was made at a hearing without notice to the respondent. The reason why the order was made without notice to the respondent was [*set out*]

   (b) The Judge read the following affidavits/witness statements [*set out*] and heard oral testimony from [*name*].

6. *(In the case of an order made following the giving of short informal notice)*

   This order was made at a hearing without full notice having been given to the respondent. The reason why the order was made without full notice having been given to the respondent was [*set out*].

7. The applicant/respondent has applied to this court for financial remedies.

8. The court must by rules 3.2 and 3.3 of the Family Procedure Rules 2010 at every stage in proceedings consider whether alternative dispute resolution is appropriate and, if so, whether to adjourn those proceedings so to enable alternative dispute resolution to take place; and has power pursuant to its general powers of management under rule 4.1 to stay the whole or any part of proceedings either generally or until a specified date or event.

…

Agreements

9. By their Form ARB1 the parties have agreed to refer to arbitration the issues described in it which include some or all of the financial remedies for which applications are pending in this court.

10. …

Undertakings to the court

11. …

12. …

IT IS ORDERED (BY CONSENT) THAT:

13. The pending application(*s*) for financial remedies is/*are* stayed pending receipt of the award in the arbitration (or until the parties may reach agreement in respect of the arbitration issues).

14. Upon receipt of the award (or upon reaching agreement) either party may in a form agreed with the other seek an order of this court to give effect to the award (or their agreement).

15. [*or if the parties cannot reach agreement upon the form of an order to give effect to the award*] Failing agreement between the parties as to the form of an order to give effect to the award either party may apply for the other to show why an order should not be made in the terms of the draft proposed.

16. Any application under either of the preceding 2 paragraphs shall be lodged together with a copy of the award, Form(s) D81 and with a draft of the order which the court is requested to make.

17. [*Provision for the costs of the stay application*]

Dated

Enforcement of arbitrator's peremptory order under section 42 Arbitration Act 1996

Enforcement of an arbitrator's peremptory order under Arbitration Act 1996 s42

In the Family Court Sitting at [Place] No:

The Arbitration Act 1996 section 42

The Marriage/Civil Partnership/Relationship/Family of XX and YY

After hearing [*name the advocate(s) who appeared*]

After consideration of the documents lodged by the parties

(In the case of an order made without notice)

After reading the statements and hearing the witnesses specified in the recitals below

ORDER MADE BY [NAME OF JUDGE] ON [DATE] SITTING IN OPEN COURT/PRIVATE

The parties

1. The applicant is XX

   The respondent is YY

   The second respondent is ZZ

   Specify if any party acts by a litigation friend

[*Where undertakings have been given*]

Notice pursuant to PD 37A para 2.1

You XX, and you YY, may be held to be in contempt of court and imprisoned or fined, or your assets may be seized, if you break the promises that you have given to the court.

Statement pursuant to PD 37A para 2.2

I understand the undertaking that I have given and that if I break any of my promises to the court I may be sent to prison, or fined, or my assets may be seized, for contempt of court.

....

XX

I understand the undertaking that I have given and that if I break any of my promises to the court I may be sent to prison, or fined, or my assets may be seized, for contempt of court.

....

YY

Definitions

2. IFLA is the Institute of Family Law Arbitrators.

3. Form ARB1 is the arbitration agreement signed by the parties of which a copy has been lodged with the court.

4. The arbitration is an arbitration which is to be conducted in accordance with the rules of the IFLA arbitration scheme.

5. The arbitrator is [*name*].

6. The arbitrator's order is a peremptory order made on [*date*] pursuant to section 41(5) of the Arbitration Act 1996 which required the respondent to comply with its terms [by [*date*]] *or* [without prescribing a date for compliance].

Recitals

7. *(In the case of an order made without notice)*

   (a) This order was made at a hearing without notice to the respondent. The reason why the order was made without notice to the respondent was [*set out*]

   (b) The Judge read the following affidavits/witness statements [*set out*] and heard oral testimony from [*name*]

8. *(In the case of an order made following the giving of short informal notice)*

This order was made at a hearing without full notice having been given to the respondent. The reason why the order was made without full notice having been given to the respondent was [*set out*]

9. *(In the case of an application commenced elsewhere than in the Family Court)*

   This application was transferred to this court from the [*specify*] Division/ Court by order of [*name of judge*] on [*date*].

10. The arbitration has commenced and is continuing.

11. The parties have by their Form ARB1 and their acceptance of the IFLA arbitration scheme rules agreed that the powers of the court under section 42 of the Arbitration Act 1996 (enforcement of peremptory orders of tribunal) are available, so mat if one of them fails to comply with a peremptory order made by the arbitrator then another party may apply to the court for an order requiring compliance.

12. The arbitrator's order is (so far as relevant to this application) in the following terms:

    [*set out in the words of the arbitrator's order*]

13. This application is for an order under section 42 of the Arbitration Act 1996 for the enforcement of the arbitrator's order and is made:

    [by the applicant.] *(or)*

    [by the arbitrator, upon notice to the parties.]

14. This court is satisfied that:
    (a) the applicant has exhausted all available arbitral process in respect of the respondent's failure to comply with that/*those* provision(*s*) of the peremptory order; and
    (b) the respondent has failed to comply with that/*those* provision(*s*) of the peremptory order [within the time prescribed by the order] *or* [within a reasonable time, no time for compliance having been prescribed].

Agreements

15. …

Undertakings to the court

16. …

IT IS ORDERED (BY CONSENT):

17. The respondent shall comply with the peremptory order by no later than [*date*].

[*or*]

18. [*Other orders*]

19. [*If applied for*] Permission to appeal against this decision is granted/*refused.*

20. [*Provision for costs*]

Dated

Order seeking the attendance of witnesses under section 43 Arbitration Act 1996

Order securing the attendance of witnesses under Arbitration Act 1996 s43

In the Family Court Sitting at [Place] No:

The Arbitration Act 1996 section 43

The Marriage/Civil Partnership/Relationship/Family of XX and YY

After hearing [*name the advocate(s) who appeared*]

After consideration of the documents lodged by the parties

(In the case of an order made without notice)

After reading the statements and hearing the witnesses specified in the recitals below

ORDER MADE BY [NAME OF JUDGE] ON [DATE] SITTING IN OPEN COURT/PRIVATE

The parties

1. The applicant is XX

   The respondent is YY

   The second respondent is ZZ

   Specify if any party acts by a litigation friend

[*Where undertakings have been given*]

Notice pursuant to PD 37A para 2.1

You XX, and you YY, may be held to be in contempt of court and imprisoned or fined, or your assets may be seized, if you break the promises that you have given to the court.

Statement pursuant to PD 37A para 2.2

I understand the undertaking that I have given and that if I break any of my promises to the court I may be sent to prison, or fined, or my assets may be seized, for contempt of court.

………

XX

I understand, the undertaking that I have given and that if I break any of my promises to the court I may be sent to prison, or fined, or my assets may be seized, for contempt of court.

………

YY

Definitions

2. IFLA is the Institute of Family Law Arbitrators.

3. Form ARB1 is the arbitration agreement signed by the parties of which a copy has been lodged with the court.

4. The arbitration is an arbitration which is to be conducted in accordance with the rules of the IFLA arbitration scheme.

5. The arbitrator is [*name*].

6. The witness/*witnesses* is/*are* [*name(s)*]

Recitals

7. *(In the case of an order made without notice)*

   (a) This order was made at a hearing without notice to the respondent. The reason why the order was made without notice to the respondent was [*set out*]

   (b) The Judge read the following affidavits/witness statements [*set out*] and heard oral testimony from [*name*]

8. *(In the case of an order made following the giving of short informal notice)*

   This order was made at a hearing without full notice having been given to the respondent. The reason why the order was made without full notice having been given to the respondent was [*set out*]

9. *(In the case of an application commenced elsewhere than in the Family Court)*

   This application was transferred to this court from the [*specify*] Division/ Court by order of [*name of judge*] on [*date*],

10. The arbitration has commenced and is being conducted in England and Wales and the witness/*witnesses* are in the United Kingdom.

11. This application is for an order pursuant to section 43 of the Arbitration Act 1996 to secure the attendance before the arbitrator of the witness/*witnesses* in order:

    [to give oral testimony] *(and/or)*

    [to produce documents or other material evidence which the witness/ *witnesses* can be compelled to produce in legal proceedings, namely [*specify*].]

12. This application is made:

    [by the applicant with the permission of the tribunal.] *(or)*

    [with the agreement of the other *party/parties* to the arbitration.]

Agreements

13. …

Undertakings to the court

14. …

IT IS ORDERED (BY CONSENT):

15. [*Insert the form of order or notice appropriate to secure the attendance of a witness in order to give oral testimony and/or to produce documents or other material evidence.*]

16. [*Other orders*]

17. [*Provision for costs*]

Dated

Arbitration – gatekeeper's initial order

Order 6.5: Arbitration – Gatekeeper's initial order

Artwork-App 2-01

In the Family Court sitting at [*Court name*]

No: [*Case number*]

[The Matrimonial Causes Act 1973] /

[The Civil Partnership Act 2005] /

[The Children Act 1989, Schedule 1]

(Adapt as necessary)

The [Marriage] / [Partnership] of [*applicant name*] and [*respondent name*] (Adapt as necessary)

After consideration of the documents lodged by the applicant

ORDER MADE BY [*NAME OF JUDGE*] ON [*DATE*] ON THE PAPERS

The Parties

1. The applicant is [*applicant name*]

   The respondent is [*respondent name*]

   (Specify if any party acts by a litigation friend)

Recital

2. Form A was filed by the [applicant] / [respondent] on [*date*].
3. [By an order dated [*date*] the proceedings initiated by the Form A were stayed in order for the parties to engage in arbitration.]
4. **(Either)**
   a. [The applicant has applied to this court in Form D11 dated [*date*] challenging an arbitral award made by [*name of arbitrator*] on [*date*].
   b. Grounds of challenge are annexed to the Form D11.
   c. A skeleton argument has been filed by the applicant.
   d. The award dated [*date*] has been filed by the applicant.]

   (OR)

a. [The applicant has applied to this court in Form D11 dated [*date*] for an order implementing an arbitral award made by [*name of arbitrator*] on [*date*].

b. A skeleton argument and a draft proposed order have been filed by the applicant.

c. The award dated [*date*] has been filed by the applicant.]

IT IS ORDERED THAT:

5. [The aforesaid stay is lifted.]

6. The procedural requirements in FPR 9.12 and 9.14 (including, but not limited to, the requirement for each party to file a Form E and to attend a first appointment) are suspended.

7. The applicant shall serve the application and accompanying papers on the respondent forthwith. The service requirements of FPR 18.8 are disapplied.

8. The respondent may within 14 days of such service file a short skeleton argument in response including grounds of challenge, if applicable, and a proposed draft order.

9. **(Either)**

   [The application and the accompanying documents will be considered by a circuit judge without a hearing not sooner than 21 days after issue of the application.]

   (OR)

   [The application and the accompanying documents shall be placed [before Mostyn J(**FOR A CASE PROCEEDING IN LONDON OR ON THE SOUTH-EASTERN CIRCUIT)**]/[before [*name of judge* **(THE RELEVANT FDLJ FOR A CASE PROCEEDING ELSEWHERE)**]] for allocation.]

10. Costs reserved.

Dated [*date]*

APPENDIX 3

Case Studies

DENNIS SHERIDAN

CASE STUDY 1 – SOLICITOR SITTING AS REPRESENTATIVE TO A PARTY

I acted for a client in a moderately valued financial claim, involving overseas property. Following discussion, it was agreed the case proceed by way of Arbitration.

Sir Peter Singer was nominated as Arbitrator and a pre-commitment meeting was held at which Arbitration and its procedure was further explained most particularly that upon signing the ARB1(now ARB1FS) the parties were committed to proceed with Arbitration. The parties confirmed their instructed Solicitors to act as their Legal Representatives throughout the Arbitration.

Following the signing of the ARB1 the Arbitrator agreed to setting a Preliminary Meeting and recommended documents and detail to be provided prior to that hearing.

At the Preliminary Hearing there was detailed discussion on what additional documents and information was required and directions were given which upon their compliance would enable preparation for a final hearing. We were directed to provide written submissions and following exchange and telephone discussion with the Arbitrator we were directed to file counter-arguments. The Arbitrator informed he had all necessary detail to prepare his award which could be given on paper or the parties to attend for him to address. Both parties opted to attend before the Arbitrator where the award was read out and matter concluded.

This Arbitration from start to finish (final award) took four months.

CASE STUDY 2 – SOLICITOR SITTING AS ARBITRATOR

The parties who were in their early 30's following the breakup of their relationship decided having read about Family Law Arbitration to have their grievances resolved through Arbitration.

Both had appointed McKenzie Friends and wished they be in attendance at every hearing. At the initial pre-commitment hearing discussion took place setting out the Mackenzie Role and with agreement as to their presence I explained the Arbitration procedure and the effect of signing the ARB1 (now ARB1FS). The parties and the Mackenzie Friends had come to this pre-commitment hearing with intent on immediately signing the ARB1 and with the wish that the Arbitration proceed without delay. Irrespective of that intent the parties were given time in separate rooms to confirm their decision and once confirmed signed the ARB1 transforming the pre-commitment hearing to a formal Directions hearing.

This was a ToLATA case covering

(a) The division of the former family home

(b) Motor vehicle – as to its ownership

(c) The joint bank account

(d) The occupational rent

Following detailed discussion, I provided extensive directions. It was explained that the directions had to be complied with within the date and time so directed enabling their wish that all issues relating to their relationship could be bought to an end as soon as possible. In consequence they complied with the directions within the time agreed. A further hearing was held at which additional documents were requested. With all directions complied with I was then able to proceed to prepare my Award. Irrespective the parties were given the option of a Final hearing but were happy to my proceeding to prepare my Award and for it to be delivered on paper

I set out in the Final Award a detailed explanation for my decision on each of the 4 issues and an explanation as to why I would not make a cost order. This complex matter from first being nominated as Arbitrator to final approval and conclusion of the matter took 6 months.

KAREN DOVASTON

CASE STUDY 1 – SOLICITOR SITTING AS ARBITRATOR

One case I dealt with was concerning a specific issue and a very small part of the overall matters. Both parties had solicitors. They had drafted a consent order aside from the issue that they referred to arbitration. Both solicitors had never arbitrated before. I had a pre-engagement conversation with both solicitors together and explained the process for arbitration. Once the ARB1FS was sent to me and I accepted the appointment, I was invited by them to make directions. Both parties wanted the matter dealt with on paper. I invited submissions in writing from both of them and the draft of the consent order agreed with a schedule of assets. I then made the arbitration award. From receipt of ARB1FS to issue of my Award was 29 days with two directions orders made.

CASE STUDY 2 – SOLICITOR SITTING AS ARBITRATOR

Another arbitration matter I dealt with on paper was a single issue. This case had two solicitors and I was invited to make directions which included the parties providing submissions and the pension report (since that was central to the issue). These matters were dealt with very swiftly, within a month of submissions being made. The parties were then able to settle the case overall.

CASE STUDY 3 – SOLICITOR SITTING AS ARBITRATOR

I have also deal with a matter with litigants in person. This matter was complicated and involved a TOLATA matter and a cross application pursuant to Schedule 1, Children Act 1989. Court proceedings had been stayed to allow for arbitration. I dealt with it remotely via Teams as the case arose during the pandemic. Since the parties were litigants in person, I held the directions appointments via Teams, taking it slowly and explaining each point. I broke the matter into two parts –first TOLATA and second Schedule 1, making it easier for the litigants to deal with the case that way. We held several directions appointments enabling the matter to be kept on track. I intervened when I was being copied into emails and could see the parties beginning to argue/go off track, this being a major benefit, in my view. Arbitration enabled all issues to be dealt with within 6 months.

NADIA BECKETT
CASE STUDY 1 – SOLICITOR SITTING AS ARBITRATOR

This was an acrimonious case involving arrangements for two young dependent children of the family and distribution of the limited assets of the marriage. The parties were living separately, the wife cohabiting with a new partner in the former matrimonial home and the husband living in rented accommodation. There were no safe-guarding issues as regards the children and the child arrangements were very close to shared care (husband had the children on 3 less nights per month).

Children

I was asked to make an interim ruling concerning arrangements for Christmas. I gave my ruling in writing following submissions. Following on from this I conducted an arbitration by Zoom with the parties present and represented by their solicitors. This first arbitration dealt with the arrangements for the children as given the extremely limited assets in the case it was necessary to resolve this issue first as parties housing needs would be dependent upon this first award.

The husband argued for shared care (50-50) which meant increasing his extra time with the children by just 3 nights. The wife vehemently argued the children should spend more time with her. On balance I determined that it was in the best interests of the children to spend their time equally with both parents particularly as I was concerned by the mother's evidence which suggested that she placed little value on the children's relationship with the father.

Finances

The financial arbitration also took place by Zoom with both partis in attendance and represented by their solicitors. The father assumed that shared care would result in a 50-50 division of the equity in the former matrimonial home (this being the only significant asset). He was wrong. The husband earned significantly more than the wife and would enjoy the benefit of a clean break. He had a mortgage raising capacity which would permit him to rehouse with a small deposit. In my view this justified a departure from equality in the wife's favour and I awarded her 62% of the available capital which I established was the minimum amount she would require to purchase a property.

The award that I made enabled both parties to re-house although it did not leave either party with what they wanted.

CASE STUDY 2 – SOLICITOR SITTING AS ARBITRATOR

I was instructed to arbitrate for an unmarried couple who were acting as litigants in person without legal advice. They had one child together and a family home which was jointly owned.

The issues in the case involved the division of the net proceeds of sale of the family home and a claim by the child's mother for lump sums to meet the child's various expenses. In addition to the family home the father owned a property in his sole name (an investment property) which he had moved into after the sale of the family home. The net proceeds of sale were being held by conveyancing solicitors and the mother was in temporary, rented accommodation.

It was intended that the child would share his time roughly, equally between the parents on an informal arrangement and the care of the child was not in dispute. I did not support the mother's claim for lump-sum payments for various expenses which appeared, in the light of the party's finances, to be unnecessary expenditure. However, I did find that the mother should have slightly more from the sale of the property than the father as she would need this to purchase a small two-bedroom flat within commuting distance of the child's school.

It was evident when taking evidence from the parties they had not considered the difficulties that would arise in sharing the care of the child if the mother's home was too far away from the school and nor close to any form of public transport. When considering location the parties had focused primarily on the cost of accommodation rather than proximity to each other's properties and the child's school.

As an arbitrator assisting two parents who did not have full benefit of legal representation, I believe I was able to add significant value by bringing to the arbitration my experience as family lawyer. I was able explore with them the unintended consequences of their proposals and the questions that they were not asking themselves.

CASE STUDY 3 – SOLICITOR SITTING AS ARBITRATOR

Acting for an unmarried couple one of whom was represented and the other a litigant in person.

They had one child together and there was a great deal of bitterness and anger. They had been separated for a considerable period of time during which the family home had been rented out (from time to time) and its value had increased significantly.

I was asked to determine i) the validity of the declaration of trust and whether the mother was entitled to a contribution of the rental income ii)to determine whether the mother should be liable for the loss of rental income as there were periods when she had refused her consent to the letting agent and iii)Validity of a loan agreement between the parties for around £50,000 owed by the mother to the father which as an isolated issue I declined as being outside my jurisdiction. However, with the mother pursing a claim under Schedule 1

Children's Act 1989 I felt it appropriate to deal with the loan having jurisdiction to make a determination under Schedule 1.

The mother's claim for periodical payments and other expenses in relation to the child were dismissed. The father was unemployed and in any event there was no CMS assessment. The mothers claims for lump sums were, in my determination, unreasonable and unjustified.

ANDRZEJ BOJARSKI
CASE STUDY I – BARRISTER SITTING AS ARBITRATOR

I. Low assets

Husband and wife had only two assets of substance. The family home in a relatively deprived part of northern England with equity of c. £60,000 and a pension in the husband's name with a CEV of less than £40,000. Both were on low incomes. They had agreed a sale of the family home but could not agree how to divide the proceeds of sale. Neither would agree to complete the sale of the property without agreement as to how to divide the proceeds of sale.

Their respective solicitors agreed that the parties were not in a position to resolve their dispute through the court. They could not afford to pay their solicitors to conduct a full court application. Furthermore, they wanted to deal with things quickly in order to keep the buyer for their family home.

They agree to invite me to arbitrate the dispute in summary fashion on the papers. I agreed to receive their combined disclosure / evidence / submissions in the form of short statements drafted by their lawyers and signed by the parties (less than 5 pages each). I wrote an award which I was able to deliver to the parties within 2 weeks of them first agreeing to approach me to arbitrate. The total cost to the parties of the process (inclusive of my fee and their own lawyers' fees) was less than £3,000, or c. £1,500 each.

CASE STUDY 2 – BARRISTER SITTING AS ARBITRATOR

Husband and wife were ex-pats living and working in Dubai. They initiated an English divorce and sought to agree financial matters through mediation conducted by an English mediator in Dubai. They agreed most matters but were stuck on a single issue. The mediator encouraged them to try mediation.

They jointly approached me to arbitrate. They were both acting in person. I invited short written submissions from them on the issue they wished me to adjudicate. Having received those submissions I was satisfied that there were no significant factual differences between them and I acceded to their request to deal with the case on the papers. I directed short s.25 statements from each party and their submissions and then delivered an award to them. The matter was concluded within 2 months of the referral from their mediator and at a combined total cost to them of £1,500, and without them having to travel to England for any hearings.

CASE STUDY 3 – BARRISTER SITTING AS ARBITRATOR

An unmarried couple separated and were unable to resolve a dispute over the ownership of their family home. They both instructed family lawyers. The lawyers did not feel comfortable dealing with proceedings in the County Court governed by the Civil Procedure Rules, and they agreed to arbitrate.

I gave directions for statements of case, disclosure and the filing of witness statements. It was agreed that there would be no 'Denton' sanctions in the event deadlines were missed, save in the event either party asked me to make an 'unless order'.

For various reasons there was considerable slippage in the time-table a few times. Each time the parties agreed that matters needed to be retimetabled and the final hearing delayed. Given that they agreed directions each time was content to approve their agreement and each time liaison between counsel's clerks allowed a new date to be fixed quite soon. The first final hearing date had been in early July but that was rearranged about a month before the hearing to a date in late July, that was then moved to early September and then again moved to late September, when it finally went ahead (although the parties settled on the morning 'at the door' of the arbitration). Had they been in the County Court not only would the adjournments possibly not been approved, but any adjournment would have been to a date several months later rather than just a few weeks later.

JAMES PIRRIE
CASE STUDY 1 – SOLICITOR SITTING AS ARBITRATOR

An arbitration involved the need to stretch limited resources, (but including a range of complex pensions, accumulated over a long marriage) between a couple with significant, changing and uncertain needs (the children's dependency coming to an end but also one party's significant health conditions).

The parties were in person and desperate to be relieved of the risk of [the costs of] future variation applications. Through various early meetings in arbitration they made clear a preference to achieve a clean break with their each then being independent with the right – and responsibility – to do what they could to make the best of their positions (earnings and spending) to improve their respective independent retirement years.

I developed for them a crude cash flow model in spreadsheet form to help them grasp a possible approach for making progress but then, at their joint request, adjourned the arbitration for them to engage with a financial planner to complete a detailed and more forensic/ accurate analysis.

I was able to support that progress and call for clarity and engagement from the financial planner where there was delay and eventually the parties were able to achieve an agreement with the FP's help, which I then drafted into court-order form for the parties to enable them to secure the pension sharing adjustments required by the work that they had completed.

I was put in mind of this case reading WL v HL [2021] EWFC B10, which has resonances: here Mr Allen QC supported the parties to bring their case to a conclusion themselves, whilst being anchored by his patient, gentle and ever-present insistence over several weeks and adjournments to progress.

CASE STUDY 2 – SOLICITOR SITTING AS ARBITRATOR

The father and mother in this matter needed a determination as to the order in which the secondary school selection would be entered on the form. The arguments and outcome are of little matter for readers, all that might be noted was the flexibility and speed of arbitration which showed itself able to deliver an outcome (including directions meeting, statements, submissions, an interview with the child and a detailed written determination) all within two and a bit days.

The parties were trying hard to reach agreement, including through engaging mediation to assist getting a structure that they could adopt over the line. Unfortunately, and with the application deadline looming they felt they had no option but to have an imposed outcome.

Given that the child was ten and had seen the relevant schools and had mature views, self-evidently, her wishes and feelings were something that needed to be incorporated within the process. We proposed the names of three experts able to speak to the child and provide a wishes and feelings report. As it turned out (given how the clock continued to run down), fortunately the parents were content to adopt the services of someone in our practice, a former probation officer, child-inclusive mediator and director of mediation, Dominic Raeside.

For reasons of transparency and proper procedure, we were careful to adopt an ethical wall between the arbitrator and our "ISW" so that the parties would be clear as to the evidence that was entering the balancing exercise. Through some excellent support from the mother's lawyer (the father was in person), we were able to manage the process at a bit of a canter as follows:

- Thursday enquiry
- Friday (after hours) confirmation that the matter was likely to proceed
- Monday arbitrator outlines possible process and provides forms
- Tuesday arbitrator sets out suggested timetabling
- Tuesday 5pm receipt of application forms and safeguarding questionnaires
- Wednesday midday arrangement for ISW to speak to child
- Wednesday 1pm both statements received and exchanged by the arbitrator
- Wednesday evening in person 'directions' meeting, refining the future steps and stages in the process, mindful in particular that the father was away from home on holiday, unrepresented and without office support.
- Wednesday evening, receipt of ISW report
- Close of business, Thursday, receipt of written submissions from each side
- Determination provided shortly before 10pm on that day. [As it happened I was keen to get it done that evening so that delivery of the outcome did not happen on the same day as the child's birthday the next day but also well before the weekend, the submission deadline so that the parties would have a chance to assimilate the decision and address with advice any points arising].

A child aged 10 does have wishes and feelings that potentially should be taken into account, in the circumstances, her voice should carry weight a child would expect to see their views taken into account and might avoid poor performance, falling back on the argument "well I never wanted to go there anyway."

HANNAH MARKHAM QC

CASE STUDY 1 – SITTING AS REPRESENTATIVE TO A PARTY

CHILD ARRANGEMENTS – Focus on living arrangements in term time only some residual minor issues.

This arbitration took place some years ago, before the lock down and was one of the first Children Act cases that was settled by way of arbitration. The parties were both highly educated and high achieving parents with the father in a semi high profile position. The final issues were as to the way in which the children would live between their parents, it being agreed that the two children (aged at the time 8 and 10) would live with both parents. M wanted less of a shared care arrangement; F sought shared care.

Arbitration was proposed by F's team at an early stage and pre proceedings. M declined.

The case was allocated to magistrates who adjourned the first hearing which application was for the appointment of an independent social worker irrespective that the parties had already agreed to this appointment at the court hearing! The Magistrates refused to deal with that agreement as part of the order and listed it for a further hearing, causing a delay of a further 3 months and at further cost to the parents.

It was at that stage that the mother agreed to arbitrate.

Following that agreement and under the structure of arbitration not only were the parties able to move final decisions forward in a prompt manner, but they were also able to start to reach agreement on issues, such as agreeing the appointment of an Arbitrator, which ISW to instruct and on management of the arbitration. Even those small agreements provided a platform for constructive co working. This meant that any residual conflict was focused and dealt with in a timely manner. Once the parties had decided to arbitrate, the arbitrator had been chosen and agreed upon within about 3 weeks. The arbitration itself took place within 4 months of the first magistrates hearing and almost within the time we would have had to wait for the hearing to appoint the ISW!

The Final Hearing was held in a comfortable suit (1GC Chambers) with sufficient rooms for pre-conference time and a much more relaxing environment; all of which assists the manner by which the parties gave their evidence and conducted themselves.

CASE STUDY 2 – QC SITTING AS ARBITRATOR

Specific issue – urgent decision required – which school v home schooling.

In this case I acted as the arbitrator in a case where an urgent decision was needed as to whether the children should remain home schooled or whether they should start school in September. I heard the arbitration in late August.

The issue arose within ongoing Children Act proceedings within a case with international issues – both whether the children who had primarily lived in Spain were habitually resident here and whether they should remain in England or return to Spain.

The children had been home schooled in Spain and had arrived for a break in England over Christmas at the eve of the pandemic. The mother then refused to move back to Spain. Children were then home schooled over lockdown. The urgent issue, pending determination of the longer-term issues was whether the children should start mainstream school in September and or remain home schooled.

The application as mentioned above arose within a hearing focusing on the wider application and the Recorder allocated to that hearing made plain that he simply had no time to hear the schooling issue. A further hearing would be required, and the likelihood was that any such hearing may fall outside of the window for a fair determination of the issue.

The parents agreed that for the children this issue needed resolving urgently. It was my understanding that one of the parties had nominated 3 arbitrators and the other that made the final choice. Enquiries were made as to whether I had availability to arbitrate a one-day arbitration and if so to provide dates. Due to the urgency the dates were limited to a specific week. My nomination was confirmed and within 48 hours the Arb 1 Form was completed. I knew from the outset that the parties needed a determination on the day of the hearing and part of the confirmation of my appointment included my being willing and able (with time allocates on the day) to consider the evidence and to form a view.

The parties requested that the arbitration irrespective of the pandemic be heard in person and arrangements for the arbitration were made that it be held at 36 Family Chambers. I was asked in opening notes to adjudicate upon whether live evidence was necessary and to determine that as a preliminary issue.

A day was agreed and the parents each wanted to give short evidence about their views. Due to the timing of the arbitration care was taken (due to Covid 19) to manage social distancing and to ensure that the parties' representatives could take part in the hearing. Using facilities at chambers we were able to provide rooms for each party on one floor and the arbitration took place in another room with just myself, the parents, and their counsel. Solicitors participated in the hearing via a live link between the rooms.

Due to the immediacy of the decision and the start of school, it was agreed that a decision would be given that afternoon with the detailed determination to follow. I made it plain in pre-hearing discussions with the parties and advocates on the day that any evidence and submissions must be concluded by lunchtime (1pm) as I would need several hours to consider the evidence, and formulate my decision which I would then give to the parties on that day in outline setting out the clear reasons for that decision which would then be written up into a long and detailed determination. With the timescale kept I had the afternoon to weigh the evidence and competing views and reach a clear and considered decision. I gave my decision to the parties at around 3/3:15pm leaving the remainder of the afternoon for the parties to take steps to make plans for the next school term which was to begin the following week.

APPENDIX 4

Remote Arbitrations
Guidance for the Conduct of a Remote Hearing in an Arbitration or Private FD

SUGGESTED GUIDANCE FOR THE CONDUCT OF A REMOTE HEARING AS ARBITRATOR OR PFDR JUDGE[1]

General

1. In the case of an arbitration hearing, the parties are in most circumstances (subject to Art. 1.4 of the relevant Rules)[2] free (pursuant to Art 9.1) to agree matters of procedure, including the form of any hearing. If they do not so agree, the question whether the hearing should proceed via videoconferencing will be a case management decision for the arbitrator as it would be for a judge in court proceedings.[3]

2. In the case of a PFDR which it is intended should proceed via videoconferencing, the parties should be asked to confirm in writing or through their solicitors that videoconferencing (i) constitutes an acceptable means of communication; and (ii) will be used as the means for conducting the hearing.

Pre-hearing preparation

3. The applicant's solicitors (or the respondent's solicitors if the applicant is not represented) ("the lead party") should be responsible for (i) the preparation of the electronic bundle of relevant documents, ordinarily in compliance with PD27A; and (ii) any electronic bundle of authorities.

4. The lead party should prepare the electronic bundle(s), usually in the following format:

1 This document includes material drawn from (i) the Civil Justice in England and Wales Protocol Regarding Remote Hearings (20th March 2020); (ii) the Protocol For Remote Hearings in the Family Court and Family Division of the High Court (23rd March 2020); (iii) the Remote Access Family Court v4 (16th April 2020); and (iv) Byron James (via Twitter).

2 Financial Scheme Rules (6th Edition, effective 1st January 2018) and Children Scheme Rules (4th Edition, effective 6th April 2020).

3 See now Re A *(Children) (Remote Hearing: Care and Placement Orders)* [2020] EWCA Civ 583.

a. PDF format is to be used;

b. all documents are to be contained, if possible, within one single PDF file;

c. the PDF file must be searchable;

d. pagination must be computer generated within the PDF and not hand-written:

   i. original pagination should be by section and page number i.e. A1, A2, A3.... B1, B2, B3 etc;

   ii. insertions should adopt 'legal' numbering (e.g. B13.1, B13.2, B13.3 to be inserted between B13 and B14); and

   e. each section of the bundle, and each individual document referenced in the index, should be separately bookmarked.

5. Unless the arbitrator/judge is to be responsible for setting up the remote hearing, the lead party should be responsible for doing so. In either case, the person so responsible should provide to all of the other parties the details required to attend the remote hearing as soon as they are available. In practice the arrangements are likely to be made by the arbitrator's/judge's/lead party's counsel's clerk.

6. Anybody attending the remote hearing should ensure that they have a good connection/signal to avoid a breakdown in connection.

7. The minimum recommended bandwidth for a successful remote video hearing is 1.5 Mbps in both directions, but ideally it should be at least 5 Mbps.

Conduct of the hearing

8. The parties should log/call into the remote platform c. 5 minutes before the hearing is due to begin.

9. Each participant's computer/tablet/phone should be set so as to identify who they are. If possible, all parties should use a computer or tablet rather than a phone.

10. Each participant should shut down all background browsers and applications on the device used for the virtual hearing (including disabling "pop up" notifications), and turn off all other devices which might either:

    a. appropriate necessary bandwidth from the device to be used to access the virtual hearing; or

    b. produce audible notifications during the hearing.

11. The arbitrator/judge should log/call into the platform at the time the hearing is due to begin.

12. Every remote hearing that is being conducted in private should start with all parties confirming that:

    a. they can see and hear everyone;

b. they are in a private space (and, so far as is possible, that they are alone and cannot be overheard);

c. everyone accessing the hearing is authorised to be there;

d. they are not relaying the hearing to any third parties;

e. subject to 15 and 16 below in the case of an arbitration hearing, they are not making any recording of the hearing; and

f. if there are any changes to the above they shall say so as soon as possible.

13. In the event that the video-conferencing fails for one of all of the participants:

a. the tribunal/parties should seek to re-establish that connection; and

b. if that is unsuccessful, the tribunal should convene a telephone hearing to determine the appropriate next steps depending on how far the hearing has progressed.

14. The following etiquette is recommended for the conduct of the hearing:

a. *"note taking"* participants (e.g. pupils or solicitors' assistants/ paralegals) should mute their feed for the entire hearing;

b. everyone should mute their microphone when not speaking, save

c. when evidence is being given, when the microphones of the witness, question-asker and tribunal should be on;

d. no-one should speak when someone else is speaking;

e. a person should only ask to speak when invited by the tribunal; and

f. if something urgent arises and a participant wishes to speak, he/she should visually indicate to the tribunal before doing so.

Arbitration Hearings

15. The person responsible for setting up the remote hearing should:

a. ensure that appropriate arrangements have been made for recording (if the hearing is going to be recorded) via Lifesize, Zoom, or Microsoft Teams; and

b. ensure that the parties know if the hearing is being recorded by the relevant platform.

16. The parties should be asked to confirm that they agree and accept that:

a. unless expressly agreed they must not record the hearing themselves;

b. it is an offence to:

i. record the hearing (save as has already been agreed as part of any directions that have been given); or

ii. make use of such a recording; and

c. any recording of the hearing in accordance with 15 above or with express agreement under 16.a above is not used for any purpose other than:

   i. the obtaining of legal advice;
   ii. court proceedings arising out of the arbitration; and/or
   iii. in accordance with the express written agreement of the arbitrator and other party to the arbitration.

17. Unless otherwise agreed, any hearing listed for a day should 'sit' from 10 am to 1 pm (with a break at a convenient moment between 11 am and 12 pm) and from 2 pm to 4.30 pm (with a break at a convenient moment between 3 pm and 3.30 pm).

18. Only documents that have been included in the bundle lodged for the hearing may be "shared" on screen without prior approval of the tribunal.

19. If oral evidence is being given the tribunal should guide witnesses in the oath or affirmation. The Mostyn J short form – *"do you swear or affirm to tell the truth, the whole truth and nothing but the truth?"* should be acceptable. There should be no expectation to hold a Holy Book.

20. Witnesses should be in a secure room, alone, with the doors closed and with measures taken to prevent interruptions and disruptions.

21. If it is not possible for witnesses to have access to a full electronic bundle consideration will need be given in advance to the documents to which the witness is likely to be referred. The parties should endeavour to agree the list of such documents (if at all possible). An electronic bundle of these copy documents should then be prepared in advance which the lead party should send to the witness.

Nicholas Allen QC
Janet Bazley QC
Andrzej Bojarski
Nigel Dyer QC
Marina Faggionato
Charles Hale QC
Suzanne Kingston
Christopher Pocock QC
6th May 2020

APPENDIX 5

Articles
Lecture to the Worshipful Company of Arbitrators (Sir Hugh Bennett)

FAMILY ARBITRATION INNER TEMPLE YEARBOOK 2015–2016

FAMILY ARBITRATION

Master Hugh Bennett discusses the advantages and perceived disadvantages of the Institute of Family Law Arbitrators scheme, in an abridged version of his lecture.

The Institute of Family Law Arbitrators (IFLA) scheme went live three years ago in March 2012. Despite the fact that arbitration concerning land and commercial disputes has been around in this country since about the 13th Century, there has never been, prior to the IFLA scheme, family law arbitration, by which I mean arbitration applying the secular family law of the state. Family litigation was seen to be the sole preserve of the courts. However, about ten or so years ago, a few brave souls decided to devise an arbitral scheme to resolve financial and property disputes between separated couples. After much perseverance and hard work, the scheme was launched.

The IFLA is responsible for the implementation and administration of the family law finance arbitration scheme. The arbitrators have all been trained in arbitral techniques and have a good working knowledge of the important and relevant parts of the Arbitration Act 1996. Each must become a member of the Chartered Institute of Arbitrators, thereby making themselves liable to its code of conduct. Solicitors, barristers, QCs and retired judges, all of whom are, or were, full-time practising family lawyers, comprise the corps of arbitrators under the scheme. They are real specialists in the field of family finance law.

The seal of approval was given by the President of the Family Division, Sir James Munby, in a recent case, *S v S* [2014] EWHC 7 (Fam). In that case, the parties had agreed to arbitrate their financial and property disputes under the IFLA scheme. The arbitrator made his award, which the parties then presented to the court for implementation. The President gave his approval, turned the award into orders of the court and said this:

> *"Although recognising that the judge is not a rubber stamp… it can only be in the rarest of cases that it will be appropriate for the judge to do other than approve the order. With a process as sophisticated as that embodied in the IFLA scheme it is difficult to contested [illegible] such a case."*

One very important part of the IFLA scheme is that its rules make it mandatory for the law of England and Wales to be applied. There is no room at all for the parties to agree that the arbitrator will apply the laws of their choosing, whether secular or religious. It is essential that the law applied by the arbitrator is the same as will be applied by the court.

In agreeing to arbitrate, the parties agree that the award is binding on them. They, not just one of them but both of them, agree to ask the court to turn the award into orders of the court. Although the award will be binding on them, each recognises that the court has a statutory discretion when turning the award into an order.

ADVANTAGES

Privacy and confidentiality

All the proceedings before the arbitrator are private and entirely confidential. This is a real bonus for parties who do not relish their family disagreements, whether great or small, being bandied about in the national or local media. With the family courts now travelling at a gallop towards hearings being heard completely in open court, those couples caught up in a broken relationship who want their disputes adjudicated in private now have that option.

When the award comes to the court for implementation, will not the parties lose their privacy and confidentiality? In *S v S*, the President simply said that he had read the necessary papers and approved the award and consequential orders Nobody was any the wiser as to the identity of the parties or the facts of the case I think the courts, following the President's lead, are going to respect the wishes of the parties, expressed in the arbitration agreement and the rules of IFLA that they opted for privacy and confidentiality throughout I see no difficulty in the judge so framing his judgment so that it does not identify the parties

Flexibility

This arbitral scheme is able to take hold of the issues which the parties want decided without the necessity to go through the whole gamut of the process in the court system. The parties can submit for arbitration those issues which they see as the stumbling block to the resolution of their financial and property disputes, and done in a way which they want. That is the ethos of the 1996 Act.

Speed

The court system can be impossibly slow, particularly for those of modest means Priority is [illegible] given to cases involving children And there is a limited pool of judges Finance cases may be adjourned almost at the last moment, because the courts are [illegible] worked, and in some courts adjourned not just once but [illegible] than once. Compare that to what can happen under the IFLA scheme According to Resolution, who collate the statistics, the longest arbitration was one year and the shortest was seven days I suggest that such speed is quite unattainable in our court system.

The arbitrator

The arbitrator must see the arbitration through to its conclusion. There is no chopping and changing of the adjudicator as can happen in the court system Further, the parties to an arbitration select the 'adjudicator' They are given the opportunity, unavailable in the court system, of choosing the person who they and their advisers consider to be the best person to decide their [illegible]routes

THE PERCEIVED DISADVANTAGES

Expense

It is said, *"The judge is free, the arbitrator must be paid."* The second part is true; the first part is only partially true. Litigants must pay court fees. But the better answer to the criticism of expense is that if parties engage in arbitration and thereby get the hearing and the award through quickly, the saving in legal fees will, I suggest, more than offset the cost of employing an arbitrator.

The belief that "arbitration is only for the rich"

Not so. Amongst the 185 qualified arbitrators are a large number who are prepared to take on arbitrations in cases of very modest means and tailor their fees accordingly and, indeed, who are happy to agree a fixed fee. In any event, no doubt the choice of arbitrator will be influenced by the fees he proposes to charge and the parties can shop around.

Some lawyers will not advise their client to consider arbitration

They say *"if I advise my client to choose X as the arbitrator but he then goes against my client in the award, I will get the blame. If, by contrast, the judge (whom I cannot choose) decides the dispute and he goes against my client, he gets the blame, not me."* I find this an extraordinary, irrational excuse, Lawyers spend their professional lives making choices. Is it not better for the lawyer and his client to have the opportunity, together with the other side, to choose the 'adjudicator'? But if that does not satisfy the anxieties, under the scheme, the parties can submit an agreed shortlist and ask IFLA to nominate one from that list, or ask IFLA to nominate an arbitrator from its panel.

No right of appeal

Despite the restricted situations in which an award can be challenged under the Arbitration Act 1996, the reality is that in family law if an arbitrator makes an award which is 'off the wall', no family court is going to turn such an award into court orders if one party were to challenge the award, because the court has a discretion whether to make the orders or not.

Inconsistent decisions

There is the risk of inconsistency, but it is more apparent than real. In family finance cases, the inconsistency is likely to arise not by reason of the discretion given to tribunals to determine the fair outcome, but by an arbitrator making a decision which is wholly outside the wide parameters of that discretion. That can be cured by the court.

The law cannot be developed in an arbitration

The vast majority of family cases involve the application of existing principles to the facts of the particular case. The very small number of cases where the law may need developing can remain in the court system

ARBITRATION IN CHILDREN'S MATTERS

There is, as yet, no secular scheme in operation for disputes about children to be arbitrated However, IFLA has set up a sub-committee under the chairmanship of HH Judge Michael Horowitz QC to consider this matter.

In my view, the first question to consider is whether there ought to be, as a matter of principle, an arbitral scheme to resolve children disputes as an alternative to that provided by the court system. Subject to certain criteria, I do not see why not. Why should parents not be able to agree to resolve their differences through a secular, arbitral mechanism? Is it not patronising and paternalistic to say that parents may not have the opportunity to agree on what method of resolution they consider is best in the circumstances of the case?

The first criteria I would suggest is that the arbitrator must apply English, secular, family law.

Secondly, there will have to be areas of children law that cannot be the subject of arbitration. Perhaps the most obvious example is public law, where the state intervenes in a family, and in the end may have to remove from one or both parents one or more of their children.

Thirdly, in an appropriate case, provision ought to be made for the child to participate directly. This will need some very careful thought, but if a child may be represented in court and thus make his or her wishes directly known to the tribunal, there seems no good reason why the same should not happen in arbitral proceedings.

Fourthly, the award of the arbitrator should be final and binding. There should be a provision that both parties, not just one of them, will apply to the court to transform the award into court orders with an express recognition that the court can exercise its own discretion.

Fifthly, those who wish to become arbitrators in children matters should undergo suitable training just as the arbitrators under the current IFLA scheme underwent and, having undergone that training, should be required to become members of the Chartered Institute of Arbitrators. It is so important for the success of any arbitral scheme that the public should see that the arbitrators are members of a reputable professional body.

CONCLUSION

We are fortunate in this country to have a good legal and judicial system. But it is under immense strain. Here for the first time is an arbitral scheme applying English law that empowers couples, suffering a terminal breakdown in their relationship, to opt to have their financial and property disputes adjudicated in the way that they consider suits them best

The full version of this lecture is available at

www.innertemple.org.uk/education/lecture-series-2015

Arbitration – A Fairer Process? (Alexis Campbell QC and Suzanne Kingston)

ARBITRATION – A FAIRER PROCESS?

Suzanne Kingston, consultant at Mills & Reeve LLP, and Alexis Campbell QC of 29 Bedford Row, suggest that following the Court of Appeal decision in Haley v Haley, family arbitration can be as closely aligned to the court system as the parties choose, now with the added assurance that even if it goes wrong, it can be put right.

As we face the global coronavirus (COVID-19) pandemic, the court system has changed beyond recognition. Many of the courts were closed and even now, as they slowly re-open, many are still operating with limited caseloads with much work is being conducted remotely. There seems to be a consensus that litigators must seriously consider alternative dispute resolution, to avoid the log-jam in courts across the country. And it is no surprise that arbitration—bespoke, private, quick to set up and able to be conducted remotely on a variety of digital platforms—is becoming increasingly popular.

The recent unanimous decision from the Court of Appeal in Haley v Haley [2020] EWCA Civ 1369, [2020] All ER (D) 110 (Oct) may well encourage practitioners and parties alike to look to arbitration much more seriously as a viable means of resolving their disputes.

What has changed? Under the Arbitration Act 1996 (AA 1996), which governs all English arbitral disputes, appeals are few and far between; the mystical white leopard. Now, the Court of Appeal has given the green light for an appeal process in financial remedy cases, which looks to transform the legal landscape for financial arbitration in family cases.

Under AA 1996, appeals are only permitted where there is lack of jurisdiction (AA 1996, s 67), there has been a serious procedural irregularity (AA 1996, s 68) (which is very narrowly interpreted), or where the arbitrator has erred in law (AA 1996, s 69). The last test also sets a very high threshold. The decision must be one which no reasonable arbitrator could have reached when applying the law properly. There is also a preliminary filter under AA 1996, ss 57 and 70, which requires the parties to apply first to the arbitrator for clarification or to correct an award (akin to the slip rule procedure) before pursuing an appeal under AA 1996.

In an impressive line of first instance authorities, starting with Munby P in S v S (financial remedies: arbitral award) [2014] EWHC 7 (Fam), [2014] 1 FLR 1257, including Mostyn J in J v B (Family Law Arbitration Award) [2016] EWHC 324 (Fam), [2016] 2 FLR 1308, and Clare Ambrose, sitting as a deputy High Court judge, in BC v BG [2019] EWFC 7, [2019] 2 FLR 337, the High Court has consistently reinforced the narrow scope of the appeal process within the family arbitration structure. In an about turn, the Court of Appeal have now said that those decisions were wrong.

What was the background?

The couple had had their two-day final financial hearing adjourned by the court at short notice due to judicial unavailability. Quickly entering into an arbitration agreement, they identified a number of issues for determination covering both capital and income division. Having heard the arbitration, the arbitrator circulated a draft award. The husband's counsel sought under AA 1996, s 57, clarification and/or explanation of 14 'substantial' points. Declining to provide clarification on the basis that the requests went beyond what was permissible, the arbitrator produced his final award. Dissatisfied, the husband sought to challenge the award and applied to the court for an order that the award not be made into a court order on a number of grounds including that the arbitrator had erred in law, had failed to give reasons for his decision, and had ignored or overlooked facts.

What did the court decide at first instance?

Clare Ambrose, sitting as a deputy High Court judge, found in favour of the wife (R v K [2020] EWHC 841 (Fam), [2020] All ER (D) 193 (Feb)), applying the hitherto accepted approach under AA 1996, that grounds for appeal from arbitral awards are extremely limited and this award was not so wrong that it should not be made into an order. She approved the award and made an order which reflected its terms. The husband appealed.

What did the Court of Appeal decide?

In a typically clear judgment, King LJ gave a full analysis of the interplay between AA 1996 and the courts, both in general civil litigation and specifically in the family arena. The civil courts, she noted, strive for certainty, an essential ingredient for successful commerce. Appeals detract from certainty and are discouraged even at the cost of fairness, ie 'when parties agree arbitration, they buy the right to get the wrong answer' (per Sir Bernard Eder on 15 December 2014, as quoted by Mostyn J in J v B [2016] EWHC 324 (Fam), [2016] 2 FLR 1308).

The family courts, by contrast, have fairness at their heart. It is not a concept that can be contracted out of. So, within the arbitration scheme and AA 1996, how does the strict civil interpretation fit in with the ethos of the family courts?

King LJ provided the answer to this 'conundrum' (para [51]): the family court must allow appeals from an arbitral award where a party can show a real prospect of success in appealing. The high threshold as applied in civil proceedings (that the decision is plainly wrong and will usually fail) does not apply. The family court will consider a complaint against an arbiter, in the same way that it would consider a complaint against a judge: where there is 'a real prospect of success' which is realistic, not fanciful (per CR v SR (Financial Remedies: Permission to Appeal) [2013] EWHC 1155 (Fam), [2014] 1 FLR 186).

In civil litigation, the parties agree to arbitrate. That contract is enforceable. In family proceedings, irrespective of the parties' agreement, whether recorded in a contract (such as a pre-nuptial agreement) or a consent order, it is unenforceable without the approval of the court applying the criteria provided by section 25 of the Matrimonial Causes Act 1973 (MCA 1973). The family court retains an inquisitorial role in approving agreements and contracts. It is required to so do to ensure those agreements and contracts are fair. If they are considered unfair, the court must decline to convert them into court orders. This remains the case when the parties sign a contract for a third party to resolve the disputes between them. Just as the parties' direct agreement is subject to assessment under the MCA 1973, so too is the arbitrator's assessment.

Permission to challenge an order based on Barder principles (mistake or supervening events) will continue to be available.

Process to challenge an arbitral award

The decision in Haley provided guidance on process for appeals from an arbitral award. A party unhappy with the outcome can apply under the notice to show cause procedure. It is not now necessary to apply under the AA 1996 routes (AA 1996, ss 67, 68 and 69) first. The application does not need to be made in the High Court. It should be made to the specialist circuit judges who hear financial remedy appeals, from district judges, or to the High Court if appropriate on the facts of the case.

On the application, the court will carry out a 'triage' process to assess what needs to be done. If the complaints do not pass the permission to appeal test, of a real prospect of success, the court should convert the award into an order, and penalise the reluctant party in costs. If the permission to appeal test is passed, the case should be remitted before a suitable judge for review (as with appeals – this is not ordinarily a re-hearing and a re-hearing is only permissible if the interests of justice require one (Family Procedure Rules 2010, SI 2010/2955, 30.12(1)(b)), with such directions as considered appropriate. The 'form and extent' of further hearings will be tailored for each case. It may be appropriate to give limited directions or list for more detailed case management, such as further updating evidence.

Is this good for arbitration?

The great fear of many practitioners, in submitting to arbitration, has been that a wrong decision from an arbitrator, unless very wrong or so wrong that it 'leaps off the page', cannot be corrected. Clients are forced to accept and live with a bad decision. Many will immediately turn to the practitioner for advising the specific arbitrator or the process in general. As an elective process it is easy to be blamed for the election. Now, a decision by the arbitrator which would be unacceptable from a judge can be properly challenged. Clients can expect arbitral awards to be policed just as judgments are capable of scrutiny. Financial remedy arbitration now stands on an equivalent footing with financial remedy litigation; whether before a public or private judge.

It may be argued that the one feature of arbitration that has attracted many supporters, the finality and the certainty, is now lost. As with commercial litigation, some cases cry out for a binary decision, which will be almost impervious to challenge and therefore offer finality. Whatever the outcome, the cost and anguish or ongoing litigation will be over. The right to pay for a wrong answer has now gone. While some may lament that loss, it is likely that more will now be prepared to embrace the possibility of arbitration, to avoid lengthy and expensive delays, knowing that even a wrong decision can be remedied.

It is hoped that arbitration will be seen as a realistic means of resolving all types of financial remedy cases, not just the for the rich and famous hoping to avoid the spotlight of the court process. Quick, simple and tailored for the needs of all cases, arbitration offers an affordable solution, which is now subject to limited, but careful review.

Practicalities

When considering arbitration, it is important to bear in mind a few practical points:

Even if an arbitration is being conducted at short notice, all of the formalities in setting it up should be complied with—it is sensible to have a pre-commitment conversation with the arbitrator to scope out the subject matter of the arbitration and practical issues such as submission of forms, timing and course if the arbitrator is from the same chambers as either of the advocates involved (and subject to any legitimate concerns a client may have) practitioners should explain to clients that this will not give rise to any bias—if there are concerns, invite the IFLA scheme to appoint an arbitrator, and arbitrated awards need to be clear, easily digestible and deal with every material point raised by the parties— when completing the ARB1 form, remember to list the headline issues, because the arbitrator only has jurisdiction to address the matters listed on the form

As a process, arbitration in financial remedy processes can be as closely aligned to the court system as the parties choose. It can also be short circuited, to limit the length and scope of disclosure. It can offer a service with great costs savings. Now with the added assurance that even if it goes wrong, it can be put right. Time will tell if there is an appetite for this level of privatisation of the court process, under the ongoing surveillance of the judicial eye.

Outlook after Hayley (Suzanne Kingston & Jonathan Tecks)

FAMILY ARBITRATION: THE OUTLOOK AFTER HALEY

The recent decision of the Court of Appeal in Haley v Haley [2020] EWCA Civ 1369 (case report at [2021] Fam Law 37) settled an important issue for family arbitration. It established that contested awards in the area of financial remedy could be reviewed by the Family Court by a process akin to an appeal against decisions made in court proceedings, and on the same basis as such an appeal: that the decision is 'wrong'.

This article assesses the significance of the decision by looking at its background and context. It sets out our understanding of the procedural implications. Finally, it identifies remaining areas of uncertainty and offers some views as to how they might be resolved.

Background

The conjunction of arbitration and the area of family law may, at first glance, seem incongruous. The essence of arbitration is the principle that disputing parties appoint a trusted third-party well-versed in their area of activity to adjudicate, on the basis that they agree to be bound by the outcome. The simplicity of this principle allows for speed and informality, suiting the process very well to areas of commercial activity which call for robust, rapid resolution. Important features are the encouragement of party autonomy – the 'ownership' of the dispute by the parties themselves; and the discouragement of court intervention, which would be likely to impede efficiency.

In contrast, family law is an area where the courts have traditionally seemed jealous of their role, perhaps because of the sensitive and personal nature of the issues to which it gives rise, and their at once immediate and general significance. A highpoint is the principle that agreements arrived at by parties themselves may not oust the jurisdiction of the court. Even less so, it would seem, should a potentially rival process such as arbitration be capable of shutting out the court's scrutiny.

Nevertheless, when the Institute of Family Law Arbitrators ('IFLA') initiated a family law arbitration scheme some 10 years ago, points of synergy were identified. In particular, a movement towards party autonomy (which arbitration would encourage) seemed to coincide with a growing willingness on the part of the courts to respect agreements freely arrived at in the area of family law, characterised, for example, by the Supreme Court's decision in Radmacher (Formerly Granatino) v Granatino [2010] UKSC 42, [2010] 2 FLR 1900.

And when it came to devising different aspects of the scheme, the remarkable flexibility afforded by the open weave of the Arbitration Act 1996 (the Act) allowed a considerable degree of integration. Non-mandatory sections of the Act facilitated rules by which a family law arbitration model for England and Wales was fashioned. Thus the 'applicable law' (s 46), which ordinarily would be a matter of choice, was delimited to the law applicable within England and Wales. Conversely, available 'remedies' (s 48), which ordinarily would be limited in range, were enlarged to encompass those frequently used in family matters. And 'costs' (s 61), which ordinarily would be allocated following a civil pattern, were specifically aligned with the family regime.

One aspect where integration was less immediately obvious concerned that of potential challenge to an award. The routes available under the Act were clear: a slip rule (s 57); jurisdictional challenge (s 67); procedural irregularity causing injustice (s 68); and error of law (s 69). Equally clear was the arbitral orthodoxy that findings of fact and overall conclusions were generally not open to challenge.

How would these sit with family law matters, where an outcome would often represent an exercise of discretion following a multitude of factual decisions? Would there be a basis for overriding an award where the arbitrator had arrived at an irrational or bizarre outcome? And how would the arbitral regime be compatible with the family law principle that the court's jurisdiction may not be ousted?

In the absence of legislative assistance or judicial direction, recourse was had to s 58 of the Act, dealing with the effect of an award. The section provides that an award is final and binding subject to the routes of challenge within the Act. Crucially, this provision is non-mandatory, so it operates 'unless otherwise agreed by the parties'. It follows that parties to family arbitrations could agree to leave the way open to some kind of further court intervention.

Since the form and extent of that intervention were not certain, the wording of the rules (and corresponding wording of the 'ARB1' arbitration agreement) was intentionally somewhat open-ended. It committed the parties, where necessary (and in virtually all financial remedy cases, it would be necessary):

- To apply to an appropriate court for an order in the same or similar terms as the award;
- To recognise that the court had a discretion as to whether and in what terms to make an order; and
- To acknowledge that the finality of the award was subject to any changes which the court making that order may require.

This formula represented a platform that would allow a court to take a range of steps from making changes purely incidental to the transformation of an award into an order (for example, by translating a party commitment in the arbitration into a formal undertaking to the court) to (we considered) changing the outcome of an award in its entirety, if possible and necessary.

Context

It remained to see how the courts would construe their role in relation to actual cases. The progress of a number of decisions was charted by the Court of Appeal in Haley, paras [51]–[64].

Perhaps unsurprisingly, those decisions adopted a general approach that adhered to the routes of challenge under the Act, but made a limited – and diminishing – acknowledgment that some residual possibility of discretionary intervention should be available. This was partly in deference to arbitral orthodoxy. However it also reflected a sense that by agreeing to refer their dispute to an arbitrator – a qualified and accredited third party who, as a matter of duty, was bound to act fairly and impartially – parties were taking a course that was less susceptible to a problematic outcome than if they simply reached agreement between themselves.

The decision under appeal in Haley represented an extension and extreme instance of the trend, asserting arbitral orthodoxy with virtually no possibility of exception.

Court of Appeal decision

The Court of Appeal's decision in Haley was that where the award concerned financial remedy of a kind that fell within the Matrimonial Causes Act 1973 ('MCA 1973') and a contested application was made to embody it in a court order, it was open to the court to review the award substantively, applying the same test as would apply in an appeal in a financial remedy case that had gone through the court procedure: was the decision 'wrong' or 'unjust' (because of a serious procedural or other irregularity in the arbitral process) [49(ii)].

Further, whilst not wishing to be seen as 'undermining the arbitration process' [72], the Court of Appeal held [71]:

> 'Given that the orders determining the enforceable legal rights of the parties following divorce are made under the MCA 1973 and not under the AA 1996, there is no requirement for the discontented party first to make an application under s 57, s 68 or s 69 AA 1996 before asking the Family Court to decline to make an order under the MCA 1973 in the terms of the arbitral award.'

Further, the Court expressly rejected the notion that an arbitrated outcome was somehow stronger than an agreement between the parties. In the latter case, the parties were committing to a known outcome; in the former, they were simply committing to a process [67].

Implications

On one view, the decision in Haley could be considered 'niche'- a decision that is simply about the process available for challenging a financial remedy arbitration award, interesting only to those who actually arbitrate, and primarily about the firm promotion of the MCA 1973 appeal route over the arbitral challenge routes.

However, it would be wrong and simplistic to consider Haley in isolation. For those who act as arbitrators and those who use arbitration there are, of course, important practical implications to be aware of, which we consider (below). Haley goes further than this though and raises significant questions that go to the heart of what arbitration means in the family law context.

(1) Changes to the IFLA Rules and ARB1 FS

It is quite clear that both the Form ARB1 FS and IFLA's Rules now need to be amended. For example, the current warning on the ARB1 FS says: 'Arbitration is a process whose outcome is generally final. There are very limited bases for raising a challenge or appeal, and it is only in exceptional circumstances that a court will exercise its own discretion in substitution for the award.' At the time of writing, work was underway to address this, with a revised edition of Rules and Forms envisaged for early 2021.

For those advising parties or clients about the arbitration process, they too will need to amend their advice about the finality of an award. No doubt this will be welcomed by family lawyers who are likely to be far more comfortable explaining the appeals test under the MCA 1973 and Family Procedure Rules 2010 than they are explaining to clients the routes of challenge available under the Act. An added complication has been that no family arbitration award has yet been successfully challenged under the Act and there is therefore no precedent on which to base advice.

A word of caution, though. The 'wrong' test may be less restrictive, but it is by no means pushing at an open door. Parties entering arbitration should continue to do so in full expectation of being bound by the eventual award made. King LJ herself warned at para [72]:

> '... parties must go into arbitration with their eyes open with the understanding that, all other things being equal, the award made at the end of the process will thereafter be incorporated into a consent order.'

(2) How does a party challenge a financial remedy arbitration award using the 'wrong' test?

Paragraphs [48] and [73] of Haley state that, unless and until otherwise indicated, practitioners need to adopt the approach set out in Part 30 FPR 2010 when it comes to challenging a financial remedy arbitration award using the 'wrong' test.

A challenge to an arbitral award will be referred to a specialist financial remedy Circuit Judge or High Court Judge. It is not necessary for such cases to be put before a High Court Judge as a matter of course. It is also not necessary for routes under the Act to be exhausted first.

The party seeking to resile from the award will need, on paper, to 'show cause' why the award should not be turned into a court order.

CR v SR (Financial Remedies: Permission to Appeal) [2013] EWHC 1155 (Fam), [2014] 1 FLR 186, Re R (A Child: Possible Perpetrator) [2019] EWCA Civ 895, [2019] 2 FLR 1033).

If the challenge does not meet the test, the Family Court will make an order in the terms of the award and has the power to penalise the resiling party in costs (para [96]).

If the challenge does meet the test, ordinarily a review hearing (and not a re-hearing) will be listed subject to case management directions which can deal with the timetable, moving forward. Those case management directions will enable the hearing to be tailored to the circumstances of the case.

In the event that the Family Court concludes that the arbitrator's award was wrong, it will substitute its own order.

It is important to remember that Haley does not sweep away the routes of challenge under the Act, nor the ability to challenge an award on the grounds of mistake or supervening events; these remain open, although it is difficult to envisage the circumstances in which a party would not opt for the FPR 2010 route.

As with appeals more generally, practitioners will need to advise their clients that where permission is granted, the appeal hearing is not an opportunity for a 'second bite of the cherry'. Unless justice demands otherwise, the appeal will be a review hearing. The approach to appeals as set out in Piglowska v Piglowski [1999] 1 WLR 1360 remains good law.

(3) What is the status of an arbitration award before it becomes a court order?

The Court of Appeal held that without orders made under the MCA 1973 following an arbitral award, parties' rights were both 'legally undetermined' [31] and 'unenforceable' [90]. This raises some doubt about the precise status of an award that has been made (and would normally be effective, at least as between the parties, following s 58), but not yet embodied in a court order. In practical terms, it means that parties to arbitrations dealing with financial remedies under the MCA 1973 are bound to make an application to court in relation to their arbitral awards, rather than that being an optional recourse.

Authorities such as S v S (Financial Remedies: Arbitral Award) [2014] EWHC 7 (Fam), [2014] 1 FLR 1257 had endorsed an approach that arbitral awards should attract less court scrutiny than, for example, agreements arrived at by the parties themselves, when presented to the court to be converted into a consent order. Indeed, in S v S, Sir James Munby (then President of the Family Division) famously said, 'the arbitral award should be determinative of the order the court makes' (para [19]).

By contrast, in Haley, King LJ said:

> 'The agreement to arbitrate is an agreement that a third party will determine the terms. It is not, at the time the agreement is reached, an agreement to any particular terms' (para [67]).

Whilst this seems highly unlikely to be a direct criticism of the arbitration process itself (King LJ commented on more than one occasion that the judgment should not be read as undermining the 'valuable service' arbitration provides (paras [5]–[6] and [72])), it is hard to simply ignore it. Should those who choose to arbitrate feel more exposed as a result?

As set out below, the Family Court does not rubber stamp consent orders. However, arbitrators should not fear greater scrutiny of their awards by the Family Court. Well-reasoned, well-structured awards, arrived at as they are by qualified, experienced specialists who are bound by a duty to act fairly and impartially with the benefit of all the evidence, will continue to carry significant weight. At para [46], King LJ concluded by saying 'Although the court still has to exercise its statutory role, it will be heavily influenced by what the parties themselves have agreed'. If greater scrutiny of awards reduces the scope for errors and helps to ensure consistently high quality awards, it is surely to be welcomed.

(4) Does Haley create a tension between the Family Court and the Act?

The Court of Appeal has firmly asserted the pre-eminence of relevant family law – the MCA 1973 – over arbitration law and orthodoxy. It has also confirmed the availability of a substantive review adopting a family law orientation. Does this tell us anything about the interplay between the Family Court and the Act?

As mentioned above, the IFLA scheme derives its authority from the Act. Some purists are likely to hold a view that when parties agree to arbitrate under the IFLA scheme, they are contracting to arbitrate under the Act as modified by the scheme's rules. And a key feature of the Act is that arbitral awards can only be challenged in very limited circumstances as highlighted in the quote at para [19]: 'Remember, when parties agree arbitration they buy the right to get the wrong answer'. So, for non-family lawyers the mere fact that an award is wrong or even unjust does not, of itself, provide a basis for challenging the award.

Being critical, one might ask, 'what makes financial remedy arbitration awards so special that they deserve a different review process, one that is less restrictive?' The writers cannot fail to be reminded of the Supreme Court decision in Prest v Petrodel Resources Ltd & Others [2013] UKSC 34, [2013] 2 FLR 732 where the Family Court had taken a different approach to their Chancery colleagues when it came to piercing the corporate veil. Lord Sumption said: 'Courts exercising family jurisdiction do not occupy a desert island in which general legal concepts are suspended or mean something different' (para [37]).

A key consideration must be that, unlike their civil counterparts, family law consent orders – the enforceable orders – derive their authority from the court and not from the consent of the parties. This is recognised on the Form ARB1 FS. Family lawyers are all too familiar with the court's inquisitorial jurisdiction not being a rubber stamp, but also 'neither being a bloodhound or a ferret' (L v L [2006] EWHC 966 (Fam)). The Supreme Court in Sharland v Sharland [2015] UKSC 60, [2015] 2 FLR 1367 made clear that the fact there is an agreement (even if it is an agreement to arbitrate and therefore put the decision-making in the hands of a third party) does not oust the court's jurisdiction and that, although the court is heavily influenced by an agreement, the court should always conduct its own assessment to enable it to discharge its statutory role.

(5) Does Haley apply to family law arbitrations other than MCA cases?

It should be noted that the scope of the IFLA Financial Scheme is not limited to financial remedies that would fall within the MCA 1973. It also accommodates cases under the Trusts of Land and Appointment of Trustees Act 1996, the Inheritance (Provision for Family and Dependants) Act 1975, the Children Act 1989, Schedule 1 and the Married Women's Property Act 1882, for example. The Court of Appeal was not asked to consider whether the Haley type of review would be available for arbitral awards in these areas.

It may be that this would depend on factors such as whether cases turned on trust and property principles rather than the exercise of a discretion; and whether the relevant court procedure was governed by the Family or the Civil Procedure Rules. Further cases will presumably clarify the position.

It seems likely that the conclusions in Haley would apply to the IFLA Children Scheme (whose scope engages for the most part with matters which could be the subject of applications to court under s 8 of the Children Act 1989). Arrangements for children would seem to be always open to review by the court in the interests of the child's welfare; however, we await further guidance.

(6) How does Haley impact on the New York Convention 1958?

Interestingly, no mention is made in the judgment of the New York Convention 1958 ('NYC'). The UK is bound by this convention, and refusing to enforce an arbitral award is a breach of it. How would an overseas court in a signatory state respond to an attempt by a party to enforce an English award for financial remedy that had not been made into a court order? Could Art V 1(e) of the NYC (which allows enforcement to be refused if 'the award has not yet become binding on the parties') be successfully invoked to resist enforcement? Whilst such an eventuality may be rare (because of the domestic orientation of IFLA arbitrations; and the commercial opt-out that precludes the entertainment of non-commercial awards in many jurisdictions) it is an area that may at some stage have to be considered and fully scrutinised.

Concluding remarks

The court system has changed beyond recognition in the wake of Covid-19. Courts, whilst open, are operating with limited caseloads, with much work being conducted remotely. Litigators have to seriously consider alternative dispute resolution to avoid the log-jam. And it is no surprise that arbitration – bespoke, private, quick to set up and able to be conducted remotely on a variety of digital platforms – has become increasingly popular.

Yet there had remained a fear that, by submitting to arbitration, a wrong decision from an arbitrator, unless very wrong, or so wrong that it 'leapt off the page', could not be challenged. By placing financial remedy arbitration on the same footing as financial remedy litigation when it comes to appeals, the Court of Appeal's decision is likely to encourage more couples to see arbitration as a viable, meaningful alternative to lengthy and expensive court proceedings.

More generally, it seems possible to regard Haley as a significant step towards a closer integration of the arbitral and family regimes, and the evolution of family arbitration as a fully developed process.

The views expressed in this article are those of the authors (and not, necessarily, those of IFLA).

Suzanne Kingston

Jonathan Tecks

Family Arbitration – The New Landscape (Suzanne Kingston, James Ewins QC, Alexis Campbell QC and Jonathan Tecks)

FAMILY ARBITRATION – THE NEW LANDSCAPE

1. Since the arrival of the global coronavirus (COVID-19) pandemic, the court system has changed beyond recognition. Many of the courts were closed and even now, as they slowly re-open, many are still operating with limited caseloads, with much work being conducted remotely. There seems to be a consensus that litigators must seriously consider alternative dispute resolution, to avoid the log-jam in courts across the country. And it is no surprise that arbitration—bespoke, private, quick to set up and able to be conducted remotely on a variety of digital platforms—is becoming increasingly popular, nowhere more so than in family disputes.

The origin of Family Arbitration (IFLA)

2. The conjunction of arbitration and the area of family law may, at first glance, seem incongruous. The essence of arbitration is the principle that disputing parties appoint a trusted third-party well-versed in their area of activity to adjudicate, on the basis that they agree to be bound by the outcome. The simplicity of this principle allows for speed and clarity, goals aligned very well to areas of commercial activity which call for robust, rapid resolution. Important features are the encouragement of party autonomy – the 'ownership' of the dispute by the parties themselves; and the discouragement of court intervention, which would be likely to impede efficiency.

3. In contrast, family law is an area where the courts are jealous of their statutory role, exemplified in the principle that not even agreements arrived at by parties themselves can oust the jurisdiction of the court. Even less so, it would seem, should a potentially rival process such as arbitration be capable of supplanting the court's scrutiny.

4. Nevertheless, when the Institute of Family Law Arbitrators (IFLA) initiated a family law arbitration scheme some 10 years ago, points of synergy were identified. In particular, a movement towards party autonomy (which arbitration would encourage) seemed to coincide with a growing willingness on the part of the courts to respect agreements freely arrived at in the area of family law, characterised, for example, by the Supreme Court's decision in *Radmacher v Granatino* [2010] UKSC 42.

5. And when it came to devising different aspects of the scheme, the remarkable flexibility afforded by the open weave of the Arbitration Act 1996 (the AA 1996) allowed a considerable degree of integration. Non-mandatory sections of the AA 1996 facilitated rules by which a family law arbitration model for England and Wales was fashioned. Thus the 'applicable law' (s.46), which ordinarily would be a matter of choice, was delimited to the law applicable within England and Wales. Conversely, available 'remedies' (s.48), which ordinarily would be limited in range, were enlarged to encompass those frequently used in family matters. And 'costs' (s.61), which ordinarily would be allocated following a civil pattern, were specifically aligned with the family regime.

6. One aspect where integration was less immediately obvious concerned that of potential challenge to an award. In the absence of legislative assistance or judicial direction, recourse was had to s.58 of the AA 1996, dealing with the effect of an award. The section provides that an award is final and binding subject to the routes of challenge within the AA 1996. Crucially, this provision is non-mandatory, so it operates 'unless otherwise agreed by the parties'. It follows that parties to family arbitrations could agree to leave the way open to some kind of further court intervention.

7. Under the AA 1996, appeals are only permitted where there is lack of jurisdiction (s.67), where there has been a serious procedural irregularity (s.68) (which is very narrowly interpreted), or where the arbitrator has erred in law (s.69). The latter test also sets a very high threshold. In effect, the decision must be one which no reasonable arbitrator could have reached when applying the law properly. There is also a preliminary filter under the AA 1996, ss.57 and 70, which requires the parties to apply first to the arbitrator for clarification or to correct an award (akin to the slip rule procedure) before pursuing an appeal under the AA 1996. Equally clear was the arbitral orthodoxy that findings of fact and overall conclusions were generally not open to challenge.

8. How would these sit with family law matters, where an outcome would often represent an exercise of discretion following a multitude of factual decisions? Would there be a basis for overriding an award where the arbitrator had arrived at an irrational or bizarre outcome? And how would the arbitral regime be compatible with the family law principle that the court's jurisdiction may not be ousted?

9. Since the form and extent of any court intervention were not certain, the wording of the scheme rules (and corresponding wording of the 'ARB1' arbitration agreement) was intentionally somewhat open-ended. It committed the parties, where necessary (and in virtually all financial remedy cases, it would be necessary):

   9.1. to apply to an appropriate court for an order in the same or similar terms as the award;

   9.2. to recognise that the court had a discretion as to whether and in what terms to make an order; and

9.3. to acknowledge that the finality of the award was subject to any changes which the court making that order may require.

10. This formula was intended to create a platform that would allow a court to take a range of steps from making changes purely incidental to the transformation of an award into an order (for example, by translating a party commitment in the arbitration into a formal undertaking to the court) to (IFLA considered) changing the outcome of an award in its entirety, if possible and necessary.

Case Law

11. The cases that launched appeals from this platform generated in an impressive line of first instance authorities: starting with Munby P in S v S *(financial remedies: arbitral award)* [2014] EWHC 7 (Fam), [2014] 1 FLR 1257, followed by Mostyn J in *J v B (Family Law Arbitration Award)* [2016] EWHC 324 (Fam), [2016] 2 FLR 1308, and two decisions of Clare Ambrose, sitting as a deputy High Court judge, in *BC v BG* [2019] EWFC 7, [2019] 2 FLR 337 and *H v W* [2019] EWHC 1897 (Fam). However, in each of these cases the High Court reinforced the increasingly narrow scope and high bar of the appeal process within the family arbitration structure, exemplified by the following extract from a lecture by Sir Bernard Eder, quoted with approval by Mostyn J in *J v B* (at §6):

> "…the general approach of the Court is one which strongly supports the arbitral process. By way of anecdote, it is perhaps interesting to recall what I was once told many years ago by Michael Kerr, a former judge in the Court of Appeal and one of the leading figures in the recent development of the law of arbitration in England, when I was complaining about an arbitration that I had just lost and the difficulties in the way of challenging the award. I told him that the award was wrong and unjust. He looked baffled and said: *"Remember, when parties agree arbitration they buy the right to get the wrong answer"*. So, the mere fact that an award is "wrong" or even "unjust" does not, of itself, provide any basis for challenging the award or intervention by the Court."

12. Mostyn J went on to conclude:

> *"An assertion that the award was "wrong" or "unjust" will almost never get off the ground: in such a case the error must be so blatant and extreme that it leaps off the page."*

13. Unsurprisingly, therefore, in the next arbitration case that came before Clare Ambrose, sitting as a deputy High Court judge, *R v K* [2020] EWHC 841 (Fam), [2020] All ER (D) 193 (Feb)), she applied the hitherto accepted approach, that grounds for appeal from arbitral awards are extremely limited, leading to the conclusion that the arbitral award before her was not so wrong that it should not be made into an order. But the parties in *R v K* were Mr and Mrs Haley. And when Mr Haley took his case to the Court of Appeal, the court decided, in a dramatic about turn, that those previous decisions were wrongly decided.

Haley v Haley

14. The recent decision from the Court of Appeal in *Haley v Haley* [2020] EWCA Civ 1369, [2020] All ER (D) 110 (Oct) has endorsed a review process in financial remedy arbitrations akin to that applicable to appeals from judicial determinations under s.25 of the Matrimonial Causes Act 1973. This has transformed the legal landscape for financial arbitration in family cases and should encourage practitioners and parties alike to look to arbitration much more seriously as a viable, often preferable, means of resolving their disputes, now with the added assurance that even if it goes wrong, it can be put right.

Background

15. Mr and Mrs Haley had had their two-day final financial hearing adjourned by the court at short notice due to judicial unavailability. Quickly entering into an arbitration agreement, they identified a number of issues for determination covering both capital and income division. Having heard the arbitration, the arbitrator circulated a draft award. The husband's counsel sought clarification and/or explanation of 14 'substantial' points under s.57 of the AA 1996. Declining to provide clarification on the basis that the requests went beyond what was permissible, the arbitrator produced his final award. Dissatisfied, the husband sought to challenge the award and applied to the court for an order that the award not be made into a court order on a number of grounds including that the arbitrator had erred in law, had failed to give reasons for his decision, and had ignored or overlooked facts. In the High Court, Clare Ambrose approved the award and made an order which reflected its terms (*R v K*).

16. The husband appealed. Although his appeal necessarily included the argument that Clare Ambrose had misapplied the AA 1996 on the facts of his case, central to the appeal was a direct challenge to the relatively high threshold faced by an appellant from an arbitral award compared to that which applied to an appeal from a judicial determination. Moylan LJ gave permission to appeal on the basis that the appeal raised an important point of principle as to the proper approach which the family court should take to arbitral awards when making a financial remedy order.

Decision

17. Subsequently, in a typically clear judgment, King LJ gave a full analysis of the interplay between the AA 1996 and the courts, both in general civil litigation and specifically in the family arena. The civil courts, she noted, strive for certainty, which is an essential ingredient for successful commerce where appeals detract from certainty and are discouraged even at the cost of fairness. King LJ noted that whilst "fairness as a concept has no place in a challenge to an arbitral award; arbitration being a procedure designed to provide certainty across the international commercial world", fairness is

nonetheless central the court's determination under s.25 of the Matrimonial Causes Act 1973 (para. [14-15]). And such "fairness" is not a concept that can be contracted out of. So how does the strict civil interpretation fit in with the ethos of the family courts in the context of arbitration?

18. King LJ provided the answer to this 'conundrum' (para [51]) which lies in the simple fact that *"family cases are different from civil cases"*. Whereas court orders embodying commercial and civil arbitration awards derive their authority from the parties' agreement, orders determining the enforceable legal rights of the parties following divorce are made under the court's jurisdiction under Matrimonial Causes Act 1973. Therefore, in the family context, arbitration cannot oust the underlying jurisdiction of the court, as is recognised by the IFLA arbitration agreement (ARB1 FS) (see paras. [68] – [72]).

19. The natural consequence of this analysis, per King LJ, is that the family court must allow a review of an arbitral award where the award was "wrong" (i.e. applying the same threshold test as appeals from judicial determinations under the Matrimonial Causes Act 1973). Consequently, the higher threshold that had previously been held to apply (i.e. requiring that the decision is "obviously wrong") does not apply to family arbitrations under s.25 of the Matrimonial Causes Act 1973. Consistently with this, the family court will consider a review of an arbitrator's award on the same basis that it would consider an appeal against a judgement (para. [72]): it will grant permission to appeal where there is 'a real prospect of success' which is realistic and not fanciful (per *CR v SR (Financial Remedies: Permission to Appeal)* [2013] EWHC 1155 (Fam), [2014] 1 FLR 186) and the ultimate test is simply: was the award "wrong" (*Re B* (*A Child*) (*Care Proceedings: Threshold Criteria*) [2013] UKSC 33).

Impact

20. It is quite clear that both the Form ARB1 FS and IFLA's Rules now need to be amended. For example, the current warning on the ARB1 FS says: 'Arbitration is a process whose outcome is generally final. There are very limited bases for raising a challenge or appeal, and it is only in exceptional circumstances that a court will exercise its own discretion in substitution for the award.' At the time of writing, work was underway to address this, with a revised edition of Rules and Forms envisaged for early 2021.

21. For those advising parties or clients about the arbitration process, they too will need to amend their advice about the finality of an award. No doubt this will be welcomed by family lawyers who are likely to be far more comfortable explaining the appeals test under the MCA 1973 and Family Procedure Rules 2010 than they are explaining to clients the routes of challenge available under the 1996 Act (with the added complication that no family arbitration award was successfully challenged under the 1996 Act and therefore there was no precedent on which to base advice).

22. A word of caution, though. The 'wrong' test may be less restrictive, but it is by no means pushing at an open door. Parties entering arbitration should continue to do so in full expectation of being bound by the eventual award made. King LJ herself warned at para [72]:

> ' ... *parties must go into arbitration with their eyes open with the understanding that, all other things being equal, the award made at the end of the process will thereafter be incorporated into a consent order.*'

Process to challenge an arbitral award

23. The decision in *Haley* provided some guidance on the process for challenging arbitral award. Paragraphs [48] and [73] of *Haley* state that, unless and until otherwise indicated, practitioners need to adopt the approach set out in Part 30 FPR 2010 when it comes to challenging a financial remedy arbitration award using the 'wrong' test.

 23.1. The party seeking to resile from the award will need, on paper, to 'show cause' why the award should not be turned into a court order.

 23.2. A challenge to an arbitral award will be referred to a specialist financial remedy Circuit Judge or High Court Judge. It is not necessary for such cases to be put before a High Court Judge as a matter of course. It is also not necessary for remedies under the 1996 Act to be exhausted first.

 23.3. The triage or filter is performed by the judge applying r.30.3(7)(a) FPR 2010 i.e. the challenge must demonstrate a real prospect of success of demonstrating that the award is wrong, a prospect that is realistic and not fanciful (CR v SR (financial remedies: permission to appeal) [2013] EWHC 1155 (Fam), Re A (a child) [2019] EWCA Civ 895).

 23.4. If the challenge does not meet the test, the Family Court will make an order in the terms of the award and has the power to penalise the resiling party in costs (para [96]).

 23.5. If the challenge does meet the test, ordinarily a full review hearing will be listed subject to case management directions which can deal with the timetable, moving forward. Those case management directions will enable the hearing to be tailored to the circumstances of the case. It may be appropriate to give limited directions or list for more detailed case management, such as further updating evidence. NB: This is not ordinarily a re-hearing; a re-hearing is only permissible if the interests of justice require one (Family Procedure Rules 2010, SI 2010/2955, 30.12(1)(b))).

 23.6. In the event that the Family Court concludes that the arbitrator's award was wrong, it will substitute its own order.

24. It is important to remember that Haley does not sweep away the routes of challenge under the Act, nor the ability to challenge an award on the

grounds of mistake or supervening events; these remain open, although it is difficult to envisage the circumstances in which a party would not opt for the FPR 2010 route.

25. As with appeals more generally, practitioners will need to advise their clients that where permission is granted, the appeal hearing is not an opportunity for a 'second bite of the cherry'. Unless justice demands otherwise, the appeal will be a review hearing. The approach to appeals as set out in *Piglowska v Piglowski* [1999] 1 WLR 1360 remains good law.

Is this good for arbitration?

26. A great fear of many practitioners when considering submitting to arbitration, has been that a wrong decision from an arbitrator, unless very wrong or so wrong that it 'leaps off the page', cannot be corrected and clients would be forced to accept and live with a bad decision. This puts enormous pressure on the choice of a specific arbitrator, leaving scope for blame for an election that results in a bad decision (although IFLA has always been able to make the selection – including from a shortlist – if asked). Post-*Haley*, a decision by an arbitrator which would be unacceptable if made by a judge can be challenged on the same basis. Financial remedy arbitration therefore now stands on an equivalent footing with financial remedy litigation, whether before a public judge or private arbitrator (and you cannot select your judge, even from a shortlist).

27. It may be argued that the one feature of arbitration that has attracted many supporters, the finality and the certainty, is now lost because the right to pay for a wrong answer has gone. It is fair to say that a small minority of cases cry out for a binary decision which will be impervious to challenge and therefore offer finality. While some may lament that loss in a small number of cases, the benefits for the vast majority of cases remain; and not only will clients be able to avoid lengthy and expensive delays, but they can now do so knowing that even a wrong decision can be remedied.

28. As noted by King LJ (para. [5]), *"There is a common misconception that the use of arbitration, as an alternative to the court process in financial remedy cases, is the purview only of the rich who seek privacy away from the courts and the eyes of the media. If that was ever the position, it is no more."* It is hoped that, now more than ever, arbitration will be seen as a realistic means of resolving all types of financial remedy cases, not just the for the rich and famous hoping to avoid the spotlight of the court process, but in more modest cases too. Whilst some arbitrators are top-flight QCs and former High Court judges charging commensurate fees, there are arbitrators whose professional practices specialise at more modest levels, and whose fees will align with an economic resolution of such cases. Arbitrations can be tailored for the needs of all cases, offering an affordable solution, which is now subject to the same fair and limited opportunity of appeal as court determined decision.

Unresolved Issues

29. It should be noted that the scope of the IFLA Financial Scheme is not limited to financial remedies that would fall within the MCA 1973. It also accommodates cases under the Trusts of Land and Appointment of Trustees Act 1996, the Inheritance (Provision for Family and Dependants) Act 1975, the Children Act 1989, Schedule 1 and the Married Women's Property Act 1882, for example. The Court of Appeal was not asked to consider whether the *Haley* type of review would be available for arbitral awards in these areas. It may be that this would depend on factors such as whether cases turned on trust and property principles rather than the exercise of a discretion; and whether the relevant court procedure was governed by the Family or the Civil Procedure Rules. Further cases will presumably clarify the position.

30. It seems likely that the conclusions in *Haley* would apply to the IFLA Children Scheme, whose scope engages for the most part with matters which could be the subject of applications to court under s.8 Children Act 1989. Arrangements for children would seem to be always open to review by the court in the interests of the child's welfare; however, further guidance is awaited.

31. Interestingly, no mention is made in the judgment of the New York Convention 1958 (NYC) – although there was some discussion at the hearing about the status of awards not made into orders. The UK is bound by this convention, and refusing to enforce an arbitral award is a breach of it. How would an overseas court in a signatory state respond to an attempt by a party to enforce an English award for financial remedy that had not been made into a court order (or was, conceivably, subject to an appeal in the English court)? Could Art.V 1(e) of the NYC (which allows enforcement to be refused if 'the award has not yet become binding on the parties') be successfully invoked to resist enforcement, especially in the light of the King LJ's dicta that without orders made under the MCA 1973 following an arbitral award, parties' rights were both 'legally undetermined' [31] and 'unenforceable' [90]?

32. While the relevance of the NYC may be remote because of the domestic orientation of IFLA arbitrations, and the commercial opt-out that precludes the entertainment of non-commercial awards in many jurisdictions, this is nevertheless an area that may at some stage have to be considered and fully scrutinised.

Conclusion

33. *Haley* is undoubtedly a case in which the Matrimonial Causes Act 1973 and the AA 1996 were pitched against each other in the Court of Appeal and the Matrimonial Causes Act 1973 came out on top. Some purists are likely to be troubled by that outcome. When the AA 1996 was passed its interaction with Matrimonial Causes Act 1973 was not considered, perhaps

understandably, since the IFLA scheme had not even been conceived at that time. Nonetheless, it will no doubt be argued that a key feature of the 1996 Act is that arbitral awards can only be challenged in very limited circumstances as highlighted in the quote at para [19]: "Remember, when parties agree arbitration they buy the right to get the wrong answer". So, for non-family lawyers the mere fact that an award is wrong or even unjust does not, of itself, provide a basis for challenging the award. They will no doubt question whether family arbitration post-*Haley* is arbitration at all.

34. Such critics might ask, 'what makes financial remedy arbitration awards so special that they deserve a different review process, one that is less restrictive?', reminding family lawyers of the Supreme Court decision in *Petrodel v Prest* [2013] UKSC 34 where the Family Court had taken a different approach to their Chancery colleagues when it came to piercing the corporate veil. Lord Sumption said: 'Courts exercising family jurisdiction do not occupy a desert island in which general legal concepts are suspended or mean something different' (para 37).

35. Nonetheless, a key consideration must be that, unlike their civil counterparts, family law consent orders – the enforceable orders – derive their authority from the court and not from the consent of the parties. The Supreme Court in *Sharland v Sharland* [2015] UKSC 60 made clear that the fact there is an agreement (which surely includes an agreement to arbitrate and therefore put the decision-making in the hands of a third party) does not oust the court's jurisdiction and that, although the court is heavily influenced by an agreement, the court should always conduct its own assessment to enable it to discharge its statutory role.

36. Such debates will no doubt continue. In the meantime, by placing financial remedy arbitration on the same footing as financial remedy litigation when it comes to appeals, the Court of Appeal's decision is likely to encourage more couples to see arbitration as a viable, meaningful alternative to lengthy and expensive court proceedings. More generally, it seems possible to regard *Haley* as a significant step towards a closer alignment of family arbitration and litigation in the wider dispute resolution landscape.

Part of this article first appeared in Family Law. The authors are grateful to Family Law for allowing it to be replicated.

Suzanne Kingston
James Ewins QC
Alexis Campbell QC
Jonathan Tecks

Global Arbitration – Right place, right time? (Suzanne Kingston, Geoff Wilson and Rachael Kelsey)

FAMILY LAW JOURNAL – OCTOBER 2021 #207

ARBITRATION

Global arbitration: Right place, right time?

Many countries have statutory provision for family law arbitration schemes and even those that don't have a statutory scheme have given careful thought to arbitration.

Suzanne Kingston, Rachael Kelsey and Geoff Wilson look at developments in arbitration in England and Wales, Scotland and Australia together with tables on arbitration schemes around the world

Mills & Reeve, SKO Family LLP & HopgoodGanim

Suzanne Kingston (top) is a consultant at **Mills & Reeve**, **Rachael Kelsey** is a partner at **SKO Family LLP**, Scotland and **Geoff Wilson** (bottom) is a partner at **HopgoodGanim**, Australia

Suzanne Kingston, Rachael Kelsey and Geoff Wilson look at developments in arbitration in England and Wales, Scotland and Australia together with tables on arbitration schemes around the world

Many countries have statutory provision for family law arbitration schemes and even those that don't have a statutory scheme have given careful thought to arbitration.

In 2012 we wrote a two-part comparative article about family law arbitration around the world ('Wide focus', *FLJ*122 and 'Global view', *FLJ*123, by Suzanne Kingston and Rachael Kelsey). This time, we are joined by our antipodean friend, Geoff Wilson, and as previously we are extremely grateful to all of the fellows of the International Academy of Family Lawyers (IAFL) who answered our call to provide information about family law arbitration in their respective jurisdictions. A comprehensive set of tables setting out details of arbitration across the Asia Pacific, Europe, Canada, the US and various other countries can be accessed via links below.

It is almost unimaginable to think how much has changed since 2012. Perhaps the most far-reaching changes have come in the last year as a consequence of Covid-19, as up until then court systems around the world functioned in the way they did but there was no impetus to modernise or to change. But the sudden onset of stay-at-home orders has meant that whole new ways of working have had to be quickly embraced. It probably comes as no surprise that individuals were able to do this much more nimbly and flexibly than institutions.

As a consequence, non-court dispute resolution has become even more popular – whether mediation, hybrid mediation/arbitration, private adjudication, early neutral evaluation or of course arbitration. In England and Wales arbitration cases increased dramatically and we saw remote arbitration hearings undertaken via platforms such as Zoom or Teams. A group of arbitrators has prepared suggested guidelines for the conduct of remote hearings as an arbitrator or private judge, to help in setting up and undertaking those hearings.

DEVELOPMENTS IN ENGLAND AND WALES

Outside of recent events, there had been notable progressive changes to the arbitration rules since 2013 and a steady evolution has occurred. One of the most significant changes has been the extension of the financial scheme to include a separate, but similar, children's scheme. The Institute of Family Law Arbitrators (IFLA) early on made the decision to start arbitration in financial cases only, so as to gain traction and to test the uptake of arbitration before launching the children's scheme. Between 2012 and 2016 it was clear that arbitration was gaining prominence and that the judiciary supported the scheme and were prepared to endorse arbitration in a number of cases and in practice guidance delivered by the president of the Family Division. Practitioners were keen to support this new way of working and many senior practitioners, whether retired judges/barristers or solicitors with at least ten years' qualification, sought to train as arbitrators.

The main issues in extending to children arbitration were to ensure that there are robust systems for safeguarding and to ascertain the wishes and feelings of the children. A great deal of thought was devoted to these two issues.

Safeguarding is dealt with in two ways:

- Art 17 of the IFLA children scheme rules clearly sets out that the arbitrator must ensure that safeguarding issues have been dealt with prior to the commencement of the arbitration and must have continuous regard for safeguarding during the course of the arbitration; and
- the originating application for arbitration, ie form ARB1CS, also sets out the requirements for safeguarding.

If the arbitrator is concerned about safeguarding issues, they may involve an independent social worker to assist them. The independent social worker fulfils another vital function, ie where the arbitrator and/or the parties need to ascertain the wishes and feelings of the children, or to have external expert help, the independent social worker can be appointed by the tribunal to undertake this role.

The scope of children arbitration is set out in the children scheme rules at Art 2 and includes both internal and external relocation to certain jurisdictions. External relocation was only added in 2019 after the scheme had been running for three years as it was felt appropriate to ensure that the scheme was fully embedded before allowing external relocation, whether on a permanent or temporary basis.

A further development has been the decision in *Haley v Haley* [2020], where the Court of Appeal effectively endorsed a review process in financial remedy arbitrations akin to that applicable to appeals from a judicial determination made under s25, Matrimonial Causes Act 1973 (MCA 1973), ie the basis for an appeal must be that the decision is 'wrong'. In *Haley,* the MCA 1973 and the Arbitration Act 1996 (AA 1996) were pitched against each other and some purists are likely to be troubled by that outcome. Critics of the decision in *Haley* might ask what makes a financial remedy arbitration award so special that it deserves a different review process, ie one that is less restrictive than that in AA 1996? But we are reminded that in other areas of the law, the family courts have taken a different approach, see for example *Prest v Petrodel Resources Ltd* [2013], when the Supreme Court disapproved of the previous approach to the 'corporate veil' in the family courts and found that there must be alignment with the approach in other divisions of the courts. On the other hand we must remember that, unlike their civil counterparts, consent orders in family proceedings derive their authority from the court and not from the consent of the parties. We are yet to see whether the decision in *Haley* is applicable to other areas of family law, including children proceedings or claims under the Trusts of Land and Appointment of Trustees Act 1996.

DEVELOPMENTS IN SCOTLAND

The Scottish family law arbitration scheme (Family Law Arbitration Group Scotland (FLAGS)) celebrated its tenth birthday earlier this year. The scheme was set up by around 20 senior family law practitioners and membership has steadily grown since then to nearly 60, which, in context, is around a fifth of the family lawyers in Scotland who specialise in or undertake a substantial amount of family law.

The scheme was created by six people (who now are a judge, two sheriffs, a QC and two solicitors, but at that time were simply a mixture of counsel and solicitors). Work started in the early 90s to try and find a way to use arbitration as a dispute resolution model in cases that needed a determination. Given the general patchwork of provision for arbitration in Scots law at that time, progress was slow, but the advent of a new legislative framework for arbitration in Scotland in 2010 saw matters reignite.

The Arbitration (Scotland) Act 2010 is a beautifully straightforward piece of legislation: it has a schedule of rules and a framework that discourages judicial involvement, other than when required to support the arbitral process. The schedule can be used as is, with certain mandatory rules that deal with the arbitral process and then discretionary rules that can be amended and/or expanded to be tailored to a particular industry or context. The FLAGS group revised the schedule for use in family law matters (child and money) and the FLAGS rules were born (now in their third edition).

The FLAGS scheme can be used for any family law dispute, for example:

- financial provision on divorce and discrete issues in financial cases, such as ascertaining the 'relevant date' (which is a significant issue in Scotland, as that is the date on which assets are valued);
- determining valuations to be used;
- dealing with the realisation (or not) of individual assets; and
- the occupation and use of property.

The scheme has also always covered child law matters (other than public law issues, obviously, which are reserved to the state, and not matters that parties can privately contract out of). The full range of child law cases from residence and contact through to specific issues like relocation, which school children should attend and medical treatment, are all capable of being determined in a FLAGS arbitration.

The latest, exciting development arises from new legislation, namely the Children (Scotland) Act 2020 (C(S)A 2020). Section 23, C(S)A 2020 obliges the Scottish government to make legal aid available for the costs associated with arbitration in child law cases that relate to parental responsibilities and rights, so residence, contact, relocation, specific issues and guardianship are all encompassed. The provisions came into force in January 2021 and the detailed arrangements are being worked on by the Scottish Legal Aid Board.

As Scotland starts to look forward to the easing of coronavirus restrictions within the next few months and, in particular, the Covid-19 recovery plan that has been put in place by the Scottish Courts and Tribunals Service (SCTS), there is going to be pressure on the civil courts, as priority is given to getting through the backlog of criminal business. The decision to make legal aid available to child law arbitration fits well with the SCTS strapline of 'Supporting justice through the pandemic and beyond', and it is to be hoped that some of the matters that would have found their way wending through the courts will instead be capable of being dealt with by FLAGS arbitration.

DEVELOPMENTS IN AUSTRALIA

The Australian Family Law Act 1975 (Commonwealth) (FLA 1975) has contained provisions for arbitration of financial matters since 1991. Family law arbitrations in Australia are governed by the contractual arrangements of the parties and the arbitrator and the provisions of FLA 1975, the Family Law Rules 2004 and the Family Law Regulations 1984 (FLR 1984).

Section 13A(1)(c), FLA 1975 provides that an object of the legislation is to:

> *... encourage people to use, in appropriate circumstances, arbitration to resolve matters in which a court order might otherwise be made, and to provide ways of facilitating that use.*

Arbitrations are either ordered by the court (with the consent of the parties) or by a private arrangement (as to relevant property or financial arbitration) between the parties. Arbitral awards may be registered by the court and have the effect as if it were a decree (ie order) made by that court.

The level of activity in arbitration in Australia was at best patchy until 2015, and for reasons that are unclear, the arbitration provisions were largely ignored despite the traditional reasons for engaging in arbitration, but possibly due to a then well-functioning family court system. Others postulated that it was partly due to perceptions about the legislative structure and concerns about the status of arbitral awards, and the narrowness of appeal rights was an important consideration for practitioners choosing whether to recommend consensual arbitration to their clients. Other reasons for a resistance to arbitration may include a natural conservatism among lawyers or clients, or just a fear of the unknown among family law professionals.

There were however some shining lights during this period, including the arbitration scheme of the Legal Aid Office of Queensland for small property matters which was a gold standard model internationally (between 2004 and 2008 under the scheme there was a total of 1,373 referrals for property arbitration) and the family court's pilot program for arbitration in Melbourne launched in November 2007.

However, family law arbitration in Australia has had a renaissance since 2016, aided by the significant delays, personnel and resourcing issues in the family law courts (the Family Court of Australia and the Federal Circuit Court of Australia). In regions that are traditionally reticent to embrace alternative dispute resolution (ADR) over litigation, such as Sydney, practitioners are reporting that the arbitration of family law property disputes has gained considerable momentum over the past six months. In addition:

- Amendments to legislation have addressed the hiatus in the existing legislation (including rollover relief for capital gains tax arising from transactions under awards, per s126-5(1)(e)(i), Income Tax Assessment Act 1977, as to disclosure, subpoena and interlocutory procedures tied to the court) and provided the necessary infrastructure for arbitration to flourish.
- Quality judges have retired and rebadged as arbitrators and currently there are at least 11 retired judges of the family law courts practising as arbitrators. There are also soon-to-retire judges who have indicated a willingness to hang their shingle as an arbitrator. The judges are well respected and trusted by family law practitioners, engendering further confidence in arbitration.
- There has been an increase in the number of trained and qualified family law arbitrators in Australia. There were 188 family law arbitrators in Australia as at 8 June 2018 on the list maintained by the Australian Institute of Family Law Arbitrators and Mediators (AIFLAM) under Reg 67B, FLR 1984. As at 2 March 2021, the number had increased to 372.
- There has been a renewed interest in private autonomy in family law, including relationship agreements for marriages and de facto relationships. The private ordering of family law in Australia is evolving tangential to traditional (public) family law litigation; financial agreements are part of ordering at the commencement or during the relationship, while mediation, collaborative practice and arbitration/private judging is part of the ordering at the end of the relationship.
- Law reform bodies, including the Australian Law Reform Commission and the Commonwealth Parliament Joint Select Committee (JSC), have endorsed and been supportive of ADR, particularly arbitration, and have recommended further substantive changes to better facilitate and increase the take-up of arbitration in Australia. This includes:
  - increasing the scope of matters which may be arbitrated such as parenting matters;
  - removing the opportunity to object to the registration of an award;
  - clarifying that superannuation splits may be effected by an arbitral award; and

- ○ providing courts with additional powers to make directions regarding the conduct of an arbitration process – the JSC went so far as to recommend that '[a] court may make an order… with or without the consent of the parties'.

Also of note is that there has been judicial activism in support of arbitration, including from the then Chief Justice of the Family Court, the Honourable Diana Bryant AO QC, and from her retirement, the Chief Justice of the Family Court of Australia and Chief Judge of the Federal Circuit Court of Australia, the Honourable William Alstergren.

The court's national arbitration list (NAL) commenced in June 2020 and Justice Wilson, as the national arbitration judge of the NAL, explained the operation of the NAL in *Seldon & Seldon* [2020] (at para 36) and *in Entezam & Devi* [2021] (at para 35). During proceedings before the court, judges are actively encouraging parties to consider arbitration, for instance Judge Neville in *Dalgleish & Dalgleish* [2020] (at para 138). There has also been an increase in support from the courts by referring matters out to arbitration by agreement, for example, by February 2020, the Federal Circuit Court of Australia at Paramatta had referred 100 matters to private arbitration.

There has also been proliferation of reported family law cases concerning arbitration since 2018 (some 30 cases between 9 July 2018 and 1 April 2021), covering a wide variety of issues including the registration of awards; objections to registration; costs; reviews of awards; the affirmation, reversal or variation of awards; the enforcement of an award; the finality principle in arbitration; family violence; screening and safety plans; the suitability of arbitration; procedural fairness and the standards applicable to an arbitrator; and the differences between international commercial arbitration rules and procedures and family law arbitrations. A recent leading case about arbitration in Australia is *Pattison & Loomis* [2021], a decision of the full court of the Family Court of Australia concerning the requisite consent of a party necessary for arbitration.

There has also been activism and advocacy by the main governing body for family law arbitration in Australia, AIFLAM, including the issue of new protocols in March 2019, the training of arbitrators, an ongoing education program with specialist accreditation initiatives and the publication of an arbitration kit with a pro forma arbitration agreement (see reference box to download). In 2018, AIFLAM conducted consultative workshops across Australia and developed a new arbitration model, the Stamford model, integrating mediation and arbitration. AIFLAM intends to pilot the Stamford model and a mediation/arbitration model in a pilot in Perth.

Also of note as to underlying reasons for the increase in arbitration in Australia are:

- the burgeoning cost of litigation, see for example paras 2.64 to 2.91 of the second interim report of the Joint Select Committee and *Simic & Norton* [2017], where the Honourable Justice Benjamin voiced his disapproval of excessively high legal fees; and

- the establishment in September 2017 of the International Family Law Arbitration Scheme (IFLAS) by Professor Patrick Parkinson (Australia) and Professor David Hodson OBE (UK), with an international stable of high-profile arbitrators waiting in the wings to undertake international family law arbitration. These include retired Australian judges of the Family Court of Australia (the Honourable Diana Bryant AO QC, former Chief Justice; the Honourable Peter Rose AM QC; and the Honourable Michelle May AM QC). IFLAS provides arbitration of forum disputes in international family law cases, providing a neutral arbitrator who hears and determines the dispute.

Finally, it should be noted that Australia is a signatory to the United Nations Convention on the Recognition and Enforcement of Foreign Arbitral Awards of 1958 (the New York Convention) and made no reservations to its accession. The International Arbitration Act 1974 (IAA 1974) was enacted in 1975 and gives effect to Australia's obligations under the New York Convention. The IAA 1974 also adopts and applies the United Nations Commission on International Trade Law's Model Law on International Commercial Arbitration (1985) (see s16, IAA 1974) as the law governing international arbitrations in Australia. Amendments to the IAA 1974 in 2010 enacted the 2006 version of the Model Law. The New York Convention and the Model Law cannot both apply. Section 20, IAA 1974 provides that the New York Convention takes precedence over the Model Law.

COMPARATIVE TABLES

As mentioned, we are very grateful to our IAFL colleagues across the globe who have contributed to the tables linked to below to answer the following questions:

- Do you have statutory provision for arbitration?
- Is arbitration strictly legally binding in your jurisdiction?
- Is arbitration much used in your jurisdiction?
- Is a mediation/arbitration hybrid used in your jurisdiction?
- Have you or your colleagues undertaken an international family law arbitration?

All of the tables can be accessed in PDF format via the following links:

- Asia Pacific
- Europe
- Canada
- US
- Rest of the world

CONCLUSION

Some of the points that we considered important from the responses we received from our colleagues around the world are:

- there continue to be issues concerning the definition of arbitration from jurisdiction to jurisdiction and it appears to us that this will make international arbitration problematic;
- we can find little evidence of cross-border arbitration, ie the arbitration of family law matters involving at least two jurisdictions, and this is something that we would like to rectify;
- many countries have statutory provision for family law arbitration schemes and even those that don't have a statutory scheme have given careful thought to arbitration; and
- many countries report that mediation is the predominant form of ADR, with mentions of mediation/arbitration hybrids, and it seems to us that this is something to keep on the radar.

References

'Suggested guidance for the conduct of a remote hearing as arbitrator or PFDR judge', Nicholas Allen QC, Janet Bazley QC, Andrzej Bojarski, Nigel Dyer QC, Marina Faggionato, Charles Hale QC, Suzanne Kingston and Christopher Pocock QC (6 May 2020)

'AIFLAM Arbitration: Practice and Approval Standards' (March 2019)

'AIFLAM Arbitration Kit' (August 2016), click to download or visit www.aiflam.org.au/aiflam-members/arbitration

UNCITRAL Model Law on International Commercial Arbitration (1985), with amendments as adopted in 2006, United Nations Commission on International Trade Law

Cases Referenced

- Dalgleish & Dalgleish [2020] FCCA 1833
- Entezam & Devi [2021] FamCA 25
- Haley v Haley [2020] EWCA Civ 1369
- Pattison & Loomis [2021] FamCAFC 41
- Prest v Petrodel Resources Ltd & ors [2013] UKSC 34; [2013] WTLR 1249 SC

- Seldon & Seldon [2020] FamCA 762
- Simic & Norton [2017] FamCA 1007

Citation reference:

Suzanne Kingston, Rachael Kelsey and Geoff Wilson, 'Global arbitration: Right place, right time?', (October 2021 #207) *Family Law Journal*,

https://www.lawjournals.co.uk/2021/09/03/family-law-journal/global-arbitration-right-place/, see footer for date accessed

APPENDIX 6

CASES

S v P [2008] 2 FLR 2040

S V P (SETTLEMENT BY COLLABORATIVE LAW PROCESS)

Family Division

Coleridge J

30 July 2008

Family proceedings – Collaborative law – Consent orders – Approved short-cut process

The parties, who had never married, negotiated a comprehensive settlement of all the issues arising on their separation using the collaborative law process. The agreement reached was contained in two documents, one dealing with finances and the other with the arrangements for the two children, who were moving to the USA with the mother. The documents set out in a great deal more detail than normal matters agreed in the course of the negotiation. The parties sought approval of these agreements as draft consent orders.

Held – approving both the form and content of the consent orders –

(1) This application for approval of draft consent orders could be dealt with in the 'urgent without notice' applications list, in order to shortcut the normal rather lengthier process of lodging consent orders through the Principal Registry and waiting for them to be approved and sent back (see para [5]).

(2) The court would usually be prepared to entertain applications of this kind in the without notice applications list before the applications judge of the day on short notice. A full day's notice must be given to the clerk of the High Court judge in front of whom it was proposed to list the case; such notice could be given by telephone. The clerk of the rules should be informed that this was taking place. Use of the shortcut process was always subject to the consent of the urgent application judge. However, provided every aspect of documentation was agreed, the hearing was not expected to last more than 10 minutes, and the documentation was lodged with the judge the night before the hearing, this process had been approved by the President for use by those who achieved collaborative law agreements, in order to provide as much encouragement as possible to people to resolve their difficulties

in this civilised and sensible way. If a flood of applications results it might be necessary to revisit the facility, but in the meantime the prospect of obtaining finalised court documentation speedily would be an incentive to negotiating an agreement (see paras [5], [6]).

Susan Todd for the applicant

Martyn Daldorph for the respondent

Cur adv vult

COLERIDGE J:

[1] This application for consent orders comes before me by an unusual route. The parties, who I do not need to identify, have negotiated a comprehensive settlement of all the issues that arise on their separation through the collaborative law process. This process, as those of us who work in this field know, is becoming increasingly popular as a means of resolving difficult and sensitive family disputes arising on separation.

[2] The result of the settlement is that before me today have been placed two documents entitled, '*Minutes of agreement for consent order reached through the Collaborative Family Law Process*'. They set out over a number of pages a comprehensive arrangement covering all possible issues between the parties relating to the mother, the father and the children. I should say this is a couple who have never married but have two children, one aged 5 and another aged just over 3.

[3] So they have reached this agreement, and it is now contained in two documents, one dealing with the finances and the other dealing with the arrangements for the children which will involve, in this particular case, the mother leaving the jurisdiction to take up residence in the USA with the children.

[4] The agreed documents in many ways have more of the character of an American style agreement which is now quite familiar to this jurisdiction. The documents set out, in a great deal more detail, than normal matters which the parties have put their minds to over the period of the negotiation. I am told by those who appear for the mother and father this morning (the solicitors who assisted them in this process) that this negotiation has gone on over a series of meetings in the period since February of this year. I have had no difficulty in approving both the form and content of the orders and they will be drawn in the form in which they have been lodged.

[5] The purpose of my making these few remarks this morning is to give such encouragement as the court can to this collaborative process. Accordingly, I have permitted the application for approval to be dealt with in the urgent without notice applications list, as this considerably shortcuts the normal rather lengthier process of lodging consent orders through the Principal Registry and waiting for them to be approved and sent back. Whilst I cannot bind the court always to allow this shortcut process to be available, I have discussed this suggestion with the President and he has given his approval to this shortcut process being used by those who achieve collaborative law agreements in this way. He has approved this in order to provide as much encouragement as possible to people to resolve their difficulties in this civilised and sensible way. Obviously, if this gives rise to a flood of such applications which puts pressure on the listing in other ways, it may be necessary to revisit this facility. However, for my own part I think every conceivable encouragement should be given to parties to negotiate by this method. I have no doubt at all that the prospect that they can obtain finalised court documentation speedily once they have reached agreement, is an incentive to them to knuckle down and negotiate to an agreed conclusion.

[6] So, as I say, the court will usually be prepared to entertain applications of this kind in the ex parte applications list before the applications judge of the day on short notice. A full days notice must be given to the Clerk of the High Court judge in front of whom it is proposed to list the case (there is one such judge allocated per week). Such notice may be given by telephone. The Clerk of the Rules should be informed that this is taking place. It is important to emphasise that such a course is subject to the consent of the urgent application judge. It is only appropriate where *every* aspect of the documentation is agreed, the hearing is not expected to last more than 10 minutes and the documentation is lodged with the judge the night before the hearing.

[7] With those few words, I readily approve the orders.

Order accordingly.

Solicitors: *Withers LLP* for the applicant

Hunters for the respondent

PHILIPPA JOHNSON
Law Reporter

S v S [2014] EWHC 7 (Fam)

Neutral Citation Number: [2014] EWHC 7 (Fam)

Case No: GU12D00692

IN THE HIGH COURT OF JUSTICE FAMILY DIVISION

Royal Courts of Justice

Strand, London, WC2A 2LL

Date: 14 January 2014

Before :

SIR JAMES MUNBY

President of the Family Division

....

Between :

S		**Petitioner**
	– and –	
S		**Respondent**

....

....

Hendersons for the Petitioner

Family Law in Partnership for the Respondent

No hearing : application dealt with on paper

....

JUDGMENT

Sir James Munby, President of the Family Division:

1. I have before me an application, transferred to me from the Guildford County Court at my direction, for the approval of a consent order which has been lodged with the court following, and intended to give effect to, an arbitral award made by Mr Gavin Smith in an arbitration conducted under the IFLA (Institute of Family Law Arbitrators) Scheme.

2. There is no doubt that in this case the court should approve the consent order, as I do. But it seemed to me appropriate to give some guidance about the proper approach of the court to such applications.

The IFLA Scheme

3. The IFLA Scheme is described by Sir Peter Singer in '*Arbitration in Family Financial Proceedings: the IFLA Scheme: Part 1*', [2012] Fam Law 1353, and '*Part 2*' [2012] Fam Law 1496. Up-to-date details about the Scheme and arbitrators accredited under it can be found on IFLA's website, ifla.org.uk.

4. For present purposes all I need say is that:
   i) IFLA is a not for profit organisation, created by the Chartered Institute of Arbitrators (CIArb), the Family Law Bar Association, and the family lawyers' group Resolution, in association with the Centre for Child and Family Law Reform;
   ii) IFLA arbitrations are conducted in accordance with the Arbitration Act 1996 and IFLA's Arbitration Rules (the Rules);
   iii) IFLA arbitrators are all Members of the CIArb, that is, MCIArb;
   iv) The IFLA Scheme covers financial and property disputes arising from relationship breakdown (Article 2 of the Rules);
   v) The Rules contain a mandatory requirement (Articles 1.3(c) and 3) that the arbitrator will decide the substance of the dispute only in accordance with the law of England and Wales.

   This last point is significant.

The facts

5. I can take the relevant facts very briefly. The parties were married in 1986 and separated in 2012. Their only child is now 19. A decree nisi on the wife's petition was granted early in 2013. In June 2013 the parties signed IFLA's Form ARB1, agreeing to arbitration in accordance with the Rules by Mr Smith in relation to their claims for ancillary relief and thereby binding themselves to accept his award. The arbitrator's Final Award is dated 7 November 2013. On 9 December 2013 the parties applied to the

Guildford County Court seeking approval of the consent order. In addition to the draft consent order they lodged the Form ARB1, the Final Award, a Joint Statement of Information in Form D81 and, marked for dismissal purposes only, their Forms A.

6. The facts relevant to the subject matter of the arbitration are set out, clearly and comprehensively, in the Final Award. They concern only the parties, so I say nothing more about them except to note that the Form D81 shows the matrimonial assets to be worth in excess of £1.5 but less than £2 million.

The legal context

7. The strong policy argument in favour of the court giving effect to an agreement that the parties have come to themselves for the resolution of their financial affairs following divorce has been recognised for a long time: see the discussion in *X v X (Y and Z Intervening)* [2002] 1 FLR 508 of the line of authorities of which *Dean v Dean* [1978] Fam 161, *Edgar v Edgar* [1980] 1 WLR 1410, *Camm v Camm* (1983) 4 FLR 577 and *Xydhias v Xydhias* [1999] 1 FLR 683 were the most prominent.

8. Thus by the turn of the Millennium it was well established that the court would not lightly permit parties who had made an agreement between themselves to depart from it. Indeed, as a matter of general policy what the parties had themselves agreed would be upheld by the courts unless contrary to public policy or subject to some vitiating feature such as undue pressure or the exploitation of a dominant position to secure an unreasonable advantage.

9. In *X v X*, para 103, I said that a formal agreement, properly and fairly arrived at with competent legal advice, should be upheld by the court unless there were "good and substantial grounds" for concluding that an "injustice" would be done by holding the parties to it. In propounding that formulation I adopted the language used by Ormrod LJ in *Edgar v Edgar* in preference to that of Thorpe J in *Smith v McInerney* [1994] 2 FLR 1077. I said that Thorpe J's references to "the most exceptional circumstances" and "overwhelmingly strong considerations" seemed to me, with respect, to put the matter perhaps a little too high. With the benefit of hindsight I was too questioning of what Thorpe J had said. Not for the first time he had seen, more clearly and presciently than others, the way in which the law was moving and, indeed, had to move.

10. There have of course been many significant developments in this area of the law since it was first set on its course by Ormrod LJ. Many have helpfully been identified by Baker J in *AI v MT* [2013] EWHC 100 (Fam), paras 20-21, 30-31. For present purposes three developments demand particular notice.

11. First, there was the identification and subsequent elaboration by Thorpe LJ of the concept of the 'magnetic factor' – the feature(s) or factor(s) which in the particular case are of "magnetic importance" in influencing or even

determining the outcome: see, for example, *White v White* [1999] Fam 304, 314 (affirmed, [2001] 1 AC 596) and *Crossley v Crossley* [2007] EWCA Civ 1491, [2008] 1 FLR 1467, para 15. We see this approach, though not the label, carried forward in the fundamentally important statement of principle by the Supreme Court in *Radmacher (formerly Granatino) v Granatino* [2010] UKSC 42, [2011] 1 AC 534, para 75:

> "The court should give effect to a nuptial agreement that is freely entered into by each party with a full appreciation of its implications unless in the circumstances prevailing it would not be fair to hold the parties to their agreement."

12. Secondly, mediation and subsequently other forms of alternative dispute resolution have become well established as a means of resolving financial disputes on divorce. As Thorpe LJ observed in *Al Khatib v Masry* [2004] EWCA Civ 1353 [2005] 1 FLR 381, para 17, "there is no case, however conflicted, which is not potentially open to successful mediation". By 2008 use of the collaborative law approach was being encouraged by the court: see the observations of Coleridge J in *S v P (Settlement by Collaborative Law Process)* [2008] 2 FLR 2040. The same year, writing extra-judicially in '*Statutory Arbitration and Ancillary Relief*', [2008] Fam Law 26, Thorpe LJ ventured the view that "to extend the Arbitration Acts to reach all financial issues created by the breakdown on relationships is surely safe territory." Indeed, there is nothing in the Arbitration Act 1996 which on the face of it would preclude arbitration as a permissible process for the resolution of disputes rooted in family life or relationship breakdown. The Family Procedure Rules 2010 now encourage resort to alternative dispute resolution procedures in this as in other areas of family law: see FPR rule 1.4(e) and FPR Part 3. It was against this background that the IFLA Scheme was introduced in February 2012.

13. Thirdly, the court has adapted and abbreviated its processes to facilitate the appropriately simple and speedy judicial approval of such agreements. Where the parties are agreed on the terms of the consent order the court has available to it the process adopted by the parties in the present case. But in the context of collaborative law, Coleridge J, with the support of Sir Mark Potter P, was willing to adopt an even more streamlined process in *S v P (Settlement by Collaborative Law Process)* [2008] 2 FLR 2040.

14. Where, in contrast, one of the parties seeks to resile, the court has long sanctioned use of the abbreviated 'notice to show cause' procedure utilised in *Dean v Dean* [1978] Fam 161, *Xydhias v Xydhias* [1999] 1 FLR 683, *X and X (Y and Z Intervening)* [2002] 1 FLR 508 and *S v S (Ancillary Relief)* [2008] EWHC 2038 (Fam), [2009] 1 FLR 254. The approach here was well captured by Thorpe LJ in *Xydhias v Xydhias* [1999] 1 FLR 683, 692:

> "If there is a dispute as to whether the negotiations led to an accord that the process should be abbreviated, the court has a discretion in determining whether an accord was reached. In exercising that discretion the court should be astute to discern the antics of a litigant

> who, having consistently pressed for abbreviation, is seeking to resile and to justify his shift by reliance on some point of detail that was open for determination by the court at its abbreviated hearing."

Moreover, in such a case the court, if need be of its own motion, can always, by the appropriately robust use of its case management powers, limit the ambit of the issues to be considered at the hearing; for example, as was done in both *Crossley v Crossley* [2007] EWCA Civ 1491, [2008] 1 FLR 1467, and *S v S (Ancillary Relief)* [2008] EWHC 2038 (Fam), [2009] 1 FLR 254, by focusing the hearing exclusively on those issues relevant to the magnetic factor(s).

15. Back of all this there is the increasing emphasis on autonomy exemplified by cases such as *MacLeod v MacLeod* [2008] UKPC 64, [2010] 1 AC 298, and *Radmacher (formerly Granatino) v Granatino* [2010] UKSC 42, [2011] 1 AC 534. As Lord Phillips PSC said in *Radmacher*, para 78:

> "The reason why the court should give weight to a nuptial agreement is that there should be respect for individual autonomy. The court should accord respect to the decision of a married couple as to the manner in which their financial affairs should be regulated. It would be paternalistic and patronising to override their agreement simply on the basis that the court knows best. This is particularly true where the parties' agreement addresses existing circumstances and not merely the contingencies of an uncertain future."

I draw attention in the present context to the last sentence. I would accordingly respectfully endorse what was said by Charles J in *V v V (Prenuptial Agreement)* [2011] EWHC 3230 (Fam), [2012] 1 FLR 1315, para 36:

> "[*Radmacher*] necessitates a significant change to the approach to be adopted, on a proper application of the discretion conferred by the MCA, to the impact of agreements between the parties in respect of their finances. At the heart of that significant change, is the need to recognise the weight that should now be given to autonomy, and thus to the choices made by the parties to a marriage … The new respect to be given to individual autonomy means that the fact of an agreement can alter what is a fair result and so found a different award to the one that would otherwise have been made".

The future

16. What, then, should be the approach in cases where there has been an arbitration award under the IFLA Scheme or something similar?

17. Two situations need to be considered: one where the parties come before the court seeking a consent order; the other where one or other party is seeking to resile from the arbitrator's award. In the present case I am, strictly speaking, concerned only with the first, but some provisional comments on the other may be helpful and not out of place.

18. The starting point in every case, as it seems to me, is that identified in characteristically arresting language by Sir Peter Singer in '*Arbitration in Family Financial Proceedings: the IFLA Scheme: Part 2*' [2012] Fam Law 1496, 1503:

> "I suggest that the 'magnetic factor' perspective provides an appropriate analogy, and illuminates how applications (whether or not by consent) for orders to reflect an IFLA award should be viewed by the court: through the wrong end of a telescope rather than through a wide-angle lens. Such an approach respects the court's jurisdiction, but gives full force and effect to party autonomy by treating the parties' agreement to be bound by the award as the magnetic factor which should lead to a reflective order. Thus an arbitral award founded on the parties' clear agreement in their Form ARB1 to be bound by the award should be treated as a lodestone (more then than just a yardstick) pointing the path to court approval".

19. While respectfully questioning whether it can ever be appropriate for a judge to look through the *wrong* end of a telescope, I agree with that approach. Where the parties have bound themselves, as by signing a Form ARB1, to accept an arbitral award of the kind provided for by the IFLA Scheme, this generates, as it seems to me, a single magnetic factor of determinative importance. As Sir Peter Singer said ([2012] Fam Law 1496, 1503):

> "The autonomous decision of the parties to submit to arbitration should be seen as a 'magnetic factor' akin to the pre-nuptial agreement in *Crossley v Crossley*".

I agree. This, after all, reflects the approach spelt out by the Supreme Court in *Radmacher* in the passages I have already quoted. In the absence of some very compelling countervailing factor(s), the arbitral award should be determinative of the order the court makes. Sir Peter had earlier suggested (1502) that:

> "The scope for backsliding, resiling and indeed any space for repentance should … be just as narrowly confined [as it was in *L v L* [2006] EWHC 956 (Fam), [2008] 1 FLR 26] where what is in question is an attempt to wriggle out of the binding effect of an arbitral award."

Again, I agree. There is no conceptual difference between the parties making an agreement and agreeing to give an arbitrator the power to make the decision for them. Indeed, an arbitral award is surely of its nature even stronger than a simple agreement between the parties.

20. It is worth remembering what the function of the judge is when invited to make a consent order in a financial remedy case. It is a topic I considered at some length in *L v L* [2006] EWHC 956 (Fam), [2008] 1 FLR 26. I concluded (para 73) that:

> "the judge is not a rubber stamp. He is entitled but is not obliged to play the detective. He is a watchdog, but he is not a bloodhound or a ferret."

21. Where the consent order which the judge is being asked to approve is founded on an arbitral award under the IFLA Scheme or something similar (and the judge will, of course, need to check that the order does indeed give effect to the arbitral award and is workable) the judge's role will be simple. The judge will not need to play the detective unless something leaps off the page to indicate that something has gone so seriously wrong in the arbitral process as fundamentally to vitiate the arbitral award. Although recognising that the judge is not a rubber stamp, the combination of (a) the fact that the parties have agreed to be bound by the arbitral award, (b) the fact of the arbitral award (which the judge will of course be able to study) and (c) the fact that the parties are putting the matter before the court *by consent*, means that it can only be in the rarest of cases that it will be appropriate for the judge to do other than approve the order. With a process as sophisticated as that embodied in the IFLA Scheme it is difficult to contemplate such a case.

22. These are the principles that I have applied in the present case in deciding whether or not to approve the consent order. I do not propose to go into the details – why, after all, in a case like this should litigants who have chosen the private process of arbitration have their affairs exposed in a public judgment? Suffice it to say that I have no hesitation in approving the consent order in the form in which it has been put before me.

23. I should add that I can see no reason why the streamlined process applied by Coleridge J in *S v P (Settlement by Collaborative Law Process)* [2008] 2 FLR 2040 in the context of a consent order which was the product of the collaborative law process should not be made similarly available in cases where the consent order is the product of an arbitral award under the IFLA Scheme or something similar. From now on, if they wish, parties should be able to avail themselves of that process[1] whether the consent order is the product of the collaborative law process or an arbitral award under the IFLA Scheme or something similar.

24. I add two points in relation to procedure. The first is that in every case the parties should, as they did here, lodge with the court both the agreed submission to arbitration (in the case of an arbitration in accordance with the IFLA Scheme, the completed Form ARB1) and the arbitrator's award.

1 The process is described in the headnote to the report as follows: "This application for approval of draft consent orders could be dealt with [by a High Court judge] in the 'urgent without notice' applications list, in order to shortcut the normal rather lengthier process of lodging consent orders … and waiting for them to be approved and sent back … The court would usually be prepared to entertain applications of this kind in the without notice applications list before the applications judge of the day on short notice. A full day's notice must be given to the clerk of the High Court judge in front of whom it was proposed to list the case; such notice could be given by telephone. The clerk of the rules should be informed that this was taking place. Use of the shortcut process was always subject to the consent of the urgent application judge. However, provided every aspect of documentation was agreed, the hearing was not expected to last more than 10 minutes, and the documentation was lodged with the judge the night before the hearing, this process had been approved by the President".

Second, the order should contain recitals to the following effect, suitably adapted to meet the circumstances:

> "The documents lodged in relation to this application include the parties' arbitration agreement (Form ARB1), their Form(s) D81, a copy of the arbitrator's award, and a draft of the order which the court is requested to make.
>
> By their Form ARB1 the parties agreed to refer to arbitration the issues described in it which encompass some or all of the financial remedies for which applications are pending in this court; and the parties have invited the court to make an order in agreed terms which reflects the arbitrator's award."

25. Where a party seeks to resile from the arbitral award, the other party's remedy is to apply to the court using the 'notice to show cause' procedure. The court will no doubt adopt an appropriately robust approach, both to the procedure it adopts in dealing with such a challenge and to the test it applies in deciding the outcome. In accordance with the reasoning in cases such as *Xydhias v Xydhias*, the parties will almost invariably forfeit the right to anything other than a most abbreviated hearing; only in highly exceptional circumstances is the court likely to permit anything more than a very abbreviated hearing.

26. Where the attempt to resile is plainly lacking in merit the court may take the view that the appropriate remedy is to proceed without more ado summarily to make an order reflecting the award and, if needs be, providing for its enforcement. Even if there is a need for a somewhat more elaborate hearing, the court will be appropriately robust in defining the issues which are properly in dispute and confining the parties to a hearing which is short and focused. In most such cases the focus is likely to be on whether the party seeking to resile is able to make good one of the limited grounds of challenge or appeal permitted by the Arbitration Act 1996. *If* they can, then so be it. If on the other hand they can *not*, then it may well be that the court will again feel able to proceed without more to make an order reflecting the award and, if needs be, providing for its enforcement.

Concluding observations

27. I have already drawn attention to the fact that the IFLA Scheme requires the arbitrator to decide the dispute in accordance with the law of England and Wales. In this context it is important to remember the fundamental principles expounded by the House of Lords in *White v White* [2001] 1 AC 596, 604-605, that in arriving at any financial order the objective must be to achieve a fair outcome and that, in seeking to achieve a fair outcome, there is no place for discrimination between husband and wife. My observations in this judgment are confined to an arbitral process such as we have in the IFLA Scheme. Different considerations may apply where an arbitral process is based on a different system of law or, in particular,

where there is reason to believe that, whatever system of law is purportedly being applied, there may have been gender-based discrimination. The proper approach in that situation will have to be considered when such a case arises.

28. There is one final matter I must mention. New and emerging forms of alternative dispute resolution highlight the need for the court's processes to keep pace with the needs of litigants and their advisers, nowhere perhaps more so than where, as in this context, the mechanism for resolving a family financial dispute is arbitration conducted in accordance with the Arbitration Act 1996. For example, and no doubt there are other such matters, we need appropriate procedures to enable the Family Court, not the Commercial Court, to deal expeditiously (and if appropriate without the need for an oral hearing) with:

    i) applications for a stay of financial remedy proceedings pending the outcome of arbitration;

    ii) applications seeking any relief or remedy under the Arbitration Act 1996, such as, for instance, under section 42 to enforce an arbitrator's peremptory order, or under section 43 to secure the attendance of witnesses.

29. Drafts of templates for such orders have been produced for consultation as part of the Family Orders Project being managed by Mostyn J. But alongside these innovations the need for procedural adaptation is becoming increasingly pressing. Whether such topics are most appropriately dealt with by rule changes (for example to the Family Procedure Rules 2010 and/or the Civil Procedure Rules 1998) or by the issue of Practice Directions or Practice Guidance is a matter for consideration. Initially, however, I would invite the Family Procedure Rules Committee to consider this as a matter of urgency.

DB V DLJ [2016] EWHC 324 (Fam)

Artwork-App 6-01

Neutral Citation Number: [2016] EWHC 324 (Fam)

Case No: FD13D05331

IN THE HIGH COURT OF JUSTICE FAMILY DIVISION

Royal Courts of Justice

Strand, London, WC2A 2LL

Date: 24/02/2016

Before:

MR JUSTICE MOSTYN

....

Between :

DB **Applicant**

– and –

DLJ **Respondent**

....

....

Martin Pointer QC and Jeni Kavanagh

(instructed by **Kidd Rapinet LLP**) for the **applicant**

Patrick Chamberlayne QC and Jacqueline Marks

(instructed by **Blake Morgan LLP**) for the **respondent**

Hearing date: 12 February 2016

....

APPROVED JUDGMENT

I direct that pursuant to CPR PD 39A para 6.1 no official shorthand note shall be taken of this Judgment and that copies of this version as handed down may be treated as authentic.

....

MR JUSTICE MOSTYN

This judgment was delivered in private. The judge has given leave for this version of the judgment to be published on condition that (irrespective of what is contained in the judgment) in any published version of the judgment the anonymity of the children and members of their family must be strictly preserved. All persons, including representatives of the media, must ensure that this condition is strictly complied with. Failure to do so will be a contempt of court.

Mr Justice Mostyn:

1. In this judgment I shall refer to the applicant as "the husband" and to the respondent as "the wife".

2. This is my judgment on the husband's application dated 7 October 2015 that the wife do show cause why an arbitral award (as supplemented) made by Mr Gavin Smith dated 2 July 2015 should not be made an order of the court. The wife resists the application. She says that the award is vitiated by a mistake about the true value of the property in Portugal allocated to her. Alternatively, she says that events have occurred since the award which invalidate the finding made by the arbitrator as to the value of that property.

Family arbitration

3. The arbitration procedure for family financial dispute resolution was launched by the Institute of Family Law Arbitrators in February 2012. A useful short guide (written by Gavin Smith and Sir Peter Singer) is to be found in Table 29 of At A Glance. It is described more fully by Sir Peter in "Arbitration in Family Financial Proceedings: the IFLA Scheme" Part 1 [2012] Fam Law 1353 and Part 2 [2012] Fam Law 1496. A recent article explaining its undoubted merits and advantages written by Duncan Brooks appears in Resolution's "The Review", Issue 180 at 32.

4. The scheme was intended to align the new family finance arbitration procedure as closely as possible with commercial arbitrations governed by the Arbitration Act 1996. Now divorcing couples were to be afforded the same advantages as had been made available to commercial people for over a century. Therefore, when parties agree to enter into arbitration they sign a document – ARB1 – which states that:

"We, the parties to this application, whose details are set out below, apply to the Institute of Family Law Arbitrators Ltd for the nomination and appointment of a sole arbitrator from the Family Arbitration Panel to resolve the dispute referred to in paragraph 2 below by arbitration in accordance with the Arbitration Act 1996 ('the Act') and the rules of the Family Law Arbitration Scheme ('the scheme')"

5. Before I examine the differences, if any, that apply, or should apply, to a family arbitration I shall set out shortly the scope for challenging a commercial award governed exclusively by the 1996 Act.

6. In his excellent paper *"Challenges to Arbitral Awards at the Seat"* given to the Mauritius International Arbitration Conference on 15 December 2014[2] Sir Bernard Eder explains at [6] that:

"…the general approach of the Court is one which strongly supports the arbitral process. By way of anecdote, it is perhaps interesting to recall what I was once told many years ago by Michael Kerr, a former judge in the Court of Appeal and one of the leading figures in the recent development of the law of arbitration in England, when I was complaining about an arbitration that I had just lost and the difficulties in the way of challenging the award. I told him that the award was wrong and unjust. He looked baffled and said: *"Remember, when parties agree arbitration they buy the right to get the wrong answer"*. So, the mere fact that an award is "wrong" or even "unjust" does not, of itself, provide any basis for challenging the award or intervention by the Court. Any challenge or appeal must bring itself under one or more of the three heads which I have identified."

7. The grounds or heads of challenge are very circumscribed indeed. In addition to the three heads mentioned by Sir Bernard (to which I will turn below) there is the facility under section 57 to ask the arbitrator to correct his award. It is noteworthy that by virtue of section 57(1) the parties are free to agree on the powers of the tribunal to correct an award or make an additional award. As will be seen, in this case the parties agreed that certain matters could and should be corrected and clarified by the Tribunal. In the absence of agreement then by virtue of section 57(3) and (4) a party may apply to the arbitrator within 28 days of the award either (a) to correct an award so as to remove any clerical mistake or error arising from an accidental slip or omission or clarify or remove any ambiguity in the award; or (b) to make an additional award in respect of any claim (including a claim for interest or costs) which was presented to the tribunal but was not dealt with in the award.

8. This power is very limited. In *Ases Havacilik Servis Ve Destek Hizmetleri AS v Delkor UK Ltd* [2012] EWHC 3518 (Comm) Hamblen J (as he then was) stated at [21]:

2 https://www.judiciary.gov.uk/announcements/challenges-to-arbitral-awards-at-the-seat-december-2014/

> "Whilst the decision in *Craske v Norfolk CC* [1991] JPL 760 indicates that the power of the arbitrator under the slip rule contained in what is now s.57 of the 1996 Act (formerly s.17 of the Arbitration Act 1950) to correct errors in the award applies to errors which were attributable to the parties, as well as errors attributable to the tribunal, it also makes it clear that it does not extend to oversights or errors in production of evidence or argument before the Arbitrator – see *White Book 2012, Vol. 2, Note 2E-226* at page 648. S.57 does not apply to second thoughts, still less to second thoughts based on fresh evidence."

9. An example of an arbitrator correcting an accidental slip or mistake is *Union Marine Classification Services LLC v The Government of the Union of Comoros* [2015] EWHC 508 (Comm) where the arbitrator had, surprisingly, completely failed to deal with the Government of Comoros's counter-claim. The corrected award dealt with that and the challenge to such amended award was dismissed by Eder J. An application for leave to appeal against that decision was, I understand, recently dismissed by the Court of Appeal.

10. Aside from this limited corrective jurisdiction the only ways of contesting an award are by:

    i) challenging an award of the arbitral tribunal as to its "substantive jurisdiction" under s67 of the 1996 Act; or

    ii) challenging an award on the ground of "serious irregularity" under s68 of the 1996 Act; or

    iii) an appeal to the Court on a "question of law" arising out of an award made in the proceedings under s69 of the 1996 Act.

    By s70, an applicant must first have exhausted all available arbitral processes of appeal and review. Further, any application or appeal must be brought within 28 days of the award.

11. There is a great deal of jurisprudence about these three heads and these are fully explained in Sir Bernard's paper. Challenges as to the tribunal's substantive jurisdiction go to the matters mentioned in section 30(1)(a) – (c) namely whether there is a valid arbitration agreement; or whether the tribunal is properly constituted; or what matters have been submitted to arbitration in accordance with the arbitration agreement. Serious irregularity is specified in nine sub-sections viz:

    (a) failure by the tribunal to comply with section 33 (general duty of tribunal to act fairly);

    (b) the tribunal exceeding its powers (otherwise than by exceeding its substantive jurisdiction: see section 67);

    (c) failure by the tribunal to conduct the proceedings in accordance with the procedure agreed by the parties;

    (d) failure by the tribunal to deal with all the issues that were put to it;

    (e) any arbitral or other institution or person vested by the parties with powers in relation to the proceedings or the award exceeding its powers;

(f) uncertainty or ambiguity as to the effect of the award;

(g) the award being obtained by fraud or the award or the way in which it was procured being contrary to public policy;

(h) failure to comply with the requirements as to the form of the award; or

(i) any irregularity in the conduct of the proceedings or in the award which is admitted by the tribunal or by any arbitral or other institution or person vested by the parties with powers in relation to the proceedings or the award.

I draw attention to (g) where, unsurprisingly, fraud is mentioned as a ground of serious irregularity entitling the court to set-aside an award.

12. An appeal on a question of law needs the leave of the court. Section 69(3) states that:

> Leave to appeal shall be given only if the court is satisfied–
>
> (a) that the determination of the question will substantially affect the rights of one or more of the parties,
>
> (b) that the question is one which the tribunal was asked to determine,
>
> (c) that, on the basis of the findings of fact in the award– (i) the decision of the tribunal on the question is obviously wrong, or (ii) the question is one of general public importance and the decision of the tribunal is at least open to serious doubt, and
>
> (d) that, despite the agreement of the parties to resolve the matter by arbitration, it is just and proper in all the circumstances for the court to determine the question.

This is a stringent test indeed.

13. What amounts to "a question of law" is, of course, capable of an expansive interpretation and might sweep up mixed questions of law and fact. However, in *Pioneer Shipping Ltd v BTP Tioxide Ltd (The Nema)* [1982] AC 724 leave to appeal was granted on the ground that an issue of frustration was a question of law. The decision of Goff J on the substantive appeal reversing the decision of the arbitrator that the charterparty in that case had been frustrated was set aside by the Court of Appeal, a decision upheld in the House of Lords, Lord Diplock proclaiming that leave to appeal ought never to have been granted and that the tide had turned in favour of finality as against "meticulous legal accuracy". Therefore, according to Sir Bernard (at [40]) "the result is that the Court will not generally give leave to appeal or substitute its own decision for that of the tribunal on points which might be said to involve a question of law (e.g., whether on the particular facts a party had wrongfully repudiated or renounced a contract) unless the Court decides that the arbitral tribunal had or might have misdirected itself in point of law".

14. The traditional grounds for challenging a financial remedy award in family proceedings are mistake, fraud, non-disclosure and supervening event.

Non-disclosure can be deliberate or innocent (see the recent decision of the Supreme Court in *Sharland v Sharland* [2015] UKSC 60, [2015] 3 WLR 1070 at [30] – [32]). Deliberate non-disclosure is a species of fraud. Innocent non-disclosure is a species of mistake (see below). Therefore, in essence, there are but three grounds of challenge in family proceedings namely mistake, fraud and supervening event.

15. Fraud, of course, is a ground of challenge under section 68(2)(g), as has been seen. An alleged mistake can only be raised if it falls within section 57, and then will not extend to an error in production of evidence. The mistake alleged here would be impossible to raise in commercial arbitration proceedings. And a supervening event is completely impossible as a ground of challenge. In *The Nema* itself the arbitrator held that the award had been frustrated by the strike in Canada. He held that it would continue indefinitely. In fact it was settled a short time after the award but no-one suggested that that unexpected development could amount to a ground of appeal.

16. It can therefore be seen that when parties sign up to arbitration under the 1996 Act they "buy" very limited rights of challenge. These rights do not extend to a challenge based on a mistake in the production of evidence or as a result of a supervening event. Mr Chamberlayne QC sought to argue that the wife could seek to argue a point of law under section 69 namely that the award had been frustrated by the later events, but this is impossible because (a) whether frustration has happened is in fact an un-appealable question of fact – see *The Nema*, and (b) the issue of law must relate to the facts as found by the tribunal – see section 69(3)(c).

17. However, I do not conclude that the door to relief is closed to the wife. This is because of certain important differences between the family and civil processes.

18. Following a civil arbitration the award is final and binding, unless the parties otherwise agree – see section 58(1) of the 1996 Act. It will amount to *res judicata* between the parties. One imagines that in the vast generality of cases no incorporating order will be sought from the court; rather, the parties will be content for their rights and obligations to speak from the award.

19. If a party does not comply with the award then it is open for the other party to apply under section 66 for enforcement by the court. Section 66(1) provides that "an award made by the tribunal pursuant to an arbitration agreement may, by leave of the court, be enforced in the same manner as a judgment or order of the court to the same effect." It might be thought that leave could be refused if the court thought that the award was wrong or unjust; but that would be a mistake. In *Middlemiss & Could v Hartlepool Corporation* [1972] 1 WLR 1643 Lord Denning MR stated at 1647:

> "I would say that it is to be used in nearly all cases. Leave should be given to enforce the award as a judgment unless there is real ground for doubting the validity of the award."

20. In contrast it is to be expected that in most family arbitration cases the parties will want an incorporating order. For example, the arbitrator may have awarded a clean break – that can only be achieved conclusively with a court order. The arbitrator may have awarded a pension share – again, that can only be achieved by a court order. It is trite law that where such an order is sought the court exercises an independent inquisitorial discretion. It is no rubber stamp: see *Jenkins v Livesey* [1985] AC 424.

21. In this case the terms of the form ARB1 signed by the parties stated:

> "5.4 We understand and agree that any award of the arbitrator appointed to determine this dispute will be final and binding on us, subject to the following:
>
> (a) any challenge to the award by any available arbitral process of appeal or review or in accordance with the provisions of Part 1 of the [1996] Act;
>
> (b) insofar as the subject matter of the award requires it to be embodied in a court order (see 6.5 below (*sic, recto* 5.5)), any changes which the court making that order may require; ...
>
> 5.5 If and so far as the subject matter of the award makes it necessary, we will apply to an appropriate court for an order in the same or similar terms as the award all the relevant part of the award. ... We understand that the court has a discretion as to whether, and in what terms to make an order and we will take all reasonably necessary steps to see that such an order is made."

22. It can therefore be seen that the parties have agreed in writing that challenges to an arbitral award would not be confined only to those available under the 1996 Act. In addition they specifically agreed that the court would retain an overriding discretion, and inferentially the parties agreed that they would each be enabled to argue that the court should not exercise its discretion to incorporate the award for reasons outwith those stated in the 1996 Act. In so doing they were agreeing, pursuant to section 58(1), an exception to the award being final and binding. In making such an agreement the parties were of course, doing no more than recognising what the general law already provided.

S v S and the Practice Guidance

23. I now need to refer to two important emanations from the President namely *S v S (Arbitral Award: Approval) (Practice Note)* [2014] 1 WLR 2299, and the *Practice Guidance (Family Court: Interface with Arbitration)* [2016] 1 WLR 59.

24. In *S v S* the President endorsed the "notice to show cause" procedure, commonly used where a party is seeking to resile from an agreement, as the appropriate procedure where a party is seeking to resile from an arbitral award: see [25], and the Practice Guidance at [15].

25. The analogy with agreement cases was not merely procedural but was substantive. Thus he stated at [21]:

> "Where the consent order which the judge is being asked to approve is founded on an arbitral award under the IFLA Scheme or something similar (and the judge will, of course, need to check that the order does indeed give effect to the arbitral award and is workable) the judge's role will be simple. The judge will not need to play the detective unless something leaps off the page to indicate that something has gone so seriously wrong in the arbitral process as fundamentally to vitiate the arbitral award. Although recognising that the judge is not a rubber stamp, the combination of (a) the fact that the parties have agreed to be bound by the arbitral award, (b) the fact of the arbitral award (which the judge will of course be able to study) and (c) the fact that the parties are putting the matter before the court by consent, means that it can only be in the rarest of cases that it will be appropriate for the judge to do other than approve the order. With a process as sophisticated as that embodied in the IFLA Scheme it is difficult to contemplate such a case."

26. In fact his observations appear to suggest that it will be even more difficult for a party to resile from an arbitral award than from a negotiated agreement. At [26] he said:

> "Where the attempt to resile is plainly lacking in merit the court may take the view that the appropriate remedy is to proceed without more ado summarily to make an order reflecting the award and, if needs be, providing for its enforcement. Even if there is a need for a somewhat more elaborate hearing, the court will be appropriately robust in defining the issues which are properly in dispute and confining the parties to a hearing which is short and focused. In most such cases the focus is likely to be on whether the party seeking to resile is able to make good one of the limited grounds of challenge or appeal permitted by the Arbitration Act 1996. If they can, then so be it. If on the other hand they cannot, then it may well be that the court will again feel able to proceed without more to make an order reflecting the award and, if needs be, providing for its enforcement."

27. This would appear to suggest that the Family Court could only refuse to make the order if a challenge or appeal under the 1996 Act could be made out. I would not go that far, as this would appear to rule out a challenge on the ground of a vitiating mistake or a supervening event. If a challenge were to be made out on one or other such ground it would in my judgment be a plainly wrong exercise of discretion for the court to incorporate an award nonetheless. I agree with Mr Chamberlayne QC in this regard. However I do agree with Mr Pointer QC that when exercising its discretion following an arbitral award the court should adopt an approach of great stringency, even more so than it would in an agreement case. In opting for arbitration the parties have agreed a specific form of alternative dispute resolution and it is important that they understand that in the overwhelming majority of cases the dispute will end with the arbitral award. It would be the worst of

all worlds if parties thought that the arbitral process was to be no more than a dry run and that a rehearing in court was readily available. Thus in the Practice Guidance at [12] the President stated:

> "Attention is drawn to my observations in *S v S (Arbitral Award: Approval) (Practice Note)* [2014] 1 WLR 2299, para 21 about the attitude likely to be adopted by the court in such cases: '[where] the parties are putting the matter before the court by consent … it can only be in the rarest of cases that it will be appropriate for the judge to do other than approve the order.'"

In *Fage UK Ltd & Anor v Chobani UK Ltd & Anor [2014] EWCA Civ 5*, in the context of an appeal against a finding of fact, Lewison LJ stated at [114(ii)] "the trial is not a dress rehearsal. It is the first and last night of the show." Even more so, in my opinion, where the first instance decision is an arbitral award.

28. My conclusion is this. If following an arbitral award evidence emerges which would, if the award had been in an order of the court entitle the court to set aside its order on the grounds of mistake or supervening event, then the court is entitled to refuse to incorporate the arbitral award in its order and instead to make a different order reflecting the new evidence. Outside the heads of correction, challenge or appeal within the 1996 Act these are, in my judgment, the only realistically available grounds of resistance to an incorporating order. An assertion that the award was "wrong" or "unjust" will almost never get off the ground: in such a case the error must be so blatant and extreme that it leaps off the page.

29. In my opinion ARB1 should be modified to make this clear.

30. I now turn to consider the law relating to invalidating supervening events and mistake in financial remedy proceedings.

Barder: supervening events

31. In *Barder v Barder (Caluori intervening)* [1988] AC 20, the House of Lords stipulated the test that must be met before a set-aside could be granted. It has four conditions:

    i) New events have occurred since the making of the order invalidating the basis, or fundamental assumption, upon which the order was made.

    ii) The new events should have occurred within a relatively short time of the order having been made. It is extremely unlikely that could be as much as a year, and in most cases it will be no more than a few months.

    iii) The application to set aside should be made reasonably promptly in the circumstances of the case.

    iv) The application if granted should not prejudice third parties who have, in good faith and for valuable consideration, acquired interests in property which is the subject matter of the relevant order.

32. In *Cornick v Cornick* [1994] 2 FLR 530 at 537 Hale J explained that "for the Barder principle to apply, it is a sine qua non that the event was unforeseen and unforeseeable." Obviously, if the parties had actually foreseen a later event then it would not be unforeseeable. So, the question is usually confined to an analysis of (un)foreseeability. I agree with Hale J that the new or later event must have been unforeseeable. If relief were granted on the basis of the arrival of a foreseeable event then that would amount to exercising a disguised power of variation on proof of a mere change of circumstances, where Parliament has specifically declined to enact such a power.

33. In *Richardson v Richardson* [2011] EWCA 79 [2011] 2 FLR 244 Thorpe LJ emphasised that the jurisdiction is highly exceptional. At [86] he stated "cases in which a Barder event … can be successfully argued are extremely rare, should be regarded by the specialist profession as exceedingly rare, and should not be thought to be extendable by ingenuity or the lowering of the judicially created bar." Earlier in *Walkden v Walkden* [2010] 1 FLR 174 Elias LJ had stated at [80]: "given the importance attached to finality in settlements of this nature, the circumstances must be truly exceptional before a capital settlement can be re-opened."

34. Even where the four conditions have been met it lies within the discretion of the court whether to grant the set-aside. A set-aside would be unlikely to be granted if alternative mainstream relief could be granted which broadly remedied the unfairness caused by the later event.

35. The test for Barder relief, as propounded by the House of Lords, is a question of law. Whether it is satisfied is a question of fact. A finding that a later event was, or was not, foreseeable is an inference drawn from primary facts. Hitherto, every case where Barder relief has been granted is an appellate decision. Lord Brandon's speech is cast in the language and procedure of an appeal. So it is important to remember that every decision made by the Court of Appeal in the field since that seminal decision is a fact-finding decision. Certainly, the legal test has been explained in the appellate decisions, but none has sought to alter it. But occasionally the fact-finding exercise seems to have been driven more by considerations of the underlying merits than a faithful application of the question of law. The old cases of *Barber v Barber* [1993] 1 FLR 476 and *Heard v Heard* [1995] 1 FLR 970 and the recent case of *Critchell v Critchell* [2015] EWCA Civ 436 may be examples of this.

Unforeseeable

36. I turn to the question of (un)foreseeability. Before I consider the Barder cases on this topic I allow myself a short excursion into this area as it arises in the civil sphere. Whether an event was reasonably foreseeable is a key question in deciding whether damages are recoverable in an action for negligence for breach of contract, negligence or nuisance, or whether they are too remote and therefore irrecoverable. The question is not whether

a future event is literally incapable of being imagined. The capacity of homo sapiens to imagine fictive things is vast. The question is posed by the court standing retrospectively in the shoes of the actors and asking itself whether the then future, but by now past, event could reasonably have been predicted. The answer is generally given by linguistic tropes rather than by numeric assessments of future probability. The use of language rather than numbers led Lord Denning MR to say that he was swimming in a sea of semantics. In *Parsons (H) (Livestock) Ltd v Uttley Ingham & Co Ltd* [1978] QB 791 he stated at 801-802:

> "Remoteness of damage is beyond doubt a question of law. In *C. Czarnikow Ltd. v. Koufos (The Heron II)* [1969] 1 A.C. 350 the House of Lords said that, in remoteness of damage, there is a difference between contract and tort. In the case of a breach of contract, the court has to consider whether the consequences were of such a kind that a reasonable man, at the time of making the contract, would contemplate them as being of a very substantial degree of probability. (In the House of Lords various expressions were used to describe this degree of probability, such as, not merely "on the cards" because that may be too low: but as being "not unlikely to occur" (see pp. 383 and 388); or "likely to result or at least not unlikely to result" (see p. 406); or "liable to result" (see p. 410); or that there was a "real danger" or "serious possibility" of them occurring (see p. 415).)
>
> In the case of a tort, the court has to consider whether the consequences were of such a kind that a reasonable man, at the time of the tort committed, would foresee them as being of a much lower degree of probability. (In the House of Lords various expressions were used to describe this, such as, it is sufficient if the consequences are "liable to happen in the most unusual case" (see p. 385); or in a "very improbable" case (see p. 389); or that "they may happen as a result of the breach, however unlikely it may be, unless it can be brushed aside as far-fetched" (see p. 422).)
>
> I find it difficult to apply those principles universally to all cases of contract or to all cases of tort: and to draw a distinction between what a man "contemplates" and what he "foresees." I soon begin to get out of my depth. I cannot swim in this sea of semantic exercises – to say nothing of the different degrees of probability – especially when the cause of action can be laid either in contract or in tort. I am swept under by the conflicting currents. …"

37. I too found myself drowning when reading the old authorities. However, in *The Heron II* Lord Reid did set out what is to my mind a most helpful odds-based analysis. At 390 he stated:

> "It has never been held to be sufficient in contract that the loss was foreseeable as "a serious possibility" or "a real danger" or as being "on the cards." It is on the cards that one can win £100,000 or more for a stake of a few pence – several people have done that. And anyone who

backs a hundred to one chance regards a win as a serious possibility – many people have won on such a chance. And the *Wagon Mound (No. 2)* could not have been decided as it was unless the extremely unlikely fire should have been foreseen by the ship's officer as a real danger. It appears to me that in the ordinary use of language there is a wide gulf between saying that some event is not unlikely or quite likely to happen and saying merely that it is a serious possibility, a real danger, or on the cards. Suppose one takes a well-shuffled pack of cards, it is quite likely or not unlikely that the top card will prove to be a diamond: the odds are only 3 to 1 against. But most people would not say that it is quite likely to be the nine of diamonds for the odds are then 51 to 1 against. On the other hand I think that most people would say that there is a serious possibility or a real danger of its being turned up first and of course it is on the cards."

38. Lord Reid is in effect saying here that in his opinion a probability of $P = 0.25$ would satisfy the test of reasonable foreseeability but a probability of $P = 0.02$ would not, although I acknowledge that he had earlier stated at 388 that "it is hardly ever possible in this matter to assess probabilities with any degree of mathematical accuracy." Thus, the test is now linguistically expressed as saying that a wrongdoer is responsible for damage which should have been foreseen by a reasonable person as being something of which there was a real risk, even though the risk would actually occur only in rare circumstances, unless the risk was so small that the reasonable person would feel justified in neglecting it or brushing it aside as far-fetched.

39. Although the numeric approach is generally eschewed one can confidently say that for damage to be held to be unforeseeable and therefore too remote the probability of it eventuating must be very low indeed (probably $P < 0.05$, I would guess). It is worth reflecting on the *Wagon Mound (No. 2)* [1967] 1 A.C. 617. The findings of Walsh J about the bunkering oil spilled from the Wagon Mound into Sydney harbour were:

> "(1) Reasonable people in the position of the officers of the Wagon Mound would regard the furnace oil as very difficult to ignite upon water. (2) Their personal experience would probably have been that this had very rarely happened. (3) If they had given attention to the risk of fire from the spillage, they would have regarded it as a possibility, but one which could become an actuality only in very exceptional circumstances. (4) They would have considered the chances of the required exceptional circumstances happening whilst the oil remained spread on the harbour waters as being remote. (5) I find that the occurrence of damage to the plaintiff's property as a result of the spillage was not reasonably foreseeable by those for whose acts the defendant would be responsible."

40. The Privy Council overturned finding No. 5. The risk may have been very small indeed but it was not such that a reasonable man would brush it aside as far-fetched. This points up just how unlikely a future event must be before it can be classed as "unforeseeable".

41. These civil cases are very important. In *Richardson v Richardson* at [53], Munby LJ stated that "the Family Division is part of the High Court. It is not some legal Alsatia where the common law and equity do not apply." Similarly, in *Prest v Petrodel Resources Ltd & Ors* [2013] UKSC 34 [2013] 2 AC 415 Lord Sumption at [37] said that "Courts exercising family jurisdiction do not occupy a desert island in which general legal concepts are suspended or mean something different." In my opinion "unforeseeable" cannot mean one thing in the Queen's Bench Division and another in the Family Division.

42. And so I turn to some of the Barder cases and their treatment of the question of the (un)foreseeability of the later event. The first group of cases concern the death of an actor shortly after the order was made. Barder itself was just such a case. Shortly after the order the wife murdered the children and killed herself. Although the press reports a handful of such tragic cases each year the probability of such a thing happening must have been tiny. In terms of probability this was far more remote than drawing the nine of diamonds.

43. In *Barber v Barber* [1993] 1 FLR 476 the wife, aged 41, suffered from severe liver disease. The evidence was to the effect that there was a "reasonable hope" that she would live for at least five years. In fact, she died within three months. The report of the judgment of Glidewell LJ does not show that he considered the question of the (un)foreseeability of a death of that ill woman within 3 months rather than five years. A similar criticism can be made of the factual findings in *Smith v Smith* [1991] 2 FLR 432 where the husband aged 62 committed suicide shortly after the order. Nothing was said about the likelihood or otherwise of this later event, although inferentially the Court of Appeal appeared to accept that it came out of a clear blue sky. An even more surprising decision is *Critchell v Critchell* [2015] EWCA Civ 436 where the later event was the death of the husband's father shortly after the order and the consequential inheritance by the husband of a sum of money of around £100,000. The report does not state the age of the father, but the inference is that he was elderly. The finding of the circuit judge was that the death of the father was "completely unforeseen"; that may have been so, but nothing was said about the requirement that it must have been unforeseeable. That crucial requirement is not mentioned in the judgment of Black LJ. It is very hard to see how this later event could have been found to be unforeseeable. Benjamin Franklin famously said that in this world nothing can be said to be certain, except death and taxes. The death of an elderly man surely cannot be regarded as anything other than foreseeable and unremarkable.

44. In contrast is the recent decision of Moor J in *WA v Executors of the Estate of HA & Ors* [2015] EWHC 2233 (Fam). There the husband committed suicide 22 days after the order which secured for him a substantial award. Moor J very carefully considered the available evidence concerning the husband's psychological condition but reached the clear conclusion that the death was not foreseeable. It is true that he did not have the civil

authorities put before him, and one can speculate whether he may have reached a different decision had they been, but what cannot be disputed is that the court made a thorough examination, on the available evidence, of the central question of whether the death was foreseeable or not.

45. In that case Moor J followed *Reid v Reid* [2004] 1 FLR 736 where the wife was aged 74 and had disclosed that she was registered blind, had high blood pressure, high cholesterol and was diabetic. She died two months after the date of the order. Wilson J found that her death was not foreseeable. At [20] he held that "notwithstanding the possibility of death at any time, there was no material which should have placed the wife's death 2 months later into the minds of the parties as being a significant, i.e. more than a theoretical, possibility." Again, I find myself in difficulty in squaring this decision with the civil authorities to which I have referred.

46. In contrast are a number of cases where a death was not found to be a Barder event. I need only cite *Richardson v Richardson* where the wife, then aged 70, died 3 months after the order. Munby LJ held that this was not a Barder event as the death did not invalidate the order. The wife had earned her share; her award was not based on needs. Although Munby LJ referred to the death as being "unexpected" he did not discuss whether it was technically "unforeseeable".

47. The next group of cases concern those where at the time of the order a thing is known and assumed but in fact later eventuates to an extent that was not expected. These are the "known unknown" cases, to use the celebrated language of Secretary Rumsfeld. Plainly it is very difficult to satisfy the test of unforeseeability in such a case.

48. In *Walkden v Walkde*n the wife sought to plead as a Barder event the fact that certain shares had subsequently been sold by the husband at a substantially higher value than, she said, had been anticipated. At [53] Thorpe LJ held that "it could not possibly be said that the sale of the husband's shares was either unforeseen or unforeseeable". At [89] Elias LJ held that "it was plainly foreseeable that an asset of this nature might fluctuate dramatically."

49. The cases were all analysed in *Richardson* by Munby LJ. In that case there was a pending negligence action against the parties' partnership; the parties assumed that it was covered by insurance. It later transpired that the claim could be for £3m whereas cover was only for £2m. Moreover, the insurers had, after the order, avoided the policy. The former development was not a Barder event; neither was the latter, but it was a vitiating mistake. The avoidance of the policy was not foreseeable. The extent of the claim and the limit of the cover (before avoidance) was not even a later foreseeable event. It was a known unknown, and the husband with due diligence could have established the true facts. At [37] Munby LJ stated:

> "The reality is that the husband, to adopt Sir Stephen Brown's words, knew 'the essential facts' and by the exercise of due diligence could – would – have discovered the limit of the insurance cover. He has only himself to blame for the fact that he did not take these obvious steps.

Faced with a known unknown he chose to proceed without further inquiry or investigation. He cannot now be heard to say that he was mistaken. There was no vitiating mistake he can rely upon. And just as in *Walkden v Walkden*, he cannot be heard to say that his discovery of the true position in relation to the limit of cover amounted to a new or Barder event. It quite plainly was not. In this case as in that the reasons which deny him relief under the one head serve equally to deny him relief under the other. But the reality is that this was simply not, and never could have been, a Barder event. The 'problem' – the limit of the indemnity under the policy – had been there all along. Its belated discovery by the husband was not a new event; it reflected no more than his failure at the proper time to ask obvious questions about the existing state of affairs. In this case, as in both *Judge v Judge* and *Walkden v Walkden*, the husband either succeeds in mistake or not at all. For the reasons I have given he has no claim based on mistake; and that is the end of it."

Mistake

50. The practice of framing what is in fact a case of mistake as a Barder event can be traced back to *Thompson v Thompson* [1991] 2 FLR 530. In *Cornick v Cornick* [1994] 2 FLR 530 Hale J, when setting out her famous categorisation at 535E, described the situation where:

> "(2) A wrong value was put upon that asset at the hearing, which had it been known about at the time would have led to a different order. Provided that it is not the fault of the person alleging the mistake, it is open to the court to give leave for the matter to be reopened. Although falling within the Barder principle it is more akin to the misrepresentation or non-disclosure cases than to Barder itself. "

51. In *Judge v Judge* [2008] EWCA Civ 1458 [2009] 1 FLR 1287 Wilson LJ at [3] explained that a case of a vitiating mistake (i.e. Hale J's category No. 2) does not fall within the Barder principles. In that case, five years after the order, the wife discovered that a tax debt which had been assumed in the proceedings to amount to about £14m had in fact eventuated at a mere £600,000. She sought to set the order aside on the ground of a vitiating mistake, alternatively on the ground of non-disclosure. Both grounds failed. As to mistake Wilson LJ at [43] stated:

> "A judge's compilation of a balance sheet, usually necessary in order to enable him to address what is now the principle of equality, often requires him to confer a spurious specificity on the value of assets, or on the size of liabilities, in relation to which, on the evidence before him, he can reach no confident conclusion: his balance sheet demands figures so he inserts into it the figures which he considers to be the most probable or, more accurately, the least improbable. There is no evidence which enables us to override the judge's conclusion that he made no mistake in 2001 in that a liability of £600,000 fell within the spectrum

of recognised outcomes. In his judgment in 2001 he expressly referred to the need to gaze into a crystal ball."

52. In *Walkden* Elias LJ said this about the mistake ground at [83]:

"The second category of case arises where the settlement is reached on the basis of a false evaluation. That may be as a result of a mistake, or some misrepresentation or non-disclosure, innocent or fraudulent. The parties (and/or the judge) reaches a view on the value of the asset in the course of agreeing or fixing an appropriate settlement, or confirming a settlement, which would have been different had the full facts been known at the material time. In this category of case it is contended that the order reflecting the settlement should be set aside because it was not correct when made. The applicable legal principles are very different to those in the *Barder* case. For misrepresentation they are the principles enunciated by the House of Lords in *Jenkins v Livesey (Formerly Jenkins)* [1985] AC 424, [1985] 2 WLR 47, [1985] FLR 813. This second category involves no supervening event at all. The settlement is reopened because it was not sound when made; had the judge been in possession of the material facts he would have made an order for a different settlement. In *Cornick* Hale J placed mistake cases (but not misrepresentation or non-disclosure) into the first category. However, as Wilson LJ pointed out in *Judge v Judge* [2008] EWCA Civ 1458, [2009] 1 FLR 1287 para [3], it does not properly fit into that category. That is because it does not rely upon new or supervening events at all."

53. In *Richardson* the court classed the avoidance of the policy as a vitiating mistake. At the time that judgment was given in that case the insurers were considering whether to avoid the policy but had not reached a decision, let alone announced it. At [80] – [83] Rimer LJ stated:

"80. Munby LJ explains, and I agree, why down to the delivery by His Honour Judge Raynor QC of his judgment on 25 September 2009 neither the husband nor the wife had actual or other relevant knowledge that there was a risk that the insurers might avoid the policy. That risk was, therefore, not something to which either could or should have disclosed to the court. What instead happened was that the trial proceeded down to judgment on the tacit assumption of both parties that the policy was an asset in the nature of an unflawed chose in action that would, if necessary, give the parties the benefit of an indemnity against any liability in the child's damages claim up to the limit of the cover.

81. In fact, the policy was not an unflawed chose in action, because at the time of the trial the insurers were already considering whether to avoid it. Had the parties known that, they would or should have disclosed it to the court and it is probable that His Honour Judge Raynor's order would have been adjusted (perhaps by the inclusion of some contingent provision) to cater for the risk that the policy would be successfully avoided.

> 82. In the event, and following His Honour Judge Raynor's order, the insurers have claimed to avoid the policy. That event has falsified the tacit assumption upon which the parties proceeded before His Honour Judge Raynor. In my view, it is analogous to the type of event that Hale J (as she then was) identified in *Cornick v Cornick* [1994] 2 FLR 530, at 536F, example (2), and which, in *Judge v Judge* [2008] EWCA Civ 1458, [2009] 1 FLR 1287, at para [3], Wilson LJ explained would nowadays be regarded not as a *Barder* event but as 'vitiating mistake'."

54. As I see it, the crucial distinction between a mistake case and a true Barder case is that in the former the relevant facts will exist at the time of the order, but will be unknown; while in the latter, the relevant facts will arise after the order. One might think that in *Richardson* the relevant fact was the announcement on 18 December 2009, after the order, by the insurer that the policy would be avoided, so that the case was in true Barder territory. But, according to Rimer LJ (and somewhat to my surprise) the true relevant and unknown fact was that at the time of the judgment on 25 September 2009 the insurers were considering avoiding the policy even if they had not by then decided to do so, let alone announced a decision. That was an "unknown unknown".

55. Where a case of mistake, as opposed to supervening event, is being advanced the question of the ability of the claimant by exercising due diligence to have discovered the true facts is critically important. In this regard the burden will be on him to show that he could not have discovered the true state of affairs.

56. The recasting of Hale J's second category of case as a case of mistake rather than one falling within the Barder principles is relatively novel. I take it that the third and fourth Barder conditions will continue to apply. The first will not apply because there will not be any new event at all. The second is more problematic although I observe that in *Judge* no-one suggested that the five year passage of time of itself defeated the claim. Questions of foreseeability just do not arise.

57. Therefore I think that applicable principles in relation to the mistake ground can be formulated as follows:

    i) The court may set aside an order on the ground that the true facts on which it based its disposition were not known by either the parties or the court at the time the order was made.

    ii) The claimant must show that the true facts would have led the court to have made a materially different order from the one it in fact made.

    iii) The absence of the true facts must not have been the fault of the claimant.

    iv) The claimant must show, on the balance of probabilities, that he could not with due diligence have established the true facts at the time the order was made.

v) The application to set aside should be made reasonably promptly in the circumstances of the case.

vi) The claimant must show that he cannot obtain alternative mainstream relief which has the effect of broadly remedying the injustice caused by the absence of the true facts.

vii) The application if granted should not prejudice third parties who have, in good faith and for valuable consideration, acquired interests in property which is the subject matter of the relevant order.

This case

58. This was a second marriage for each of the parties. Both parties have children by their first marriages; they are now adult. The parties were married on 24 July 1999. They have a daughter who was born on 26 January 2005. They separated in November 2013. Both parties and their daughter are based in Portugal. The wife commenced divorce proceedings on 31 October 2013. Decree Nisi was pronounced on 16 April 2014; it has not yet been made absolute. (I am asked to grant the husband permission to make the decree absolute.) The wife commenced her claim for financial remedies on 10 January 2014. The parties signed ARB1 on 16 January 2015. The financial remedy proceedings were stayed to allow the arbitration to proceed.

59. Gavin Smith heard evidence on 27, 28 and 29 April 2015. Final submissions were made on 15 May 2015. Mr Smith circulated his award in draft on 2 June 2015. He invited submissions as to corrections and clarifications. These were duly supplied and on 2 July 2015 he promulgated his award and a supplemental award. I shall refer to the two awards collectively as "the award".

60. The award was a thorough, conscientious and clear piece of work. Its quality is a testament to the merit of opting for arbitration. Mr Smith decided that the parties' property and cash should be shared equally. In order to achieve equality this required the husband to pay a lump sum of £158,142. This has been paid. Mr Smith decided that the pensions should be shared equally. This would require a court order. He decided that the husband's business (in which he was a 70% shareholder) should be shared 60:40 to reflect the fact that it was well established at the time that the parties commenced their relationship. The wife would receive her 40% share on the sale by the husband of his shareholding in the business. No end date was provided for that, so the wife might have to wait a long time before she received that further payment, and of course the actual amount could only be speculated about. Pending payment the wife was to receive periodical payments of £36,000 a year. Those would end when she received her payment from the business. The periodical payments were specifically made extendable, as the arbitrator could not foresee whether at the point of payment of her share of the business the wife could adjust without undue hardship to termination. Therefore, it was open to the wife to apply for an

extension if she perceived that her payment from the business would not represent an adequate replacement for her loss of periodical payments. In fact, she has already applied for just such an extension.

61. The effect of the arbitrator's award was as follows:

	Husband	Wife
Property and cash	409,866	409,866
Pensions	274,709	274,709
Business	741,420	494,280
	1,425,995	1,178,855
	55%	45%

The business valuation was, of course, the present value. The property and cash figures were after the payment of the lump sum. Within the wife's figure for property and cash was the value of her home in Portugal. The arbitrator referred to that property as QP, and I shall do likewise. The net figure for QP taken by the arbitrator was £375,797. The wife says that the correct figure at the time of the award was in fact £152,306, a fall of £223,491. Therefore there is a vitiating mistake. Alternatively, she says that by virtue of later events the value has fallen to £152,306, and this fall invalidates the basis of the award. Mr Chamberlayne QC says that the fall of £223,491 has "devastated" and "decimated" her financial position.

62. If the wife's new figure for the value of QP is right, and if the award is not disturbed by me, then the effect is as follows:

	Husband	Wife
Property and cash	409,866	186,375
Pensions	274,709	274,709
Business	741,420	494,280
	1,425,995	955,364
	60%	40%

If the award is modified by me so that the new value of QP is used, but the arbitrator's technique otherwise maintained, then the figures become:

	Husband	Wife
Property and cash	298,121	298,121
Pensions	274,709	274,709
Business	741,420	494,280
	1,314,250	1,067,110
	55%	45%

Thus, based on her new figures, the wife seeks an additional lump sum award of £111,746 (£298,121 – £186,375). It is worth reflecting, in the context of the overarching requirement of exceptionality, that the wife's ambition is to recover a further £111,746 out of a total pool of assets (on her new figures) of £2,381,360.

63. I have seen a transcript of the wife's evidence to Mr Smith. Under cross-examination she stated she wished to keep QP and to will it to her children eventually. She stated:

> "…it belonged to me in my previous marriage and my first husband and the children have spent a great deal of time there. They are very attached to it, and it's my wish that they should inherit it. And it's also my first husband's wish. He agreed to the settlement, hoping that they would inherit it."

Earlier she had stated:

> "I don't know what my future plans are, other than to return to the UK for [our daughter's] education. In that case, if there was funds to put (sic) just a small property here so she could be educated in England, I may let it, to help maintain it but I can't do that until I have the legalisation, the habitation certificate, and a tourism licence is now required."

64. In his award Mr Smith made the following findings. At para 47(b) he dealt with its value as follows:

> "For the purpose of these proceedings [QP] has an agreed value of €660,000. This value assumes that the house will have the benefit of a 'habitation licence' which the wife has been in course of applying for some years. It is her case that without it the property cannot be sold. Costs of sale are agreed at 5%. There is an issue as to the CGT, if any, which should be set against the net equity, and as to the building and other costs which the wife will or should reasonably incur in obtaining the habitation licence. I deal with these issues below. Ignoring CGT, there is a net equity of £445,000."

Later in his award, and in the attached schedule of assets, Mr Smith dealt with the deductions and arrived at the net figure of £375,797.

65. Mr Smith dealt with the wife's future housing needs as follows:

> "97. The wife's future is at present uncertain and it is thus difficult for her to quantify her housing need. She wishes to return to the UK with [the daughter] and to buy a home in Oxfordshire, and for [the daughter] to attend school there, probably at [school named]. That is a school which she and the husband had previously identified as one which [the daughter] might in the future attend. The wife has produced estate agents' details of 3 bedroomed houses costing in the bracket £500,000-£650,000. However, she is not in a position at the moment to relocate with [the daughter], as she requires either the permission of the husband, which is not currently forthcoming, or the permission of the Portuguese court. She has not yet issued her application and has been advised not to do so until next year. The husband's Portuguese lawyer has said that if an application were issued now it would not be heard until after June 2016.

> 98. I cannot predict or second-guess the order that may be made by the Portuguese court. I cannot assume that the wife will receive permission to relocate.
>
> 99. What is clear in my judgment is that her housing need are currently met at QP and would be if she remains in Portugal. If she is successful in obtaining leave to remove, she may well have to lower her sights in terms of accommodation in England and/or use some of the pension funds with which to rehouse herself.
>
> 100. She is very attached to QP and wishes to retain it if at all possible. However, it is not in my view realistic for the wife to envisage retaining QP while at the same time buying a property in England that would be suitable for her and [the daughter] if she obtained leave to remove, but that of course is a matter for her."

66. At para 132(h) Mr Smith determined that the wife should receive periodical payments of £36,000 annually, and he concluded that she could adjust without undue hardship to termination of those payments once she receives her interest in the business on final disposal. However at para 132(f) he had held:

> "On the sale of [the husband's] shares the wife should receive a lump sum equal to 40% of the proceeds after tax and the husband the balance and at that point there should be a clean break. I shall not order a s28(1A) direction. This will be to provide a safety net in case the wife's share is substantially less than the current value would suggest and does not meet her needs."

67. It follows that the safety net is available if the wife's capital is not sufficient to meet all her needs, whether for housing or income, at the point of the sale of the business. If the value of one element of her estate has fallen, whether it be the value of QP or her share in the business, then the safety net is there to ensure that her needs in the long-term are met.

68. In my judgment, the existence of the safety net inevitably leads me to refuse to interfere with the arbitrator's award, even if the threshold requirements for proof of mistake or supervening event are demonstrated. If the notional loss of £223,491 in the value of QP – which the wife is presently not in fact intending to sell, and which she wishes to leave to her children – in fact eventuates in hard money terms then the court will have the facility to bring into operation the safety net both in relation to quantum and duration of periodical payments. I have mentioned that the wife has already applied for an extension of the term of periodical payments. The husband has applied, in effect, for a capitalisation of the periodical payments in that following receipt of the draft award he has tendered to her the sum of £494,280, which is the present value taken by the arbitrator of the wife's 40% share in the business. In his supplemental award Mr Smith rightly refused to deal with the husband's de facto capitalisation application. This would have to be heard as a fresh application either by means of arbitration or in court. At all events, there are now pending cross-applications for variation of

the wife's award of periodical payments. In those proceedings the wife's assertions as to the fall in value of QP will fall to be adjudicated. If those assertions are found proved then I imagine that the arbitrator or court will wish to reconsider whether the periodical payments should terminate on receipt by the wife of her share of the business when it is sold.

69. However, I will deal with the wife's primary case as it may be that others disagree with my view that the existence of the safety net inevitably means that the discretion to set aside the award should not be exercised.

70. I take the facts largely from Mr Chamberlayne's skeleton argument. These are not seriously disputed.

71. In 1992 the wife acquired QP, a Portuguese farmhouse sited on agricultural land. The original house was built prior to 1951 and does not require legalisation (planning consent). In the 1970s its previous owners constructed a separate annex (bedroom kitchenette and swimming pool) and in the late 1980s they extended the main house. Planning consent was not granted for either additional construction. The total area of building construction is now 401.65 m^2.

72. In 2007 the parties jointly engaged the services of an architect, Jaime Coutinho, to secure the necessary planning consent to legalise the property and to obtain a habitation licence. A habitation licence is required in order to be able to sell the property to a third party. A notary will not sign a deed of transfer of title without there being such a licence in existence.

73. Two applications for planning have been submitted. The first application had been refused by the council on 4 October 2011 because "the main building and pool were in conditions to be legalised but not the annex, for the main reason that [it] was located at a distance less than 5m from the boundary" and "the annex is separated from the main building".

74. In 2012 or 2013 the parties acquired a strip of land from a neighbour to overcome the issue regarding the distance from the boundary. The second application for planning had been submitted by the architect on 27 November 2014 but had not been determined at the time of the arbitration. The wife had obtained quotations from two builders for the construction of a physical link – a "pergola" – between the main building and the annex. The amounts involved were relatively small – £11,000.

75. A SJE chartered surveyor, Ian Rostrum, was instructed to provide the market value of the property. He provided an initial valuation in his report dated 31 August 2014 and an updated valuation in a letter dated 2 April 2015 to take account of an increase in property prices. His evidence, which included his consideration about the issue of the likely legalisation of the property, was unchallenged.

76. In summary Mr Rostrum's opinion was that once the property obtained a habitation licence it would be worth €660,000. Without the legalisation licence, but on the assumption that planning would be granted in due course, he valued the property at €630,000. The small difference in effect

reflected the 'hassle factor' of having to obtain the licence, because, of course, the property could not be sold without it. He reports that based upon his discussion with the architect, all that was required by the council to grant a licence was a physical link between the main property and the annex. He stated:

> "The local authority has so far raised two conditions that need to be addressed before they will consider approval. One was that the detached annex was within 5m of the original southern boundary and the other was that a physical connection by way of a pergola was needed between the detached annex and the main house. They are applying the conditions set out on the Plano Director Municipal (PDM) the master plan that deals with planning regulations.
>
> A strip of land has already been purchased from the neighbouring property ensuring that the structure is five metres from the boundary and the construction of a pergola is simple and relatively inexpensive.
>
> Arq. Jaime Coutinho has advised that he is convinced that when these two conditions have been met that no more conditions will be applied by the local authority. However he has qualified this advice by adding that no one can be 100% sure that it will be approved. As a result two valuation figures have been provided for this property."

77. The evidence, accepted by all, was that the habitation licence would in all likelihood be forthcoming, subject only to the construction of a structure deemed suitable by the council to connect the main house to the annex. The precise characteristics required by the council of the structure were all that was awaited according to emails from Mr Coutinho that formed part of the evidence at the hearing.

78. As stated above at [64] Mr Smith therefore attributed to the property the full value of €660,000 but deducted as a liability the building costs and fees that the wife would have to incur in obtaining the necessary planning consent. After deduction of other expenses this resulted in a net value to the wife of £375,797.

79. The award was promulgated on 2 July 2015. On 20 July 2015 the council determined the planning application by refusing it. The decision states that the permitted planning parameters for the built area are 300 m^2 and that the existing and proposed built area exceeds this limitation (401.65 m^2).

80. On 17 August 2015 the architect Mr Coutinho sent an email to the wife clarifying the decision. He stated that the main house together with the extension was already bigger than the permitted area (324.20 m^2), let alone the annex. Mr Coutinho stated "this means that now even the main villa may not be totally approved due to excess of area". On 16 October 2015 Marta Lopes from Mr Coutinho's office advised that "the only way to continue the process to obtain a habitation licence is to reformulate the process and proceed with the demolition of the annex and the excess area of the villa to accommodate the PDM requirement."

81. In the light of these developments the wife obtained new expert evidence from Peter Densham MRICS. She has adduced his evidence in these proceedings without having obtained the court's permission under FPR 25.4(2) although no strong objection was raised by Mr Pointer QC to my being referred to it. Obviously the status of the evidence is no more than indicative. It cannot be taken to be conclusive in circumstances where the rules have not been complied with. Further, if fresh valuation evidence was to have been relied on in any definitive way then it ought to have derived from a single joint expert: see PD25D para 2.1, which provides that "wherever possible, expert evidence should be obtained from a single joint expert instructed by both or all the parties".

82. In his letter dated 23 October 2015 Mr Densham has valued the property without planning consent at €225,000 but states that "the probability of achieving a sale at all is doubtful". The value of the property with a habitation licence with it reconstructed and with reduced size will be €400,000, in his opinion.

83. The cost of reducing the property in size, digging up the pool and making good the works is set out in a table in the statement of the wife's case. This calculates the current net residual value as £152,306.

84. It is not accepted by the husband that any of these gloomy predictions will come to pass. He asserts that this issue has been "rumbling on" for nearly 10 years and that there is no firm or reliable evidence either way as to its eventual outcome.

85. I deal first with the contention that the decision of the council on 20 July 2015 was an unforeseeable later event which invalidated the decision of the arbitrator. I cannot agree that it was. The application was pending and although everyone was confident that it would be granted it must have been recognised that it might be refused. To my mind the decision, albeit unwelcome, was eminently foreseeable in the sense described by the House of Lords and the Privy Council in the cases to which I have referred. Even if the decision was unforeseeable I do not agree that it "invalidated" the arbitrator's decision in circumstances where the scale of the loss, assuming that Mr Densham's evidence is correct, would reduce the wife's overall share of the capital from 45% to 40%. A 40% overall award was well within Mr Smith's discretion and to my mind invalidation is only demonstrated where it can be shown that the consequence plainly falls outside the discretionary band. A claim for a further lump sum of £111,746 out of a total pool of assets of £2,381,359 does not come close to meeting the requirement of exceptionality.

86. The wife's case on mistake is stronger and has similarities to the case of *Richardson*. It would certainly seem to be undeniable that on 2 July 2015 the council were considering refusing the application, just as in *Richardson* on 25 September 2009 the insurers were considering avoiding the policy. However, I am not satisfied on the evidence that the wife with due diligence could not have discovered that the council might well adopt a much

harder line about unauthorised building developments. I have been given no evidence of any efforts made by her to find out what the council were actually contemplating. There seems to have just been a blithe assumption that all would be well. The possibility of rejection was specifically referred to by her architect and it is surprising in those circumstances that she was content to allow the arbitrator to proceed to judgment without nailing down the point one way or another.

87. I therefore reject the wife's case on mistake.

88. But either way, the wife's claim fails because there is available to her alternative mainstream relief which can broadly remedy any injustice caused to her by a fall in value in QP, if that actually eventuates.

89. The husband's application is therefore granted and the order as drafted by Mr Smith will be made by me. I further allow the husband to make absolute the Decree Nisi so that the order can take immediate effect.

Two procedural points

90. In this case the husband's notice to show cause was issued in the Central Family Court and came before Recorder Campbell on 27 October 2015. She transferred the matter to be heard by a High Court judge, but it has taken some time for this hearing to be listed. In the future any notice to show cause why an arbitration award should not be made an order of the court must, for London and the South Eastern Circuit, be issued in the Royal Courts of Justice and immediately placed before me for allocation to a High Court judge for speedy determination. If the application is issued outside London or the South Eastern Circuit then it must be immediately placed before the Family Division Liaison Judge who will arrange for it to be heard speedily by him or her or another High Court judge (including a section 9 judge). It is important for the promotion of the arbitration system that litigants should know that if a challenge to an arbitration award is raised that it will be heard by a High Court judge at the soonest opportunity.

91. Finally, I wish to deal with a procedural point which is in fact not material to this case and therefore what I say is strictly speaking obiter. In *CS v ACS* [2015] EWHC 1005 (Fam) the President decided that an application to set aside an order on the basis of non-disclosure (or fraud or mistake) could, pursuant to FPR 4.1(6) and section 31F(6) Matrimonial and Family Proceedings Act 1984, be made to the original court and did not have to be made by way of appeal. He left open the question whether a Barder application could be made to the original court or whether it had to be by way of appeal. In my judgment, for the reasons set out in Financial Remedies Practice 2016 (Class Publishing) at paragraphs 4.12 to 4.20, a Barder application can be made to the original court.

Haley v Haley [2020] EWCA Civ 1369

Artwork-App 6-01

Neutral Citation Number: [2020] EWCA Civ 1369

Case No: B6/2020/0587

IN THE COURT OF APPEAL (CIVIL DIVISION)

ON APPEAL FROM HIGH COURT OF JUSTICE

(FAMILY DIVISION)

Deputy High Court Judge Ambrose

BV18D11995

Royal Courts of Justice

Strand, London, WC2A 2LL

Date: 23/10/2020

Before:

LADY JUSTICE KING
LORD JUSTICE MOYLAN

and

LORD JUSTICE POPPLEWELL

....

Between:

Russell Haley **Appellant**

– and –

Kelly Haley **Respondent**

....

....

James Ewins QC and William Tyzack (instructed by **Levison Meltzer Pigott Solicitors**) for the **Appellant**

David Walden-Smith (instructed by **Nockolds Solicitors**) for the **Respondent**

Hearing dates: 22 July 2020

....

APPROVED JUDGMENT

Lady Justice King:

1. The issues in this appeal arise from an arbitral award made on 23 October 2019 by Mr Howard Shaw QC. The underlying litigation concerned applications for financial remedies in the Family Court sitting at Chelmsford, between Kelly Haley ("the wife") and Russell Haley ("the husband"). The husband believed that the award made by Mr Shaw was unfair. He therefore made an application to the High Court seeking either to appeal the arbitral award or, alternatively, for an order to be made by which the court would decline to make an order under the Matrimonial Causes Act 1973 ("MCA 1973") in the terms of the award and would instead exercise its discretion anew.

2. On 27 February 2020, Deputy High Court Judge Ambrose ("the judge") dismissed the appeal and refused the application to interfere with the award. The judge accordingly made an order in the terms of the arbitral award.

3. It is against this order that the husband now appeals. In giving permission to appeal in this case, Moylan LJ identified an important point of principle as to "the proper approach which the family court should take to arbitral awards when making a financial remedy order."

Arbitration in Family Cases

4. Unlike commercial arbitration, the availability of arbitration in financial remedy cases is relatively recent. The Family Law Arbitration Financial Scheme operates under the Institute of Family Law Arbitrators ("the IFLA Scheme"). The scheme was launched in February 2012 as a collaboration between Resolution, the Family Law Bar Association, the Chartered Institute of Arbitrators and the Centre for Child and Family Law Reform. The ILFA Scheme's authority derives from the Arbitration Act 1996.

5. There is a common misconception that the use of arbitration, as an alternative to the court process in financial remedy cases, is the purview only of the rich who seek privacy away from the courts and the eyes of the media. If that was ever the position, it is no more. The court was told during the course of argument, that it is widely anticipated that parties in modest asset cases (including litigants in person) will increasingly use the arbitration process in the aftermath of the Covid-19 crisis as the courts cope with the backlog of cases, which is the inevitable consequence of "lockdown".

6. It goes without saying that it is of the utmost importance that potential users of the arbitration process are not deterred from using this valuable service; either, on the one hand, because the outcome is not seen as sufficiently certain or, on the other, because arbitration is regarded as providing no adequate remedy in circumstances where one of the parties believes there to have been an unjust outcome.

7. In the present case, the wife's application for financial relief following the breakdown of the marriage went through the normal court process, including an unsuccessful financial dispute resolution hearing. The parties were unable to settle the case and the matter was set down for trial to be heard in front of a District Judge for two days and to commence on 19 September 2019. Only a week before the trial, on 12 September 2019, the parties were told that there would be no judge available to hear the case and that the matter would have to be listed for an unspecified date in the future. It was in those unhappy circumstances that, on 13 September 2019, the parties – anxious to have the case heard, and it being ready for trial – signed an arbitration agreement on the ARB1 FS form provided under rules governing the IFLA Scheme. Mr Howard Shaw QC was named as the arbitrator.

8. The arbitration hearing took place on the same days as those which had been already set aside by the parties and their legal teams for the trial, the 19 and 20 September 2019. In due course a draft award was circulated to counsel. Counsel for the husband sought clarification as to certain matters, but this request was declined by Mr Shaw. On 23 October 2019, Mr Shaw produced his final award in substantially the same terms as the draft award, save that he had increased the figure which he awarded by way of periodical payments for the wife.

9. The husband subsequently made the following applications to the court:

   i) An order setting aside the award for serious irregularity under s68 Arbitration Act 1996 ("AA 1996") (Challenging the award: serious irregularity);

   ii) Permission to appeal under s69 AA 1996 (Appeal on a point of law);

   iii) An order that the award should not be made into a final order by the court under the MCA 1973.

10. The judge dismissed the applications under s68 and s69 AA 1996. No further appeal was made in relation to s68 AA 1996, and it is common ground that, after the judge refused the application under s69 AA 1996, the Court of Appeal had no jurisdiction to grant permission to appeal from that refusal (see *The Northern Pioneer* [2003] 1 Lloyd's Rep 212).

11. The judge held that the test to be applied in determining whether to refuse, in the exercise of her discretion, to make an order in the terms of the arbitral award, was akin to the test under s68 and s69 AA 1996. Further, she held that if she was wrong as to the correct test to be applied, the award made by the arbitrator was "not wrong."

12. This appeal is limited, therefore, to a consideration as to the test to be applied where one party declines to consent to or challenges the making of an order under the MCA 1973 in the terms of the arbitral award following family arbitration under the IFLA Scheme. The questions to be determined are as follows:

   i) Did the judge apply the wrong test, namely one which was akin to that applied under the AA 1996?

ii) If so, is the correct test that which was characterised by Counsel as the 'appeals test' applicable under the MCA 1973?

iii) If the appeals test is the appropriate test, then if properly applied is there a real prospect that the first instance court would have concluded that the arbitral award was wrong;

iv) If so, should the matter be remitted to a first instance court or is this court able to substitute its own order?

13. It is useful before examining the IFLA Scheme and the appeals process under the MCA 1973, to identify in broad terms the differing approach and philosophy that apply to a challenge to an arbitral award under the AA 1996 on the one hand, and an appeal under the MCA 1973 on the other.

14. The principal routes of challenge to an arbitral award are that the arbitrator "lacked substantive jurisdiction" (s67 AA 1996); or there was "serious irregularity affecting the tribunal, the proceedings or the award" (s68 AA 1996); or that the award was wrong on a question of law (s69 AA1996). As set out at [22] – [26] below, the test under section 69 (which is the route most commonly used in an attempt to challenge an award) is applied on the basis of the facts as found by the arbitrator. The party challenging the award requires leave and must show that the decision on the question of law was "obviously wrong", unless the question is one of general public importance, in which case it must be shown to be at least open to serious doubt. Fairness as a concept has no place in a challenge to an arbitral award; arbitration being a procedure designed to provide certainty across the international commercial world.

15. By contrast, where there has been a contested financial remedy trial heard in court (which would have been the preferred option of the parties) then leave, as with a challenge under s69 AA 1996, will be required. However, permission will be given if the judge concludes that there is a real prospect that the proposed appellant can satisfy the appeal court that the order made was: (a) wrong; or (b) unjust because of a serious procedural or other irregularity in the proceedings in the lower court. Fairness will be central to the court's determination.

16. The judge in the present case held that the proper test, where the challenge is in respect of a family arbitration under the terms of the IFLA Scheme, is "closely aligned" to that provided under the stringent terms of the AA 1996, save where there has been a supervening event or mistake.

The Arbitration Agreement

17. As noted in the judgment at [13], the parties each signed the ARB1 FS form. By paragraph 6.4 of the form, the parties confirm that they:

> "...understand and agree that any award of the arbitrator appointed to determine this dispute will be final and binding on us, subject to the following:

(a) any challenge to the award by any available arbitral process of appeal or review or in accordance with the provisions of Part 1 of the Act;

(b) insofar as the subject matter of the award requires it to be embodied in a court order (see 6.5 below), any changes which the court making that order may require;

(c) insofar as the award provides for continuing payments to be made by one party to another, or to a child or children, a subsequent award or court order reviewing and varying or revoking the provision for continuing payments, and which supersedes an existing award;

(d) insofar as the award provides for continuing payments to be made by one party to or for the benefit of a child or children, a subsequent assessment by the Child Maintenance Service (or its successor) in relation to the same child or children.

6.5 If and so far as the subject matter of the award makes it necessary, we will apply to an appropriate court for an order in the same or similar terms as the award or the relevant part of the award. (In this context, 'an appropriate court' means a court which has jurisdiction to make a substantive order in the same or similar terms as the award, whether on primary application or on transfer from another division of the court.) We understand that the court has a discretion as to whether, and in what terms, to make an order and we will take all reasonably necessary steps to see that such an order is made."

18. At the end of the form, immediately above the signatures of the parties or their legal representatives, appears the following:

IMPORTANT

Parties should be aware that:

- **By signing this form they are entering into a binding agreement to arbitrate (within the meaning of s.6 of the Arbitration Act 1996).**
- **After signing, neither party may avoid arbitration (unless they both agree to do so). Either party may rely on the arbitration agreement to seek a stay of court proceedings commenced by the other.**
- **Arbitration is a process whose outcome is generally final. There are very limited bases for raising a challenge or appeal, and it is only in exceptional circumstances that a court will exercise its own discretion in substitution for the award.**

Challenges under the Arbitration Act 1996

19. As referred to above, an arbitral award can be challenged only on the grounds that: (i) the tribunal lacked substantive jurisdiction (s67 AA 1996); (ii) that

there was a "serious irregularity affecting the tribunal, the proceedings or the award" (s68 AA 1996); or (iii) "there is a question of law" arising from the award (s69 AA 1996).

20. There is, within s57 AA 1996, a corrective jurisdiction which allows the tribunal to "correct an award so as to remove any clerical mistake or error arising from an accidental slip or omission or clarify or remove any ambiguity" (section 57(3)(a)); or to "make an additional award in respect of any claim [...] which was presented to the tribunal but was not dealt with in the award" (Section 57(3)(b)). By s70 AA 1996, no application or appeal may be brought until any available recourse under s57 AA 1996 has been exhausted.

21. As was properly recognised by the judge at [60], s68 AA 1996 relates to process and is not designed to address the issue as to whether the tribunal reached the right result. This was emphasised by Flaux J (as he then was) in *Sonatrach v Statoil* [2014] 2 Lloyd's Rep 242 at [11], where he said:

> "...As the DAC Report states, and numerous cases since have reiterated, the section is designed as a long-stop available only in extreme cases where the tribunal has gone so wrong in its conduct of the arbitration that justice calls out for it to be corrected."

22. Section 69 AA 1996 deals with challenging an award on a point of law arising out of the award. Such a challenge involves an initial requirement for leave to appeal, followed by a substantive hearing on the merits of the appeal. Leave is ordinarily dealt with on paper by way of a triage type process, and:

> "(3) Leave to appeal shall be given only if the court is satisfied—
>
> (a) that the determination of the question will substantially affect the rights of one or more of the parties,
>
> (b) that the question is one which the tribunal was asked to determine,
>
> (c) that, on the basis of the findings of fact in the award—
>
> (i) the decision of the tribunal on the question is obviously wrong, or
>
> (ii) the question is one of general public importance and the decision of the tribunal is at least open to serious doubt, and
>
> (d) that, despite the agreement of the parties to resolve the matter by arbitration, it is just and proper in all the circumstances for the court to determine the question."

23. The Commercial Court is constantly alert to attempts to present challenges to findings of fact as points of law under section 69.

24. In his judgment in *J v B (Family Law Arbitration: Award)* [2016] EWHC 324 (Fam), [2016] 1 WLR 3319 (also known as *DB v DLJ*) (herein *J v B*), Mostyn J quoted with approbation a passage from a lecture by Sir Bernard Eder:

> "6. In his excellent paper *'Challenges to Arbitral Awards at the Seat'* given to the Mauritius International Arbitration Conference on 15 December 2014 Sir Bernard Eder explains at [6] that:
>
> > '...the general approach of the Court is one which strongly supports the arbitral process. By way of anecdote, it is perhaps interesting to recall what I was once told many years ago by Michael Kerr, a former judge in the Court of Appeal and one of the leading figures in the recent development of the law of arbitration in England, when I was complaining about an arbitration that I had just lost and the difficulties in the way of challenging the award. I told him that the award was wrong and unjust. He looked baffled and said: *"Remember, when parties agree arbitration they buy the right to get the wrong answer"*. So, the mere fact that an award is "wrong" or even "unjust" does not, of itself, provide any basis for challenging the award or intervention by the Court. Any challenge or appeal must bring itself under one or more of the three heads which I have identified.'"

25. This robust approach simply mirrors the approach of the Commercial Court to the various ingenious efforts on the part of disgruntled parties to dress up what they regard as perverse findings of fact, as points of law. The case of *Geogas S.A v Trammo Gas Ltd.* [1993] 1 Lloyds Rep 215, on appeal from [1991] 1 WLR. 776 *(The Baleares),* was a case decided under the earlier Arbitration Act 1979, but is still regarded as a classic statement of the proper approach to appeals on a point of law under the statutory arbitration regime. In this case, Lord Justice Steyn said:

> "This is an appeal under section 1 of the Arbitration Act 1979 on [...] a question of law arising from an arbitration award[...] For those concerned in this case that is a statement of the obvious. But it matters. It defines the limits of the jurisdiction of the court hearing an appeal under the 1979 Act. The arbitrators are the masters of the facts. On an appeal the court must decide any question of law arising from an award on the basis of a full and unqualified acceptance of the findings of fact of the arbitrators. It is irrelevant whether the court considers those findings of fact to be right or wrong. It also does not matter how obvious a mistake by the arbitrators on issues of fact might be, or what the scale of the financial consequences of the mistake of fact might be. That is, of course, an unsurprising position. After all, the very reason why parties conclude an arbitration agreement is because they do not wish to litigate in the courts. Parties who submit their disputes to arbitration bind themselves by agreement to honour the arbitrators' award on the facts. The principle of party autonomy decrees that a court ought never to question the arbitrators' findings of fact.
>
> From time to time attempts are made to circumvent the rule that the arbitrators' findings of fact are conclusive. Such attempts did not cease with the enactment of the Arbitration Act 1979. Subsequently, attempts were made to argue that an obvious mistake of fact by arbitrators may constitute misconduct. It is clear that such a challenge is misconceived.

[…] This catalogue of challenges to arbitrators' findings of fact points to the need for the court to be constantly vigilant to ensure that attempts to question or qualify the arbitrators' findings of fact, or to dress up questions of fact as questions of law, are carefully identified and firmly discouraged."

26. *Demco Investments and Commercial S.A. and Others v SE Banken Forsakring Holding Aktiebolag* [2005] EWHC 1398 (Comm), [2005] 2 Lloyd's Rep 650 *(Demco)* was an important case concerned with the alleged mis-selling of pensions to individuals who had either failed to join, or opted out of occupational pension schemes, which had otherwise been available to them. Mr Justice Cooke considered the proper test to be applied in an application for permission to appeal under s69 AA 1996. Cooke J applied the "obviously wrong" test at s69 (3)(c)(i) emphasising the opening words of s69(3)(c), that leave will only be given *"on the basis of the findings of fact in the Award"*. After considering some seemingly conflicting dicta at [43] that are not of relevance here, Cooke J concluded that Steyn LJ's dictum in *The Baleares* set out above "takes full force and effect."

Financial Provision upon divorce

27. It is common ground that in the family context arbitration cannot oust the jurisdiction of the court, as is properly recognised at para 6.5 of ARB1 FS, which says that the court "has a discretion as to whether, and in what terms, to make an order."

28. In my judgment, it is helpful briefly to consider the nature of that discretion, and how it is framed when an application for financial remedy has been made through the courts, when considering whether – as the judge and as Mostyn J effectively suggest (see below at [59]-[60]) – that discretion should be limited almost to vanishing point where a party seeks to challenge an arbitral award. This is so, given the stringency of the test under s68 and s69 AA 1996 and the rarity of cases that succeed where mistake or supervening event are pleaded.

29. At the end of a marriage, amidst potential distress and recriminations, two important matters have to be resolved, namely the arrangements for any minor children, and the separation of the finances of the parties. Rightly, the welfare of any children is the court's "first consideration" when it exercises its jurisdiction in deciding how to utilise its powers in relation to financial provision (section 25(1) MCA 1973).

30. The making of financial provision orders upon divorce (or dissolution of a civil partnership) are governed by the MCA 1973 which imposes a statutory duty upon the court to have regard to all the circumstances of the case (s25(1) MCA 1973). In broad terms, section 23 MCA 1973 provides for the making of periodical payments and lump sum orders; section 24 for property adjustment orders; section 24A for orders for the sale of property; and section 24B- section 24F for pension sharing orders.

31. These orders, or a combination of them, provide an enforceable route for the division of a couple's matrimonial assets, regardless of whether they are of modest means or, at the other end of the spectrum, wealthy with complex financial affairs involving trusts, companies and international assets. Without the appropriate orders being made, under the MCA 1973 following an arbitral award, the parties' rights will remain legally undetermined and they cannot take advantage of the bespoke provisions available under the MCA 1973, and crucially, their enforceability.

32. The couple with whom this court is concerned fall into the former category. The husband, by virtue of a demanding commute and by working long hours, has a substantial income, but the parties' capital assets amount to less than £400,000.

33. Where a couple are unable to reach agreement, one or other of them has to make an application for financial remedy to the court. The judge will then have regard to the mandatory criteria found in section 25(1) and (2) of the MCA 1973, when making orders under sections 23(1)*(a)*, *(b)* or *(c)*, 24, 24A, 24B or 24E.

34. Regardless of where a couple's assets fall on the spectrum of wealth, section 25 MCA 1973 sets out: "Matters to which the court is to have regard in deciding how to exercise its powers under ss23, 24, 24A, 24B and 24E."

35. Although familiar to all practitioners, it is worth for the purposes of this judgment rehearsing the mandatory criteria found in section 25(2) of the MCA 1973 as they apply whenever a court makes an order for financial provision, whether by consent or otherwise:

> "(2) As regards the exercise of the powers of the court under section 23(1)*(a)*, *(b)* or *(c)*, 24, 24A, 24B or 24E above in relation to a party to the marriage, the court shall in particular have regard to the following matters—
>
> (a) the income, earning capacity, property and other financial resources which each of the parties to the marriage has or is likely to have in the foreseeable future, including in the case of earning capacity any increase in that capacity which it would in the opinion of the court be reasonable to expect a party to the marriage to take steps to acquire;
>
> (b) the financial needs, obligations and responsibilities which each of the parties to the marriage has or is likely to have in the foreseeable future;
>
> (c) the standard of living enjoyed by the family before the breakdown of the marriage;
>
> (d) the age of each party to the marriage and the duration of the marriage;
>
> (e) any physical or mental disability of either of the parties to the marriage;

(f) the contributions which each of the parties has made or is likely in the foreseeable future to make to the welfare of the family, including any contribution by looking after the home or caring for the family;

(g) the conduct of each of the parties, if that conduct is such that it would in the opinion of the court be inequitable to disregard it;

(h) in the case of proceedings for divorce or nullity of marriage, the value to each of the parties to the marriage of any benefit which, by reason of the dissolution or annulment of the marriage, that party will lose the chance of acquiring."

Agreements

36. Where, however, the parties have been able to reach agreement, the Family Procedure Rules 2010 ("FPR") set out, at r 9.26, the requirements for obtaining a consent order with agreed terms. One of the requirements is for the filing of a statement of information.

37. By FPR PD 9A, paras 7.1 – 7.3, the statement of information must be in the prescribed form, setting out personal and financial information so that the court can undertake its inquisitorial jurisdiction when considering whether to approve an agreement.

38. Section 33A of the MCA 1973, as inserted by section 7 of the Matrimonial and Family Proceedings Act 1984, provides that:

> "the court may, unless it has reason to think that there are other circumstances into which it ought to inquire, make an order in the terms agreed on the basis only of the prescribed information furnished with the application."

39. The court, therefore, scrutinises the statement of information, with the list of factors from s25 MCA 1973 at the forefront of its judicial mind. The proper exercise of the court's inquisitorial jurisdiction, in relation to the making of consent orders, was graphically described in *L v L* [2006] EWHC 956 (Fam), [2008] 1 FLR 26 at [73], as being not "a rubber stamp" but that, whilst the court must always exercise a discretion, it should not be to the extent of acting as "a bloodhound or a ferret."

40. In *Sharland v Sharland* [2015] UKSC 60, [2015] 2 FLR 1367, the Supreme Court considered the relationship between the court and parties who wish to resolve their financial dispute following divorce by way of a consent order. Baroness Hale said:

> "18. It has long been possible for a married couple to make a binding agreement about the financial consequences of their present separation. However, it is not possible for such an agreement to oust the jurisdiction of the court to make orders about their financial arrangements. This was a rule of public policy, because of the public interest in ensuring that

> proper provision is made for dependent family members: see *Hyman v Hyman [1929] AC 601*. ……
>
> 19. Thus it is impossible for the parties to oust the jurisdiction of the court, but the court also possesses powers to achieve finality (a "clean break") in the parties' financial arrangements which the parties cannot achieve for themselves. For those reasons, it is now much more common for separating or divorcing spouses to negotiate with a view to embodying their agreed arrangements in a court order than to make a formal separation agreement. If they do this, the fundamental principle is that 'an agreement to compromise an ancillary relief application does not give rise to a contract enforceable in law'. Furthermore, 'the court does not either automatically or invariably grant the application to give the bargain [the] force of an order. The court conducts an independent assessment to enable it to discharge its statutory function to make such orders as reflect the criteria listed in section 25 of the Matrimonial Causes Act 1973 as amended': see *Xydhias v Xydhias* [1999] 2 All ER 386, per Thorpe LJ at 394.
>
> 20. Although the court still has to exercise its statutory role, it will, of course, be heavily influenced by what the parties themselves have agreed. …"

41. *Sharland* makes it abundantly clear that the fact of an agreement cannot oust the jurisdiction of the court and that, although the court is heavily influenced by an agreement (a matter reflected in the words of section 7 of the Matrimonial and Family Proceedings Act 1984), the court conducts an independent assessment to enable it to discharge its statutory function to make such orders as reflect the criteria listed in section 25 MCA 1973. Baroness Hale continued:

> "27. Family proceedings are different from ordinary civil proceedings in two respects. First, in family proceedings it has been clear, at least since the House of Lords' decision in *de Lasala v de Lasala [1980] AC 546*, that a consent order derives its authority from the court and not from the consent of the parties, whereas in ordinary civil proceedings, a consent order derives its authority from the contract made between the parties: see, eg, *Purcell v FC Trigell Ltd [1971] 1 QB 358* , CA. Second, in family proceedings there is always a duty of full and frank disclosure, whereas in civil proceedings this is not universal.
>
> 29. It follows that the majority in the Court of Appeal in this case were correct to say that matrimonial cases were different from ordinary civil cases in that the binding effect of a settlement embodied in a consent order stems from the court's order and not from the prior agreement of the parties. It does not, however, follow that the parties' agreement is not a sine qua non of a consent order. Quite the reverse: the court cannot make a consent order without the valid consent of the parties. If there is a reason which vitiates a party's consent, then there may also be good reason to set aside the consent order. The only question is whether the court has any choice in the matter."

42. So much for agreements which the parties wish to be incorporated into a court order. What of those agreements which have been entered into either in contemplation of marriage or at the end of the marriage?

43. The Supreme Court considered agreements made in contemplation of marriage in *Radmacher v Granatino* [2010] UKSC 42, [2010] 2 FLR 1900, quoted in both *S v S* and *Sharland* above. The Supreme Court said at [75]:

> "*White v White* and *Miller v Miller* establish that the overriding criterion to be applied in ancillary relief proceedings is that of fairness and identify the three strands of need, compensation and sharing that are relevant to the question of what is fair. If an ante-nuptial agreement deals with those matters in a way that the court might adopt absent such an agreement, there is no problem about giving effect to the agreement. The problem arises where the agreement makes provisions that conflict with what the court would otherwise consider to be the requirements of fairness. The fact of the agreement is capable of altering what is fair. It is an important factor to be weighed in the balance. We would advance the following proposition, to be applied in the case of both ante- and post-nuptial agreements, in preference to that suggested by the Board in *MacLeod:*
>
>> 'The court should give effect to a nuptial agreement that is freely entered into by each party with a full appreciation of its implications unless in the circumstances prevailing it would not be fair to hold the parties to their agreement.'"

44. Lord Philips, between [77] and [84], moved on to consider the circumstances in which it would not be fair to hold parties to their agreement. These included the welfare of the children [78] and the parties' needs. At [81], the court said:

> "The parties are unlikely to have intended that their ante-nuptial agreement should result, in the event of the marriage breaking up, in one partner being left in a predicament of real need, while the other enjoys a sufficiency or more, and such a result is likely to render it unfair to hold the parties to their agreement."

45. In relation to agreements reached between parties upon divorce, the principles have long been established in the *Edgar v Edgar* [1980] 1 WLR 1410, (1981) 2 FLR 19 (*"Edgar")* line of cases, where Ormrod LJ said at [25]:

> "To decide what weight should be given in order to reach a just result, to a prior agreement not to claim a lump sum, regard must be had to the conduct of both parties, leading up to the prior agreement, and to their subsequent conduct, in consequence of it. It is not necessary in this connection to think in formal legal terms, such as misrepresentation or estoppel; *all* the circumstances as they affect each of two human beings must be considered in the complex relationship of marriage. So, the circumstances surrounding the making of the agreement are relevant. Undue pressure by one side, exploitation of a dominant position to secure an unreasonable advantage, inadequate knowledge, possibly

bad legal advice, an important change of circumstances, unforeseen or overlooked at the time of making the agreement, are all relevant to the question of justice between the parties. Important too is the general proposition that, formal agreements, properly and fairly arrived at with competent legal advice, should not be displaced unless there are good and substantial grounds for concluding that an injustice will be done by holding the parties to the terms of their agreement. There may well be other considerations which affect the justice of this case; the above list is not intended to be an exclusive catalogue."

46. The legal position in relation to agreements is, therefore, crystal clear. Regardless of whether the parties apply to the court to make an order by consent, having reached an agreement, or whether the court is faced with a party who wishes to renege on an agreement made in contemplation of marriage or upon divorce. In each case:

    i) The family proceedings with which the court is concerned are different from ordinary civil proceedings as the order made under the MCA 1973 derives its authority from the court and not from the consent of the parties. This is in contrast to ordinary civil proceedings where the consent order derives its authority from the contract made between the parties;

    ii) Although the court still has to exercise its statutory role, it will be heavily influenced by what the parties themselves have agreed.

Appeals

47. If the matter is not resolved by agreement the matter will go to trial. In the event that either party is dissatisfied with the outcome, that party can make an application for permission to appeal (save for an appeal from the magistrates to the district judge where no permission is required). Whilst the rules governing the procedure differ, depending upon whether the appeal is to a circuit or high court judge on the one hand (FPR r 30.3 and FPR PD 30A), or the Court of Appeal on the other (CPR 1998 r52), the approach and principles that apply are the same (see *CR v SR (Financial Remedies: Permission to Appeal* [2013] EWHC 1155 (Fam), [2014] 1 FLR 186 at [6]). Permission to appeal will only be granted if there is a "real prospect of success"- that is to say, the applicant must show a realistic, rather than fanciful, prospect of success (*CR v SR* at [8]).

48. For the purposes of this appeal, I refer only to the FPR, given that Mr Ewins QC, on behalf of the husband, submits that the approach of a court where a party is dissatisfied with the outcome of an arbitration should mirror that where a litigant is dissatisfied following a financial remedy hearing before a court.

49. Where permission to appeal has been granted, the appeal hearing is not an opportunity for a "second bite of the cherry." It should be borne in mind that:

i) The appeal is limited to a review of the lower court's decision unless a rehearing is permitted for a particular class of appeal, or the court considers it to be in the interests of justice to hold a rehearing (FPR 30.12(1)(a) and (b));

ii) An appeal will only be allowed where the decision of the lower court was (a) wrong or (b) unjust because of a serious procedural or other irregularity in the proceedings in the lower court (FPR 30.12);

iii) The test to be applied on appeal is whether the decision of the lower court is "wrong" as opposed to "plainly wrong" (*Re B (A Child) (Care Proceedings: Threshold Criteria)* [2013] UKSC 33, [2013] 1 WLR 1911 at [46]; see also *Prescott v Potamianos* (also known as *Re Sprintroom Ltd*) [2019] EWCA Civ 932 at [72] – [78]);

iv) The approach to appeals, as elucidated by Lord Hoffman in *Piglowska v Piglowski* [1999] 1 WLR 1360, [1999] 2 FLR 763, has withstood the test of time, and continues to be the authoritative statement as to the proper approach to an appeal. At [1372] Lord Hoffman said:

> "The appellate court must bear in mind the advantage which the first instance judge had in seeing the parties and the other witnesses. This is well understood on questions of credibility and findings of primary fact. But it goes further than that. It applies also to the judge's evaluation of those facts. If I may quote what I said in *Biogen Inc v Medeva plc [1997] RPC 1*, 45:
>
> > 'The need for appellate caution in reversing the trial judge's evaluation of the facts is based upon much more solid grounds than professional courtesy. It is because specific findings of fact, even by the most meticulous judge, are inherently an incomplete statement of the impression which was made upon him by the primary evidence. His expressed findings are always surrounded by a penumbra of imprecision as to emphasis, relative weight, minor qualification and nuance … of which time and language do not permit exact expression, but which may play an important part in the judge's overall evaluation.'"

50. It can be seen, therefore, that whilst a rigorous approach is taken to both the granting of permission and the conduct of appeals, the approach taken by the courts to a review of what may have been an unjust outcome following a court hearing, is significantly less restrictive than that following an arbitration.

The Conundrum

51. The question, therefore, is what is the test to be applied by the court in those cases where the parties have agreed to arbitration but are dissatisfied with the award?

i) Is it limited to those matters in the AA 1996, save where there has been a supervening event or mistake (per Mostyn J in *J v B*, see below); or,

ii) Is it the appeals test under the MCA 1973?

52. If the appeals test is the proper approach, where does the fact that the parties signed a contractual agreement fit in?

53. These issues have been considered, to a limited degree, in several first instance cases. First in time was *S v S (Arbitral Award: Approval)* [2014] EWHC 7 (Fam), [2014] 1 WLR 2299 *(S v S)*. This was a case where parties were coming before the court seeking a consent order following arbitration. Sir James Munby P made, what he described as, some "provisional comments" that might be "helpful and not out of place", in cases where one party wishes to resile from an arbitrator's award, rather than seeking the court's approval of a consent order in the same terms as the arbitral award. Sir James said at [19]:

> "19. …Where the parties have bound themselves, as by signing a Form ARB1, to accept an arbitral award of the kind provided for by the IFLA Scheme, this generates, as it seems to me, a single magnetic factor of determinative importance. As Sir Peter Singer said ([2012] Fam Law 1496, 1503):
>
>> 'The autonomous decision of the parties to submit to arbitration should be seen as a 'magnetic factor' akin to the pre-nuptial agreement in *Crossley v Crossley'*.
>
> I agree. This, after all, reflects the approach spelt out by the Supreme Court in *Radmacher* in the passages I have already quoted. In the absence of some very compelling countervailing factor(s), the arbitral award should be determinative of the order the court makes."

54. In relation to the fact that the parties have made an agreement to arbitrate, Sir James went on:

> "There is no conceptual difference between the parties making an agreement and agreeing to give an arbitrator the power to make the decision for them. Indeed, an arbitral award is surely of its nature even stronger than a simple agreement between the parties."

55. It is within those parts of his judgment where Sir James deals specifically with consent orders, that one finds the origin of the phrase "leaps off the page", a phrase which has become almost a term of art in this context:

> "20. It is worth remembering what the function of the judge is when invited to make a consent order in a financial remedy case. It is a topic I considered at some length in *L v L* [2006] EWHC 956 (Fam), [2008] 1 FLR 26. I concluded (para 73) that: 'the judge is not a rubber stamp. He is entitled but is not obliged to play the detective. He is a watchdog, but he is not a bloodhound or a ferret.'

> 21. Where the consent order which the judge is being asked to approve is founded on an arbitral award under the IFLA Scheme or something similar (and the judge will, of course, need to check that the order does indeed give effect to the arbitral award and is workable) the judge's role will be simple. *The judge will not need to play the detective unless something leaps off the page to indicate that something has gone so seriously wrong in the arbitral process as fundamentally to vitiate the arbitral award.* Although recognising that the judge is not a rubber stamp, the combination of (a) the fact that the parties have agreed to be bound by the arbitral award, (b) the fact of the arbitral award (which the judge will of course be able to study) and (c) the fact that the parties are putting the matter before the court *by consent*, means that it can only be in the rarest of cases that it will be appropriate for the judge to do other than approve the order. With a process as sophisticated as that embodied in the IFLA Scheme it is difficult to contemplate such a case." (my emphasis)

56. Sir James went on to make his obiter observations about those cases where one party opposes the making of an order in the terms of the arbitral award. Having first said at [25] that the proper procedural route is via the "notice to show cause route", Sir James said:

> "26. Where the attempt to resile is plainly lacking in merit the court may take the view that the appropriate remedy is to proceed without more ado summarily to make an order reflecting the award and, if needs be, providing for its enforcement. Even if there is a need for a somewhat more elaborate hearing, the court will be appropriately robust in defining the issues which are properly in dispute and confining the parties to a hearing which is short and focused. In most such cases the focus is likely to be on whether the party seeking to resile is able to make good one of the limited grounds of challenge or appeal permitted by the Arbitration Act 1996. *If* they can, then so be it. If on the other hand they can not, then it may well be that the court will again feel able to proceed without more to make an order reflecting the award and, if needs be, providing for its enforcement."

57. This was followed up in *Practice Guidance (Family Court: Interface with Arbitration)* [2016] 1 WLR 59, issued by Sir James, where he stated at [12]:

> "Attention is drawn to my observations in *S v S (Arbitral Award: Approval) (Practice Note) [2014] 1 WLR 2299*, para 21 about the attitude likely to be adopted by the court in such cases: '[where] the parties are putting the matter before the court by consent … it can only be in the rarest of cases that it will be appropriate for the judge to do other than approve the order.'"

58. The Practice Note makes no reference to cases where one party opposes the making of an order in the terms of the arbitral award.

59. In *J v B* (reference at [24] above), Mostyn J considered the issue of whether a mistake or supervening event should have an impact on an arbitrator's award. For his part, Mostyn J, at [27], in considering Sir James' observations set out at [56] above, said that he would not go so far as Sir James did in *S v S*, which would, he believed, have resulted in the court necessarily ruling out any challenge on the ground of a vitiating mistake or supervening event. Mostyn J said: "If a challenge were to be made out on one or other such ground it would in my judgment be a plainly wrong exercise of discretion for the court to incorporate an award nonetheless." He went on:

> "….when exercising its discretion following an arbitral award the court should adopt an approach of great stringency, even more so than it would in an agreement case. In opting for arbitration the parties have agreed a specific form of alternative dispute resolution and it is important that they understand that in the overwhelming majority of cases the dispute will end with the arbitral award. It would be the worst of all worlds if parties thought that the arbitral process was to be no more than a dry run and that a rehearing in court was readily available."

60. Mostyn J went on to extend the application of the 'leap off the page' yardstick to those cases where one party wished to challenge the award as wrong rather than limiting it, as Sir James did, to those circumstances where a judge should refuse to make a consent order in the same terms as an arbitral award. More broadly Mostyn J said:

> "My conclusion is this. If following an arbitral award evidence emerges which would, if the award had been in an order of the court entitle the court to set aside its order on the grounds of mistake or supervening event, then the court is entitled to refuse to incorporate the arbitral award in its order and instead to make a different order reflecting the new evidence. Outside the heads of correction, challenge or appeal within the 1996 Act these are, in my judgment, the only realistically available grounds of resistance to an incorporating order. *An assertion that the award was "wrong" or "unjust" will almost never get off the ground: in such a case the error must be so blatant and extreme that it leaps off the page.*" (My emphasis).

61. Where an order has been made after 3 October 2016, a party may, pursuant to FPR 2010 r.9.9A(2) and FPR PD9A 13.1 – 13.9, apply to set aside a financial remedy order, where no error of the court is alleged. This is the case regardless of whether the order in question was made following a contested hearing or by consent. By PD9A 13.5, guidance is given as to the likely grounds on which an application for the setting aside of a financial remedy order will be made:

> "An application to set aside a financial remedy order should only be made where no error of the court is alleged. If an error of the court is alleged, an application for permission to appeal under Part 30 should be considered. The grounds on which a financial remedy order may be set aside are and will remain a matter for decisions by judges. The grounds

include (i) fraud; (ii) material non-disclosure; (iii) certain limited types of mistake; (iv) a subsequent event, unforeseen and unforeseeable at the time the order was made, which invalidates the basis on which the order was made."

62. It can be seen, therefore, that the exclusions which Mostyn J had in mind, that might lead a court to decline to make an order in the terms of an arbitral award, relate to matters extraneous to the judicial function as they arise in circumstances where no error of the court is alleged, whether in relation to the evaluation by the judge of the evidence before him or the exercise of the wide discretion afforded to him by s25 MCA 1973.

63. For completeness, I should note that Deputy High Court Judge Ambrose in *BC v BG (Financial Remedies)* [2019] EWFC 7, [2019] 2 FLR 337, again sat in a case where there was before her an application that an arbitral award should not be made into an order. DHJ Ambrose held, at [54], that the grounds of challenge are limited to supervening event, mistake, or those found within the Arbitration Act 1996.

64. It can be seen, therefore, that the test has become increasingly strict, and the basis for challenge correspondingly increasingly narrow; Sir James' obiter comments in *S v S* were couched in terms such as "likely" and "in most cases", or "may well be." He said that, where parties sought a consent order, only if an error "leapt off the page" would the court interfere. That has now developed to the extent that the phrase 'leapt off the page' has become some sort of a measure (as applied by the judge in the instant case), of how wrong a decision has to be in order to invoke the jurisdiction of the court; not only in cases where a consent order is sought, but equally when one party submits that the arbitral award is unfair.

The Arbitration Agreement

65. Sir James was of the view that "there is no conceptual difference between the parties making an agreement and agreeing to give an arbitrator the power to make the decision for them". The fact of the agreement he regarded as a "magnetic factor".

66. Mostyn J was of the view that the test for interference in an arbitral award should be even more rigorous than that applied in those cases where a party seeks to go behind the terms of an agreement. An argument that an award was 'wrong' or 'unjust' would, he said, rarely succeed and the error would have to be 'so blatant' that it 'leaps off the page'.

67. Both Sir James and Mostyn J were of the view that an agreement to arbitrate carries even more weight than that given by a court to an agreement reached between the parties themselves. With respect, I would disagree. The agreement to arbitrate is an agreement that a third party will determine the terms. It is not, at the time the agreement is reached, an agreement to any particular terms. An agreement as between the parties themselves is, albeit often reached with the assistance of legal advisors, by contrast

an agreement to the actual terms; the parties, therefore, know precisely the outcome and have agreed to it. That is not the case in an arbitration, where the parties have agreed to nominate a third party to determine fair terms intended to be final and binding, but subject to the court's ultimate discretion.

68. Even if I am wrong about that, the fact remains, as highlighted by Baroness Hale in *Sharland,* that family cases are different from civil cases. Court orders embodying the terms of commercial and civil arbitrations awards derive their authority from the arbitration agreement, and the enforcement of that agreement under the mandatory provisions of the AA 1996. The enforceable order following family arbitration ultimately derives its authority from the court and not from the arbitration agreement as is recognised on the face of the ARB1 FS.

69. A court can decline to make an order in the terms of an agreement negotiated by, or on their behalf, in circumstances where (to borrow the words of Lord Philips in *Radmacher*) there are "good and substantial grounds for concluding that an injustice will be done by holding the parties to the terms of their agreement"; or where "it would not be fair to hold them to their agreement". It must, in my view, equally follow that where the agreement, albeit contractual, is for a third party to decide the terms that are in dispute, the court can decline to make the order where there are good and substantial grounds for concluding that an injustice will be done if an order is made in the terms of the arbitral award.

70. It follows that, with great respect, I do not agree with the approach of either Sir James in *S v S* or Mostyn J in *J v B,* whose respective approaches limit challenges to an arbitral award in family cases to the statutory challenges found under the AA 1996 or mistake or supervening event.

71. Given that the orders determining the enforceable legal rights of the parties following divorce are made under the MCA 1973 and not under the AA 1996, there is no requirement for the discontented party first to make an application under s.57, s.68 or s.69 AA 1996 before asking the Family Court to decline to make an order under the MCA 1973 in the terms of the arbitral award. It follows that in my judgment the judge was in error in saying at [91] that "An assertion of unfairness or extreme error is likely to be rejected summarily if a party has, without justification, failed to invoke the remedies under the 1996 Act".

72. In saying this, I would emphasise that I do not wish it to be thought that I am in any way undermining the arbitration process or the fact that the parties have signed the ARB1 FS. On the contrary, parties must go into arbitration with their eyes open with the understanding that, all other things being equal, the award made at the end of the process will thereafter be incorporated into a consent order.

73. In my view, the logical approach by which to determine whether the court should decline to make an order in the terms of the award, is by reference to the appeal procedure and the approach found in the FPR 2010. In other

words, when presented with a refusal on the part of one party to agree to the conversion of an arbitral award into a consent order, the court should, at an initial stage, 'triage' the case with the reluctant party having to 'show cause' on paper why an order should not be made in the terms of the arbitral award. Such approach would be similar to the permission to appeal filter found at FPR rule 30(7) where the trial has taken place under the MCA 1973. If the judge is of the view that there is a real prospect of the objecting party succeeding in demonstrating that the arbitral award is wrong, then the matter can be set down for a hearing. That hearing will, as with an appeal, be confined to a review and will not be a rehearing, subject to any case management directions which the judge may make in relation to updating or other evidence and subject to, as under FPR 30.12(1)(b), the court considering that "it would be in the interests of justice to hold a re-hearing".

74. The court will, thereafter, only substitute its own order if the judge decides that the arbitrator's award was wrong; not seriously, or obviously wrong, or so wrong that it leaps off the page, but just wrong.

75. It follows that, in my judgment, the wording found in the bold box at the foot of the ARB1 FS is itself wrong and goes too far in saying that "it is only in exceptional circumstances that a court will exercise its own discretion in substitution for the award".

The Judgment

76. Turning then to the judgment which led to the making of the order which is the subject of this appeal. The judge, unsurprisingly, concluded that there had been no serious procedural irregularity that could lead to a successful appeal under s68 AA 1996 and, equally unsurprisingly, there is no appeal against that conclusion.

77. The judge dealt with the application under s69 AA 1996 at some length. As was necessary to satisfy the requirements of the section, those representing the husband had to characterise their complaints as errors of law which satisfied the "obviously wrong" test. The reality was that the challenges largely related to submissions that the arbitrator had failed to give adequate consideration to relevant matters, and that he had erred in the discretionary exercise. The judge, by reference to the "obviously wrong" test, considered between [38] – [54] the arguments raised by the husband in support of his application. For example, the arbitrator's treatment of the parties' housing needs [47] and the wife's earning capacity [44].

78. The judge refused permission to appeal on the basis: (i) that the suggested errors of law were in fact "questions of mixed fact and law as to how the discretionary exercise of sharing assets under the 1973 Act should be" applied; and (ii) permission will only be granted under s69 if the award was one which no reasonable (or rational) arbitrator could make (see *The Nema* [1982] AC 724 at 744). The judge concluded at [55]:

> "The arbitrator had identified the right legal test and his exercise of discretion was not obviously wrong, and indeed not even open to serious doubt."

79. The judge, having dismissed those applications made on behalf of the husband, turned, more briefly, to the husband's application that no order be made in the terms of the arbitral award by reason of its overall unfairness. The judge concluded at [55] that:

> "… Even applying the simple test of 'wrong' under Part 30 FPR permission to appeal would have been refused."

80. The judge set out between [84] – [92] "a number of threads" that she said were relevant to the court's discretion to make an order reflecting the arbitrator's award. These can be summarised as follows:

    i) The court retains its overriding discretion to make, or decline to make, orders under s25 MCA 1973. The court's discretion is not governed by the AA 1996;

    ii) The exercise of the court's discretion must take account of the award, the parties' agreement to arbitrate, and the scope of the court's grounds for setting aside under the AA 1996. In most cases, the discretion will be applied consistently with the statutory framework in the 1996 Act (*see S v S*, at [26]);

    iii) The test for not making an order giving effect to the award is high. It has been repeatedly emphasised that the court would only intervene in rare and extreme cases, where something has gone so seriously wrong that it *leaps off the page* (see Mostyn J in *J v B* at [28] and *S v S* at [21];

    iv) There is some analogy with the court's exercise of discretion in giving effect to a settlement agreement or a pre-nuptial agreement. However, the same test does not apply since the court must take into account that the parties have agreed to refer their dispute to a neutral and independent arbitrator. An arbitration award is given effect not only by consent, but also by statute and international treaty; it would, therefore, be wrong to equate its binding effect with that of a settlement agreement or pre-nuptial agreement;

    v) The parties have elected to "have their day in court" before an arbitrator, and the AA 1996 deals with procedural irregularity and errors of law. The court's discretion is not intended to allow them to re-run or improve their case, and to ask the court to be a new tribunal of fact.

81. Putting together these features, the judge concluded at [90] and [91] that the practical effect is that the s25 MCA 1973 discretion will usually be exercised in a similar way to the court's discretion to grant relief under a challenge to an award under the 1996 Act. The test for intervention, the judge said, is "closely aligned and similarly robust". The judge then concluded:

> "91. It would be rare to find a situation where a party who has not succeeded in challenging an award under the 1996 Act can persuade the court to refuse to make that award into an order by reason of its discretion under s25. If a party has failed to challenge the award under the 1996 Act (or been unsuccessful in doing so) then as a matter of statute (s58 of the 1996 Act) the award is final and binding. This is likely to be a very significant consideration and the onus would lie on the party seeking relief to explain why the court should exercise its discretion in not giving effect to that award notwithstanding its binding effect. An assertion of unfairness or extreme error is likely to be rejected summarily if a party has, without justification, failed to invoke remedies under the 1996 Act. Most complaints are properly dealt with by the 1996 Act, especially complaints regarding the procedure of the decision-making since this is not engaged by s25. The court's discretion can operate as a safety net for exceptional cases but it is unlikely to be exercised to deprive an award of binding effect unless the matter is extreme or the complaint is outside the scope of the 1996 Act (for example supervening circumstances, or matters involving third parties – such matters may also fall outside the scope of the arbitration agreement).
>
> 92. As explained above, the judge should generally not allow the exercise to be treated as an opportunity for one party to re-open the facts and introduce new evidence. It may be sufficient to start by considering whether the decision is wrong. In most cases this will be enough to determine the matter (and the answer will be consistent to that given under the 1996 Act). *Whether a decision is "seriously" or "obviously" wrong or such that the error "leaps off the page" is usually a measure of how confidently and promptly a judge can form a view as to whether it is wrong.* The test reflects the nature of the exercise: the court's role is not to re-hear the matter or search out potential errors and it should resist any attempt by the parties to achieve this (c.f. *Piglowska v Piglowski*)." (my emphasis).

82. It is clear that, whilst the judge referred to a test of "wrong", she in fact imbued the word with adverbs which served to heighten the test to "seriously wrong" or "obviously wrong" or as being a decision where the error "leaps off the page". The judge, therefore, identified a similarly high bar before a court should be permitted to exercise its s25 jurisdiction where one party is dissatisfied with an arbitration award, as to that which undoubtedly applies in relation to applications made under s68 or s69 AA 1996. Having set out her test of "seriously" or "obviously wrong" or an error which "leaps off the page", the judge went on to consider whether, in her view, the arbitrator's award would, in fact, be consistent with the court's discretion under s25. The judge said that she "put to one side the 1996 Act", and that she was satisfied that from a pure s25 MCA 1973 perspective, the award made by Mr Shaw was "not wrong". DHJ Ambrose said at [93]:

> "It [the award] reflects a fair allocation of assets taking account of the relevant considerations and is firmly within the range of right outcomes.

> Another tribunal may have been more generous to the husband on some points but it could also have gone in the other direction [...] I am satisfied that I should approve the order attached to the Award."

83. In my judgment, the judge's reference to "not wrong" can only be looked at against the backdrop of the previous paragraph, where she clearly states that she regards the "obviously wrong" test to apply to the discretionary exercise under s25 where there has been a previous arbitration award. This view is reinforced by the fact that her substantive consideration of the case, and its outcome, was considered by the judge as part of her s69 AA 1996 analysis and was effectively adopted by her for the purposes of the husband's submissions, in relation to the use of the judge's residual discretionary jurisdiction under the MCA 1973.

The Parties' submissions

84. Mr Ewins, on behalf of the husband, submits that there is conflicting High Court authority, and confusion within the profession, concerning the proper approach where a party wishes to challenge an arbitral award. In any event, he says, the husband in the present case has not had a fair determination of the wife's claims. As a consequence, by reason of the overall unfairness of the award and measured against the court's duty under s25 MCA 1973, the award's failure properly to meet the husband's needs and to take into account his contributions, means that the award is not one that the court could properly approve, pursuant to its duty under s25 MCA 1973.

85. For the detailed reasons set out in his skeleton argument, and expanded upon orally, Mr Ewins submits that the judge was in error in considering that the award was fair and "not wrong". On a proper reading of the judge's judgment, Mr Ewins submits, the reality is that, notwithstanding her reference to "wrong", the judge in reality imposed a higher test as is clear from her references at [92]. The judge approached the application of "wrong" by reference to the stringent test for the 1996 Act, and by the application of the gloss of "seriously", "obviously" or an error that "leaps off the page".

86. Mr Walden-Smith, on behalf of the wife, submits that the judge was correct in her application of the law and as to the proper test, namely one that is synonymous with s68 and s69 AA 1996. However, even if the judge was in error, and the proper test is as submitted on behalf of the husband, in fact the "appeals test" as it would be applied under the MCA 1973 rather than a higher test aligned to s68 and s69 AA 1996, the first instance (arbitral award) was not open to realistic challenge.

87. The essence of this appeal, Mr Walden-Smith submitted, is the identification of the circumstances in which a judge of the Family Court should decline to make an arbitral award, notwithstanding the failure of any appeal pursuant to ss67, 68 or 69 of the AA 1996. That being so, he submits the effect of the decision of Mostyn J in *J v B,* is that the only circumstances in which

a Family Court is justified in refusing to make an order in the terms of the arbitral award, absent a successful challenge under ss67, 68 or 69, are in cases where there has been a vitiating mistake or a supervening event.

88. Mr Walden-Smith submits that, although the making of an arbitration agreement does not oust the jurisdiction of the court, the fact that the parties have agreed to refer the matter to binding arbitration is centrally relevant to the exercise of discretion in deciding whether or not to make an order in the terms of the award.

Discussion

89. With respect, in my judgment, Mostyn J's reliance on Sir Bernard Eder's view (para. [23] above) that, where parties have entered into an arbitration agreement, "the mere fact that an award is "wrong" or even "unjust" does not, of itself, provide any basis for challenging the award or intervention by the Court", cannot be justified in the context of family proceedings.

90. Further, in order for an arbitration award to become enforceable, the parties have to issue an application and obtain orders for financial provision, the authority for those orders coming from the court.

91. In the present case, for example, the wife needs a periodical payments order in her favour, made pursuant to s23 MCA 1973. If the parties submit a consent order that is, in the mind of the district judge, unjust, having taken into account the section 25 criteria and the fact that the parties had agreed to submit themselves to arbitration, then that district judge will not rubber stamp the order, he will decline to make it. Similarly, where one party says, as here, that the proposed order does not meet his or her needs, how can a judge exercising his or her jurisdiction under the MCA 1973 metaphorically shrug his or her shoulders and say that the disgruntled party has "[bought] the right to get the wrong answer", and that (failing mistake, or a supervening event) the potentially unfair order that fails to meet the needs of one of the parties will nevertheless be made?

92. In my judgment, such an approach cuts across the fundamental tenet of "fairness", which has informed every decision made by the courts since the landmark case of *White v White* [2000] UKHL 54. In his opening remarks, Lord Nicholls said:

> "Everyone would accept that the outcome on these matters, whether by agreement or court order, should be fair. More realistically, the outcome ought to be as fair as is possible in all the circumstances. But everyone's life is different. Features which are important when assessing fairness differ in each case. And, sometimes, different minds can reach different conclusions on what fairness requires. Then fairness, like beauty, lies in the eye of the beholder."

93. "Fairness" is the constant reprise of Lord Nicholls; a concept, which he refers to as, "the underlying objective of securing fair financial arrangements".

Fairness continues to be the lodestar by which all financial remedy hearings are guided *(see H v T (Judicial Change of Mind)* [2018] EWHC 3962).

94. In my judgment, for the statutory duty found in s25 MCA 1973 to operate effectively, a person has to be able to put before the court the reason(s) why they believe the order is unjust.

95. The practical effect of the submissions made on behalf of the wife can be demonstrated by reference to the facts of this case; had the court found a deputy district judge who was available to hear the case then, in the event that either of them felt the outcome to be unfair, either the wife or the husband would, subject to leave, have an appeal to the circuit judge on the usual terms (see *Piglowska* v *Piglowski* etc). Where, however, no deputy district judge becomes available and the parties turn to arbitration as a last resort, there is no appeal and, in line with the submissions of Mr Walden-Smith and the approach of the judge, whilst the jurisdiction of the Family Court has not been ousted by the making of the arbitration award, the court's inquisitorial jurisdiction is limited to the stringent terms of the AA 1996, designed originally for civil and commercial cases.

96. Rightly, para [6.5] of the ARB1 FS form (quoted at [16] above) highlights that the parties "understand that the court has a discretion as to whether, and in what terms, to make an order and [we] will take all reasonably necessary steps to see that such an order is made". In my judgment, a party who believes the arbitral award which follows an arbitration hearing is wrong can, through the 'notice to show cause' process put their objections before the court. If the court at the triage/paper stage takes the view that the objection made to the award by one of the parties would not pass the permission to appeal test, it can make an order in the terms of the arbitral award without more ado and penalise the reluctant party in costs.

97. It follows that I do not think it necessary for these rare cases to be put before a High Court judge as a matter of course. It seems to me that they will be allocated to either the specialist circuit judges who hear financial remedy appeals from the district judges sitting in the financial remedies court or to the High Court, whichever is appropriate on the facts of the case.

Outcome of the Appeal

98. In my judgment, notwithstanding her lengthy and careful judgment, the judge applied the wrong test and the proper test is the appeals test. The judge went on specifically to hold that even had the appeals test been the proper approach, there was no basis for the court to interfere with the award.

99. A substantial part of the submissions of Mr Ewins were occupied with his detailed arguments to the effect that on the facts of the case, the arbitrator's award was wrong. Mr Ewins submitted that the judge was in error in assessing in particular: the housing budget for each of the parties and the realistic ability of the husband to rehouse himself to an acceptable standard,

the distribution of the parties' pensions and the quantum of periodical payments made to the wife by virtue of the award.

100. Mr Walden-Smith, for his part, adopted the approach of the judge; namely that, whilst another judge may have been more generous to the husband, the award made was within the discretionary bracket and the court should not, therefore, interfere.

101. In my judgment in applying the appeals test, I am satisfied that the husband would have a real prospect of succeeding in an appeal against the award made for the reasons submitted by Mr Ewins. In order to avoid appearing to express any view as to outcome, I do not intend to elaborate further or even to set out the facts and terms of the order, given that, in my judgment, the inevitable consequence of my view is that the matter must now be remitted to a circuit judge.

102. If my Lords agree, I would therefore allow the appeal and remit the matter for a case management hearing (in part because of the lapse of time since the arbitral award) before a circuit judge ticketed to hear financial remedy appeals to determine the form and extent of the hearing required to determine these proceedings.

Postscript

103. Both Moylan LJ at the permission stage, and myself at the conclusion of the appeal hearing, implored the husband and wife to settle this case. I dare not guess how little (if any) of the modest capital which was available to rehouse each of these parties is now left.

104. I can only hope that renewed efforts will be made by the parties to resolve the matter without recourse to the further litigation anticipated by this judgment.

Lord Justice Moylan:

105. I agree.

Lord Justice Popplewell:

106. I also agree

A v A (Arbitration: Guidance) [2021] EWHC1889 (Fam)

This judgment was delivered in private. The judge has given leave for this version of the judgment to be published. This version of the judgment has been anonymised and redacted and should be referred to as *A v A (Arbitration: Guidance)*. In no publication of the judgment may the identities of the parties or the contents of the redactions be revealed. Breach of this direction will amount to a contempt of court.

Neutral Citation Number: [2021] EWHC 1889 (Fam)

Case No: BD19D07750 and CC-2021-LDS-000005

IN THE HIGH COURT OF JUSTICE

FAMILY DIVISION

Royal Courts of Justice

Strand, London, WC2A 2LL

09/07/2021

Before:

MR JUSTICE MOSTYN

....

Between:

A **Applicant**

– v –

A **Respondent**

Joseph Rainer (instructed by Charles Russell Speechlys) for the Applicant
Sally Harrison QC (instructed by Jones Myers) for the Respondent

Hearing dates: 23-24 June 2021

....

HTML VERSION OF JUDGMENT APPROVED

....

MR JUSTICE MOSTYN:

1. The applications before me concern an arbitral award ("the award") made by Christopher Pocock QC ("the arbitrator") on 21 December 2020.

2. The wife has issued an application for the husband to show cause as to why he should not be held to the terms of the award. I also have before me an application made by the husband to challenge the award pursuant to s.68 of the Arbitration Act 1996 ("the 1996 Act"), as well as an application for leave to appeal on a point of law under s.69. Those applications have been transferred to the Family Division from the Money and Business Court in Leeds. The husband also in his counsel's skeleton argument of 16 February 2021 invited the Family Court to decline to make an order in the terms of the award. So there were four separate applications bringing issues about the award before the court. The Family Court does not have jurisdiction to hear the 1996 Act applications. Therefore it has been necessary to transfer the Family Court applications to the High Court.

3. These disordered procedural steps, together with my knowledge of similar procedural chaos in other cases, has led me to formulate guidance about the correct procedure to be adopted where one party wishes to challenge an arbitral award, or where a party wishes to implement an arbitral award in the face of opposition from the other party. The guidance, together with a proposed *pro forma* order, is set out in the (Appendix) to this judgment and is issued with the authority and approval of the President.

[4. Redacted]

5. The parties are both aged 63. They married in September 1979, and separated in 2018, making this a 39 year marriage. On 8 February 2019, they both signed the ARB1 form, agreeing to go to arbitration to resolve their financial situations following separation and divorce. Specifically, they agreed in writing:

> "The parties are applying for a determination as to how their assets should be divided between them."

6. Financial remedy proceedings were not commenced in the FRC at that stage. Both parties issued petitions for divorce in July 2019, and following the wife's petition being withdrawn by consent, decree nisi was pronounced in March 2020 and decree absolute in November 2020.

7. An initial directions hearing took place via telephone before the arbitrator on 1 November 2019. The final arbitration hearing had been due to commence on 11 May 2020, but at another hearing before the arbitrator on 8 April 2020, at which the husband successfully applied for an adjournment, it was relisted to begin on 14 December 2020.

8. On 1 September 2020, however, the parties reached a broad overall agreement in correspondence, but there remained several ancillary issues on which they were at odds. For the purposes of this judgment it is not necessary for me to set out in full the details of that agreement, save to

note that under its terms the husband received 52% of the circa £17 million matrimonial asset base, and the wife 48%.

9. Consequently, the parties requested that the arbitrator determine only the outstanding matters in dispute at the final arbitration hearing. A working draft order was placed before the arbitrator containing the provisions that had been agreed at that point. The final arbitration hearing took place on 14 December 2020.

10. The arbitrator then handed down his written award on 21 December 2020. This was a 32 page document much like a court judgment, which set out the reasons for the arbitrator's decisions, and it contained a section at the end entitled 'Award' summarising and declaring what had been awarded ("the declaration").

11. Following receipt of the award, the wife amended the working draft order to include the arbitrator's decisions on the matters in dispute, and invited the husband to agree it. On 18 January 2021, however, the husband made an application under s.57 of the 1996 Act for clarification and correction of the award. The arbitrator dismissed that application on 19 January 2021. The husband subsequently did not agree for the amended draft order to be converted into a consent order.

12. As a result, on 21 January 2021 the wife filed both a Form A and an accompanying Form D11 at court, in which she made her notice to show cause application against the husband. On 16 February 2021, the husband made his application under the 1996 Act to the Business and Property Court in Leeds (which had to be transferred to the Family Division), under which he presented effectively four grounds of challenge, each of which is discussed in turn below. On 1 June 2021, the husband made his Part 18 application in relation to the sale of X.

13. The final hearing of the various applications took place remotely before me on 23 and 24 June 2021.

Challenge to an arbitral award: principles

14. In *Haley v Haley* [2020] EWCA Civ 1369 King LJ ruled at [73] and [96] that, substantively, a challenge to a financial remedy arbitral award should be dealt with in broadly the same way, and subject to the same principles, as a financial remedy appeal in the Family Court from a district judge to a circuit judge.

15. The effect of the judgment of King LJ is to make a challenge to a financial remedy arbitral award under s.68 of the 1996 Act, or an appeal against such an award under s.69, entirely redundant.

16. I have to decide if the arbitral award is "wrong". King LJ at [74] emphasised that the test is "not seriously or obviously wrong, or so wrong that it leaps off the page, but just wrong". If I am so satisfied then I will make different provision to that within the arbitral award.

17. It is important that I approach the husband's challenge as if I were hearing an appeal by him from a judgment of a district or circuit judge. If this were an appeal I would have wide powers. I would have all the powers of the lower court (FPR 30.11(1)). I could affirm, set aside or vary any order or judgment of the lower court; refer any application or issue for determination by the lower court; order a new hearing; make orders for the payment of interest; and/or make a costs order (FPR 30.11(2)).

18. If this were an appeal and I reached the decision that the judge below fell into error in relation to part of his order, then I would have power to vary other parts of the order without a respondent needing to seek and obtain permission to appeal. That power is wide enough to encompass those matters which are consequential to a successful appeal and which are necessary in order for the court to do justice in the appeal which is before it: see *Phillimore v Hewson* [2020] EWHC 499 (QB), [2020] 1 WLR 2175. In that case, notwithstanding the lack of a cross-appeal, the appeal court varied (for the benefit of the respondent to the appeal) the order of the judge below so as to give effect to the judge's intention, there being no resulting prejudice to the appellant.

19. I myself have recently dismissed an appeal but have gone on to make consequential corrections to mathematical errors in order to give effect to the first instance judge's intentions: see *AZ v FM* [2021] EWFC 2.

20. In this case I propose to exercise my powers analogously to those I would have available to me if this were an actual appeal.

The first ground of challenge

21. The husband first seeks to challenge the award by arguing that there was uncertainty or ambiguity as to the effect of the award in relation to what was intended or meant by 'capital costs'.

22. The issue of these 'capital costs' arises because the wife currently remains in occupation at X. In the overall agreement reached on 1 September 2020, the husband agreed to pay £4,500 per month for ongoing running costs of the property for a period of six months while the wife remained in occupation (with the wife to be solely responsible for all running costs after that six month period while she remained in occupation, and with the parties to bear the running costs equally once the wife vacated the property). The husband also agreed to pay £12,000 towards capital costs that needed to be paid in relation to the property.

23. However, a dispute then arose about who should pay for any additional capital costs that might come to light after the agreement was reached on 1 September 2020, but while the wife remained living in the property.

24. It is the wife's occupation of X that appears to be the sticking point for the husband, for he has openly accepted that he will pay 50% of any capital costs that arise once the wife has left X. Incidentally, I am told that the

husband has not paid any of the £4,500 monthly instalments to the wife for the running costs since the agreement was reached.

25. I have to express my surprise and disappointment that an issue as banal as this should not have been the subject of agreement.

26. The arbitrator was therefore asked to determine the issue of who should pay for additional capital costs that arose after 1 September 2020 whilst the wife remained in occupation of X.

27. The arbitrator agreed that a term of the overall agreement was that the husband's contribution to the capital costs that were known as at 1 September 2020 was to be £12,000. He determined that over and above that figure, the parties should meet capital costs in equal shares. Specifically, he ruled that (a) any capital costs that became apparent or necessary after 1 September 2020, but before the wife vacated the property, would be met equally, and (b) in the event that capital costs which were known as at 1 September 2020 transpired to be more expensive than budgeted for, any surplus would be met equally.

28. Ms Harrison QC, on behalf of the husband, submitted that the terms of the award in relation to capital costs are ambiguous and uncertain, since the arbitrator failed to define what 'saleable or lettable' condition meant, and failed to define the meaning of 'capital costs'. Ms Harrison QC said that this uncertainty will cause significant injustice to the husband, who is bound to pay an uncertain amount for an indefinite period of time in relation to a property from which he is excluded for as long as the wife chooses to live there.

29. Mr Rainer submitted that no such uncertainty or ambiguity exists. He stated that the parties had already virtually entirely agreed how 'capital costs' should be defined in the working draft order. Indeed, the agreed part of the relevant paragraph in the draft order says:

> 'The 'long term capital costs' shall mean the capital expenditure required to maintain X in a lettable and saleable condition as advised and evidenced by the property managing agent.'

Mr Rainer said that neither the husband nor the wife invited the arbitrator to go into further detail in defining 'capital costs', save that the arbitrator added to the definition, at the wife's request (opposed by the husband), the words 'this shall include any ongoing costs of maintenance and decoration'. Mr Rainer noted an irony: it was the wife who at the final arbitration hearing invited the arbitrator to give more detail in the definition, while the husband resisted that further particularity. Mr Rainer further argued that the arbitrator had rightly put in place a mechanism to minimise the potential for debate over what would constitute a 'capital cost'.

30. The mechanism the arbitrator had put in place for future disputes was as follows. The starting point for any dispute was to be the definition provided by the parties in the draft order, set out above. To this the arbitrator added at paragraph 99 of the award, under the title 'Definitions', that:

> 'a) On the face of the comparison document, there is a dispute as to whether ongoing "maintenance and decoration" should be specified as a potential cost.
>
> b) It should not matter. If the agent advises (and it is for the agent, as provided here) that some maintenance and redecoration be undertaken, it should be undertaken.
>
> c) For clarity, it should be recorded here.' (original emphasis)

31. The definition in the amended draft order which the wife invited the husband to agree therefore reads:

> 'The 'long term capital costs' shall mean such capital expenditure required to maintain X in a lettable and saleable condition as advised and evidenced by the property managing agent excluding the costs listed as 'Immediate Capital Costs' above. Insofar as any of the 'Immediate Capital Costs' are estimated figures and the actual cost of the work/item is higher, the difference between the actual cost and the estimated cost above shall fall within the definition of 'long term capital costs'. For the avoidance of doubt, and subject to the above caveats, this shall include any ongoing costs of maintenance and decoration.'

32. Mr Rainer next pointed to the arbitrator's examples of the sort of costs that might fall within the definition at paragraph 87 of his award. Mr Rainer stated that the point of this guidance was to assist the parties in agreeing between themselves what should fall within the definition, and to aid the court in determining any future dispute. At paragraph 87 the arbitrator said:

> 'These are not ordinary, regular (i.e. recurring) running costs (water and electricity bills, running maintenance/servicing contracts, alarm or "brain" maintenance contracts, pool maintenance). Those are "running costs" within the agreed definition (order paragraph 1.j)). These are capital costs required to "enable the property to be let". They would include the repair of damage to the property, maintenance of the structure of the property, and replacement of its fixtures and fittings (a refrigerator has been mentioned, as has an air conditioning unit), so as to keep the property (and its fixtures and fittings, which are part and parcel of what may well, in the case of this property, be let or sold with it) in a lettable/saleable condition…' (original emphasis)

33. Mr Rainer next referred to paragraph 89 where notwithstanding this guidance the arbitrator stated:

> 'If there is any dispute as to whether something is necessary to keep the property in a saleable or lettable condition, the parties should be led by the property agent who, after all, will be marketing the property from now on…'

34. And finally, Mr Rainer submitted that the arbitrator ruled at paragraph 90 that as a backstop there should be a specific liberty to apply clause 'in relation to both the necessity and level of such costs in the event that even with the agent's advice, the parties are unable to agree'.

35. In fact, in his s.57 application, the husband asked the arbitrator to 'clarify and provide a more limited definition of what would be deemed to be capital expenses to keep the property in a 'saleable and lettable condition,' as it currently is, whilst the Wife is in occupation'. After pointing out that it seemed to him that what the husband was doing was actually requesting that he change his mind, the arbitrator responded that there was set out in the award 'as much clarity as can be achieved for the purposes of my award in those agreed definitions and conclusions'. He stressed that if there were to be a dispute about what a relevant capital cost was, the court would determine the dispute either if a party made an application for the making of an order reflecting the award, or on a later application pursuant to the liberty to apply clause.

36. Mr Rainer argued that the arbitrator had been correct in his response, and that there was as much clarity as there could be in the award given the lengthy guidance and detailed mechanism he had set out. Consequently, Mr Rainer submitted that the award cannot possibly be said to be so uncertain or unambiguous such as to make it appealably wrong.

37. In my judgment, there is no relevant uncertainty or ambiguity in this regard, and the first ground of challenge thus fails on the basis that the award was not wrong. These are my reasons.

38. First, if one reads the arbitrator's award in full, it is plain that at paragraph 87 the arbitrator went into some considerable detail about what he considered should be classed as a necessary capital cost. I accept Mr Rainer's submission that it would not have been possible for the arbitrator to specify every single item that could possibly constitute a capital cost, and in circumstances where specific examples were given by the arbitrator I unhesitatingly reject Ms Harrison QC's submission that there was no attempt to define or limit 'capital costs' such that the award was uncertain or ambiguous.

39. Secondly, I agree with Mr Rainer that the mechanism the arbitrator put in place was designed to reduce any uncertainty or disagreement as to what might constitute a capital cost, in that the parties would be guided first by the award, second by their marketing agent, and only if they could not reach an agreement following that guidance would they have to go to court. The arbitrator therefore did everything he could to reduce the uncertainty and ambiguity over what might constitute a 'capital cost' for the parties.

The second ground of challenge

40. The second ground of challenge advanced by Ms Harrison QC is that the arbitrator failed adequately to provide for a mechanism for the resolution of any dispute over future capital costs and for the determination of any liability on the part of the husband. Specifically, she submitted that the arbitrator was wrong not to direct that quotes be obtained for any work said to constitute necessary capital costs, along with a letter from the marketing

agent dealing with the issue of necessity. It was said that this will cause significant injustice to the husband because there will be uncertainty as to the method by which any expenses are to be determined.

41. Mr Rainer argued in response that the husband did not argue at the final arbitration hearing that the arbitrator should direct that quotes should be obtained. He submitted that in any event, a failure on the part of the arbitrator to direct that quotes should be obtained for any work in advance cannot conceivably render the award wrong.

42. I agree with Mr Rainer. It was perfectly legitimate for the award to state that the parties should pay for capital costs without having to procure quotes beforehand, and the fact that the arbitrator did not direct the parties to obtain quotes in advance cannot be said in any way to be wrong.

43. Furthermore, for the reasons I have set out above, I do not agree that the arbitrator failed to put in place an appropriate mechanism to resolve future disputes, and I do not agree that the mechanism was uncertain or ambiguous. The arbitrator set out a comprehensive mechanism in the award, giving the parties a clear path to follow to resolve any future disputes over capital costs. This ground of challenge therefore fails. I have come close to describing it as hopeless.

The third ground of challenge

44. The husband's third ground of challenge relates to documentation the husband believes the wife has at X and which he will require in order to prove to HMRC that on sale and remittance of his share of the proceeds no capital gains tax liability arises. During the parties' negotiations leading up to the overall agreement, the husband had proposed that the wife undertake to provide any and all records confirming the acquisition and construction costs referable to X to him. The wife said she could not give that undertaking because she had already delivered up these materials, so that they were no longer in her possession or control, and that as far as she was aware, there were no more documents at X.

45. The arbitrator determined that the wife should simply confirm (through Mr Rainer) that she had provided all such documents, and in the event that she did discover further documents, should provide copies to the husband. The wife agreed to that.

46. That decision of the arbitrator is said by Ms Harrison QC to be a failure to deal with the issue which is so gross as to render the award not only wrong, but also a serious irregularity under s.68(2)(d) of the 1996 Act. She says that this failure to deal with the issue has resulted in an award that will not ensure compliance by the wife and will cause significant injustice to the husband, who as explained above will not have the necessary documentation required to eliminate a potential capital gains tax liability in respect of X when he repatriates his share of the net proceeds of sale to the UK.

47. Mr Rainer submitted that this ground is demonstrably unarguable on the basis that no mechanism for the return of the documents over and above that suggested by the arbitrator was pursued by the husband at the hearing, and that the husband did not invite the arbitrator to make a finding that the wife's contention that she had already sent the documents she had and no longer had any in her possession was false.

48. I agree with Mr Rainer. There was no failure to deal with the issue, since the arbitrator specifically put in place a mechanism to deal with the husband's concerns about the documents by inviting the wife to confirm she did not have any documents in her possession, but that if she found any, she would deliver them up. The arbitrator's decision was therefore neither wrong, nor was there a serious irregularity. This ground of challenge fails.

49. When analysed the husband's complaint is no more than that he would prefer the wife to be subjected to the fiercer language of Ms Harrison QC when her obligation came to be expressed. I do not agree that his preference for fiercer language constitutes a valid ground of challenge. However, the order as drafted merely recorded an agreement by the wife, without any element of compulsion. In my judgment the wife's obligation should be incorporated in an undertaking. If she were to refuse to give an undertaking, her obligation should be made the subject of a mandatory injunction.

The fourth ground of challenge

50. The fourth ground of challenge put forward by the husband is that the arbitrator was obviously wrong to decide that the husband should be liable for 50% of the capital costs that became manifest and necessary after 1 September 2020, and that he should contribute equally to any expenditure in excess of the budget for the capital costs known as at 1 September 2020.

51. Ms Harrison QC submitted that this decision was wrong because it was 'outwith the amount he agreed to pay in respect of capital costs'. That sum was £12,000, and it was in respect of the known costs as at 1 September 2020 while the wife was in occupation of X. Ms Harrison QC said that rather than seeking to fill the gap created by the parties' inability to agree who should pay capital costs in excess of that sum of £12,000 whilst the wife remained in occupation of the property, the arbitrator should have directed simply that the parties would litigate any future dispute, since that is what they had agreed to do, and he should not have imposed any obligation on the husband in respect of those extra costs. She said that the husband had consented only to the terms of the agreement, and that in the agreement there was no suggestion that the husband would be fixed with an open-ended and unquantified liability for capital costs of X throughout the wife's occupation there, which was the situation he was left in as a result of the award. She also argued that the arbitrator wrongly applied *S v S (Ancillary Relief)* [2009] 1 FLR 254 as authority for the proposition that he was able to make an award outwith the parties' agreement.

52. Mr Rainer submitted in response that it was never agreed that the husband's contribution to capital costs known as at 1 September 2020 would be limited to £12,000 while the wife remained in occupation, since the wife's solicitors had sent an email on 1 September 2020 making clear that the wife did not agree to meet any and all further capital costs arising alone. Mr Rainer said that Ms Harrison QC conceded this point at the final arbitration hearing, which he said was evidenced by the fact that at paragraph 81 of the award, it was recorded that Ms Harrison QC submitted that the wife's solicitors' email left the door open to an argument that the husband should contribute to capital expenses that came to light after that date. Furthermore, Mr Rainer submitted that *S v S* is part of a long line of authorities which says that the court is not bound by the terms of a deal struck between parties.

53. The question I must answer is therefore whether the arbitrator had the power to do more than the parties had agreed. It is clear that he did. An arbitrator is given, by the agreement of the parties in Form ARB1, all the powers of a judge, and the authorities are clear that a judge, when presented with an agreement reached between parties, is not confined to a binary choice of either accepting that agreement in its entirety, or jettisoning the agreement in its entirety. On the contrary, the court not only has the power to approve those parts of an agreement it considers to be fair and just, but also to make changes to any parts of an agreement which it thinks ought to be amended in the interests of fairness. It is entirely appropriate for a court, when considering an agreement, to go beyond the terms of that agreement. It is also entirely legitimate for a judge to fill in gaps which are left open in an agreement and to correct numerical errors.

54. In this case, the gap was the issue of what to do about capital costs while the wife remained in occupation of X. The parties had agreed no more than the principle that there would be liberty to apply about any disagreement. There was therefore no substantive agreement on the issue; all the parties had done was to agree to litigate in the future. Plainly, an arbitrator should not have his hands tied by a so-called agreement that the parties will have to go to court. Plainly, it is clearly lawful, proportionate and just for the arbitrator, exercising the powers of a judge, both to fill in the gap and make his own decision about who should pay the capital costs. It was equally lawful and proportionate for him to set down a framework of indicative non-binding principles which might enable the parties to reach a compromise rather than going to court. In those circumstances, the arbitrator's decision and mechanism were wholly legitimate and in line with the authorities.

55. They were also consistent with the overriding objective, which requires the court to allot to an individual case an appropriate share of the court's resources. This must apply equally to an arbitrator. He has to consider, when faced with an impasse such as that in the present case which the parties, or at least one of them, was maintaining could only be resolved by future litigation, whether it is an appropriate use of the court's resources to allow such litigation. In my judgment it would have been wrong for the

arbitrator, faced with such intransigence and folly, not to have done his utmost to devise a scheme to avoid future litigation.

56. It is trite law that the court can fill in the gaps of an agreement where it is presented with only a framework, and can change the terms of an agreement if it thinks it is necessary. As Thorpe LJ said in *Xydhias v Xydhias* [1999] 1 FLR 683 at 692:

> 'In consequence, it is clear that the award to an applicant for ancillary relief is always fixed by the court. The payer's liability cannot be ultimately fixed by compromise as can be done in the settlement of claims in other divisions. Therefore the purpose of negotiation is not to finally determine the liability (that can only be done by the court) but to reduce the length and expense of the process by which the court carries out its function…Finally in every case the court must exercise its independent discretionary review applying the section 25 criteria to the circumstances of the case and to the terms of the accord.'

57. He had stated earlier at 691:

> 'An even more singular feature of the transition from compromise to order in ancillary relief proceedings is that the court does not either automatically or invariably grant the application to give the bargain in the force of an order. The court conducts an independent assessment to enable it to discharge its statutory function to make such orders as reflect the criteria listed in section 25 of the Matrimonial Causes Act as amended.'

58. He went on to cite the well-known dictum of Butler-Sloss LJ in *Kelley v Corston* [1998] 1 FLR 986 at 1013:

> 'The court retains the duty laid upon it under section 25 in respect of consent orders as well as contested proceedings. It has to scrutinise the draft order and to check, within the limited information made available, whether there are other matters which require the court to make enquiries. The court has the power to refuse to make the order although the parties have agreed it. The fact of the agreement will, of course, be likely to be an important consideration but would not necessarily be determinative. The court is not a rubber stamp.'

59. Given the long-established principle that the court (or arbitral tribunal) is not bound by parties' agreements, but must consider the s.25 factors in determining whether or not an agreement is fair, and can fill in gaps which are left open in an agreement, it was not wrong for the arbitrator to hold that the husband should contribute over and above the £12,000 he had agreed to pay towards capital costs. Such a decision was wholly within the arbitrator's power to make, and squarely within the bounds of discretion open to him. His hands were not tied. In my judgment the arbitrator's decision in this regard was not wrong but was right.

60. This ground therefore also fails.

The fifth ground of challenge

61. Although this did not form a separate ground in the grounds of challenge document initially prepared on behalf of the husband, Ms Harrison QC at the hearing before me further criticised the award for containing internal inconsistencies, which I treat now as a discrete fifth ground.

62. She submitted the first inconsistency is that paragraph 89 of the award says that until the wife vacates X, she will meet the ongoing running costs of the property. However, the declaration says at paragraph 133 that pending the wife's vacation of X, she would meet the ongoing running costs of the property, but that the husband would pay £4,500 per month for six months from 1 October 2020, after which he would pay half the running costs. Ms Harrison QC therefore argued that the two paragraphs are inconsistent.

63. In relation to this alleged inconsistency, Mr Rainer pointed out firstly that the husband did not actually raise the issue as a point of clarification in his s.57 application to the arbitrator. He said that the reason is that it was understood by the parties that part of the overall agreement they had reached was that the husband would pay £4,500 towards the running costs for six months, and that after that period, if the wife remained in the property, she would bear the running costs on her own. However, it was agreed that once the wife left the property, the running costs would be split equally again. Mr Rainer pointed out that the agreement that the husband would contribute £4,500 per month for six months to the running costs was first recorded at paragraph 72(d) of the award. Thus its absence at paragraph 89 and its reappearance at paragraph 133 is not an inconsistency when the award is read as a whole, as was intended.

64. I agree with Mr Rainer. As he put it, Ms Harrison QC's "island-hopping" approach of looking at individual paragraphs in the judgment ignores the fact that the award was written to be read in full from start to finish. Although it is true that the award could perhaps have been clearer in respect of whose obligation the running costs would be at various points in time, I do not accept that there is an appealable inconsistency.

65. Secondly, Ms Harrison QC argued that the arbitrator wrote at paragraph 90 of his award that the parties would have liberty to apply to the court in the event they could not agree about capital costs in the future, but that in the part of the declaration which refers to the capital costs issue, there is no reference to there being liberty to apply (at paragraphs 132 and 133). Again, Ms Harrison QC said this is an inconsistency.

66. Mr Rainer accepted that the omission in the declaration of the parties having liberty to apply was unhelpful, but submitted that it was not an omission of such moment as to render the award wrong.

67. I agree with Mr Rainer. Although it is unfortunate that liberty to apply was specifically mentioned at paragraph 90 but not in the declaration, if the award is read as a whole as was intended, there can be no doubt that the fact that the parties would have liberty to apply was implicit in the declaration. There is no appealable inconsistency.

68. Thirdly, Ms Harrison QC submitted that at paragraph 82 there is a list of specific capital expenses the wife alone had to bear, along with a recording of the fact that the husband would make a contribution of £12,000. Some of the figures given for the specific costs the wife would bear were estimates. However, at paragraph 132, the declaration says that in fact insofar as the specific expenses the wife would bear are estimates, the husband would meet one half of any cost in excess of the estimate. Ms Harrison QC said that no such stipulation was made at paragraph 82 and thus again there is doubt as to what the award actually intended.

69. Mr Rainer argued in response that once again a reading of the award in full makes it clear what the arbitrator intended.

70. I agree with Mr Rainer. While it is true that at paragraph 82 there is no mention of the husband paying one half of any costs in excess of what was estimated, paragraph 89 says explicitly that the parties would share equally the capital costs which were known as at 1 September 2020, but for which costs were underestimated. Thus, by the time the reader reaches paragraph 132 and the declaration, which says the husband would meet one half of any costs in excess of any estimate, there is no inconsistency at all.

71. Fourthly, Ms Harrison QC criticised the fact that the list of what might constitute a capital cost at paragraph 87 forms no part of paragraphs 132 or 133, the paragraphs of the declaration dealing with capital costs. Again, she said this leads to an internal inconsistency.

72. Mr Rainer submitted that paragraph 87 was not so much part of the substance of the award, but was more of a signpost for a future court should the parties invoke the liberty to apply clause, having been unable to reach an agreement on what constitutes a necessary capital cost. He argued there was therefore no inconsistency in it not being incorporated as part of the final declaration.

73. I agree with Mr Rainer that not including the list of what might constitute a capital cost in the declaration is not an appealable inconsistency. The final declaration is a concise summary of precisely what was being awarded to each of the parties. That is its purpose. It is therefore not in the least surprising that a contemplative list of suggestions as to what might or might not constitute a necessary capital cost was not included in the concise summary of the award.

74. In my judgment Ms Harrison QC's attack on the award under this ground amounts to a narrow textual analysis enabling her to claim that the arbitrator had fallen into error. This approach was criticised by Lord Hoffmann in *Piglowska v Piglowski* [1999] 1 WLR 1360 at 1372. As he said, the exigencies of daily court room life are such that reasons for judgment will always be capable of having been better expressed. There is no doubting in this case what the arbitrator intended. The inconsistencies do not detract from the clear meaning of the arbitrator's reasoning and do not amount to appealable errors.

Conclusion on the challenges to the award

75. The husband's challenges to the award are therefore dismissed.

76. I do not certify any of the challenges as having been totally without merit although some of them have been very close to the line.

[77 – 86 Redacted]

87. I have seen the working composite order agreed by counsel which sets out the few drafting differences between the parties. I am expecting that counsel will be able to agree the necessary wording in the light of this judgment.

88. I will deal with the costs of the proceedings before me separately and without a hearing. Counsel are directed to file written submissions not exceeding five pages concerning costs.

89. That is my judgment.

APPENDIX

1. In this Appendix to my judgment I shall refer to the dissatisfied party who is seeking to challenge the arbitral award as "P" and for convenience I shall use male pronouns for that party. I shall refer to the satisfied party seeking to uphold the arbitral award as "D" and for that party I shall use female pronouns. I shall use female pronouns for the circuit judge who hears the dispute.

2. In *Haley v Haley* [2020] EWCA Civ 1369 King LJ ruled at [73] and [96] that in substance a challenge to a financial remedy arbitral award should be dealt with in the same way, and subject to the same principles, as a financial remedy appeal in the Family Court from a district judge to a circuit judge. Thus, a challenge to an arbitral award by P should be placed before a specialist circuit judge who hears financial remedy appeals. That judge should then conduct a "triage/paper" exercise applying the permission to appeal test. If she takes the view that the objection made by P would not pass that test then she can make an order in the terms of the arbitral award without more ado and penalise P in costs: see [96].

3. If the circuit judge is satisfied at the "triage/paper" stage that the permission to appeal test is passed then she will set the application down for an *inter partes* hearing at which the court will decide whether the arbitral award is wrong. King LJ at [74] emphasised that the test is "not seriously or obviously wrong, or so wrong that it leaps off the page, but just wrong". If the circuit judge is so satisfied then she will make different provision to that within the arbitral award. The arbitral award will then be reduced to the status of a mere relic, superseded by the court's order.

4. The effect of the judgment of King LJ is to make a challenge to a financial remedy arbitral award under section 68 of the Arbitration Act 1996, or an

appeal against such an award under section 69, entirely redundant. For the future all challenges to a financial remedy arbitral award should be undertaken in accordance with the new procedure.

5. There are certain aspects of the new procedure which need to be clarified.

6. The first end is to determine exactly how the challenge is brought before the court. In the proceedings before me there has been a plethora of applications which betray the confusion into which the procedure has fallen. The husband has applied to challenge the award under section 68 of the Arbitration Act 1996. He has also sought permission to appeal pursuant to section 69. Those applications have been transferred to the Family Division. He has further informally applied for an order that the arbitral award should not be made into an order of the court. The wife has issued a notice for the husband to show cause why the award should not be made an order of the court.

7. This kind of confusion is all too prevalent. For example in *BC v BG* [2019] EWFC 7 the dissatisfied wife issued "A Letter to the Court and Judge at the High Court" with a personal note, and a Form D11 and N8 including grounds for appeal out of time. In that case I directed that her application should be issued and treated as an application that the award is not made an order of the court.

8. In *S v S (Arbitral Award: Approval)* [2014] EWHC 7 (Fam), [2014] 1 WLR 2299 Sir James Munby P held at [25] that "where a party seeks to resile from the arbitral award, the other party's remedy is to apply to the court using the 'notice to show cause' procedure". This procedure finds its origin in agreement cases where it has been used for decades: see *S v S* at [14]. For example in *Dean v Dean* [1978] Fam 161 just such a procedure was used.

9. *Haley v Haley* itself presupposes that this procedure will be used. At [96] King LJ stated:

> '…a party who believes the arbitral award which follows an arbitration hearing is wrong can, through the 'notice to show cause' process put their objections before the court.'

10. A contested application to the court will therefore most commonly be made by P, seeking to challenge an arbitral award. Less commonly the application will be made by D, seeking to implement the award in an order of the court, but not having the consent of P to do so.

11. Very commonly, the parties will be jointly applying for a consent order implementing the award. In such circumstances the application for a consent order will follow the normal path in FPR 9.26 and PD 9A para 7.1.

12. The guidance I give in this judgment is confined to contested cases. Its terms have been approved by the President.

13. An issue with the "notice to show cause" procedure is that it presupposes that D will make the running by applying to the court. This is the opposite

of what would happen on an appeal. On an appeal the dissatisfied party, the appellant, applies to the court for permission to appeal, and if permission is granted advances the appeal. The notice to show cause procedure is not literally apt where it is P who wishes to mount a challenge to the award, although I accept that efforts have been made to adapt it so that P can proactively challenge an award.

14. A further issue with a "notice to show cause" application is that no rule or practice direction within the FPR allows a financial remedy claim to be initiated in this way. It is a judicial invention which has not been reproduced in the rules. FPR 9.9B(2) and FPR PD 9A paras 1.2 and 1.2A mandatorily state that an application for a financial remedy must be dealt with under the standard procedure unless it is for periodical payments, variation of periodical payments (but not capitalisation) or for relief under Schedule 1 of the Children Act 1989 (or under the Domestic Proceedings and Magistrates' Courts Act 1978, or under article 10 of the 2007 Hague Convention), in which case it must be dealt with under the fast-track procedure. Neither track allows a financial remedy claim to be initiated by a "notice to show cause". FPR 5.1(1) and PD 5A Tables 1 and 2 stipulate that an application for a financial order must be made in Form A.

15. It is therefore axiomatic that a Form A needs to be filed. It may be that a Form A was filed previously and stayed pending arbitral proceedings. But before an application can be made by P challenging an award, or by D seeking to implement an award, there must be a Form A on the file.

16. The filing of a Form A in these circumstances does not give rise to a requirement to attend a MIAM. An arbitral award is of the character of an agreement: see *S v S* at [19] where Sir James Munby P stated:

> 'There is no conceptual difference between the parties making an agreement and agreeing to give an arbitrator the power to make the decision for them. Indeed, an arbitral award is surely of its nature even stronger than a simple agreement between the parties.'

Therefore, pursuant to FPR PD 3A para 13(2)(b), the proceedings do not fall within FPR PD 3A para 11 to which the MIAM requirement applies: see *Practice Guidance (Family Court: Interface with Arbitration)* [2016] 1 WLR 59 at [18].

17. Once there is a validly issued Form A on the court file the application by P, challenging the award, or by D, seeking to implement the award, should be made in Form D11 – the standard application notice – using the Part 18 procedure.

Application by P

18. Where P challenges the arbitral award and seeks that different provision should be made by the court, he should file in his local FRC zone hub a Form D11 as follows:

i) Box 3 should contain the statement:

This is a challenge to an arbitral award dated [date] made by [name of arbitrator]. The grounds of challenge are annexed at page 7.

ii) If there is already a Form A on the file which is stayed in favour of arbitration the statement in Box 3 should further seek that the stay be lifted.

iii) At page 7 the grounds of challenge should be annexed.

19. The Form D11 should be filed within 21 days of the date of the arbitral award in its final form.

20. The grounds of challenge should set out succinctly, and in the same manner as grounds of appeal would be pleaded, P's complaints about the arbitral award. They should specify in respect of each ground whether the ground raises a challenge against a point of law or a challenge against a finding of fact, or an allegation of procedural irregularity (c.f. FPR PD 30A para 3.2(b)).

21. In addition, P should file along with the Form D11:

i) a skeleton argument not exceeding 20 pages in length (c.f. FPR PD 30A para 5.13 – 5.22 and PD 27A para 5.2A.1);

ii) the award; and

iii) a draft of the initial gatekeeper's order (see below).

22. On the issue of the Form D11 the gatekeeper should immediately issue an order:

i) disapplying the procedural requirements in FPR 9.12 and 9.14 (including, but not limited to, the requirement for each party to file a Form E and to attend a first appointment) which would otherwise have been triggered by the filing, or un-staying, of the Form A;

ii) disapplying the service requirements in FPR 18.8 and providing that on service of the application and accompanying papers on D she may within 14 days of such service file a short skeleton argument in response (c.f. CPR PD 52C paras 19 and 20(1)) and a draft order which she wishes the court to make in the event that it determines that the permission to appeal test is not passed;

iii) lifting any stay on an existing Form A; and

iv) directing that the application and the accompanying documents will be considered by a circuit judge without a hearing not sooner than 21 days after issue of the application.

23. Pursuant to the gatekeeper's initial order, but subject to para 30 below, the papers should be placed before a circuit judge authorised to hear financial remedy appeals not sooner than 21 days after issue (thereby allowing time for D to file a skeleton argument in response). That judge will then conduct the "triage/paper" exercise without a hearing and will decide whether the permission to appeal test has been passed.

24. If the judge decides that the permission to appeal test has not been passed then she will make the order drawing on the draft provided by D, and will likely penalise P in costs. If she decides that the permission to appeal test has been passed then directions will be given by her for the application to be heard *inter partes.*

Application by D

25. Sometimes D has to bring the matter before the court because P, while rejecting the award, is refusing to cooperate in the making of a consent order that implements it. In that case the above procedure should be followed save that Box 3 of the Form D11 should contain the statement:

> **This is an application for an order implementing an arbitral award dated [date] made by [name of arbitrator]. The grounds in support, and a draft order, are annexed at page 7.**

26. In this scenario D should:

    i) annex to the Form D11 a draft order which implements the award;

    ii) file a skeleton argument;

    iii) file the award; and

    iv) file a draft of the initial gatekeeper's order (see below).

27. The gatekeeper's initial order will be in the same terms as para 22 above save that sub-para (ii) is to be read as providing that P should file any skeleton argument in response, together with any grounds of challenge to the arbitral award, within 14 days of service.

28. Subject to para 30 below, the papers should then be placed before the circuit judge who will decide whether the objections of P pass the permission to appeal test. If they do not pass that test she will make the order drawing on the draft provided by D. If the objections do pass the permission to appeal test, directions will be given by the circuit judge for the application to be heard *inter partes*.

29. In this scenario there should not be a time limit within which D must make her application to the court. It is easy to imagine negotiations about the terms of an implementing consent order breaking down after weeks of discussion.

Allocation to High Court judge level

30. If either P or D considers that the application seeking to challenge or uphold the arbitral award should be allocated within the Family Court to High Court Judge level then a written request to that effect should be made at the time of making the application. This will be considered by the gatekeeper, and if granted the initial order should provide under para 22(iv) above that the papers should be sent to Mostyn J (for a case proceeding in London or on the South-Eastern circuit), or to the relevant FDLJ (for a case

proceeding elsewhere), for assignment to a specific High Court judge to conduct the "triage/paper" exercise.

Conclusion

31. If the above procedure is followed, I believe that the intention of King LJ to align as much as possible a challenge to an arbitral award with an appeal in the Family Court is achieved. Obviously, variations demanded by the facts of the individual case can be made to the above process. But the process should be followed as far as possible.

32. On an appeal costs will normally follow the event. The same principle should apply on an application seeking to challenge, or implement, an arbitral award. The general rule of no order as to costs in FPR 28.3(5) will not apply to such an application: see *BC v BG* at [90].

33. I attach a *pro forma* initial gatekeeper's order. It will be added to the Compendium of Standard Orders as Order No. 6.5.

In the Family Court sitting at [*Court name*]

No: [*Case number*]

The Matrimonial Causes Act 1973

The Civil Partnership Act 2005

The Children Act 1989, Schedule 1

(ADAPT AS NECESSARY)

The [Marriage] / [Partnership] / [Relationship] of [*applicant name*] and [*respondent name*]

(ADAPT AS NECESSARY)

After consideration of the documents lodged by the applicant

ORDER MADE BY [*NAME OF JUDGE*] ON [*DATE*] ON THE PAPERS

The Parties

1. The applicant is [*applicant name*]

   The respondent is [*respondent name*]

   (SPECIFY IF ANY PARTY ACTS BY A LITIGATION FRIEND)

Recital

2. Form A was filed by the [applicant] [respondent] on [date].

3. By an order dated [date] the proceedings initiated by the Form A were stayed in order for the parties to engage in arbitration.

4. **EITHER**

   a. The applicant has applied to this court in Form D11 dated [date] challenging an arbitral award made by [name of arbitrator] on [date].

   b. Grounds of challenge are annexed to the Form D11.

   c. A skeleton argument has been filed by the applicant.

   d. The award dated [date] has been filed by the applicant.

   OR

   a. The applicant has applied to this court in Form D11 dated [date] for an order implementing an arbitral award made by [name of arbitrator] on [date].

   b. A skeleton argument and a draft proposed order have been filed by the applicant.

   c. The award dated [date] has been filed by the applicant.

IT IS ORDERED THAT:

5. The aforesaid stay is lifted.

6. The procedural requirements in FPR 9.12 and 9.14 (including, but not limited to, the requirement for each party to file a Form E and to attend a first appointment) are suspended.

7. The applicant shall serve the application and accompanying papers on the respondent forthwith. The service requirements of FPR 18.8 are disapplied.

8. The respondent may within 14 days of such service file a short skeleton argument in response including grounds of challenge, if applicable, and a proposed draft order.

9. **EITHER**

   The application and the accompanying documents will be considered by a circuit judge without a hearing not sooner than 21 days after issue of the application.

   OR

   The application and the accompanying documents shall be placed [before Mostyn J] **[FOR A CASE PROCEEDING IN LONDON OR ON THE SOUTH-EASTERN CIRCUIT]** [before X J] **[THE RELEVANT FDLJ FOR A CASE PROCEEDING ELSEWHERE]** for allocation.

10. Costs reserved.

Dated [*date*]

WL v HL [2021] EWFC B10

Case No: BV 17 D 30182

IN THE FAMILY COURT SITTING AT

THE CENTRAL FAMILY COURT

Date: 5th March 2021

Before:

RECORDER ALLEN QC

....

Between:

WL		**Applicant**
	-and-	
HL		**Respondent**

....

....

Ms Cecilia Barrett instructed by Goodman Derrick LLP for the applicant

Ms Felicity Goldsbrough instructed by Shakespeare Martineau LLP for the respondent

Hearing date: 16th December 2020

JUDGMENT

IMPORTANT NOTICE This judgment was delivered in private. The judge has given leave for this version of the judgment to be published on condition that (irrespective of what is contained in the judgment) in any published version of the judgment the anonymity of the parties and members of their family must be strictly preserved. All persons, including representatives of the media, must ensure that this condition is strictly complied with. Failure to do so will be a contempt of court.

1. On 1st June 2018 His Honour Judge Meston QC made a final order by consent in financial remedy proceedings between WL and HL following their short marriage which lasted between February 2015 and separation in October 2017.

2. The financial order contained an obligation that HL pay WL for the benefit of the parties' child, CL, born in February 2017, one-half of her nursery costs and, from the date that CL started primary education, one half of her reasonable childcare costs.

3. In June 2020 CL's full-time nanny, who she had had since birth, resigned. Thereafter WL engaged more *ad hoc* childcare including a local childminder, a friend's au pair, a school friend's nanny, and a babysitter. HL ceased making childcare payments. This led to WL issuing an enforcement application in Form D50K on 20th August 2020 seeking (as at that date) £758.00.

4. This application came before me on 16th November 2020. The sum claimed had increased to £3,788.50 as at the end of October 2020. With some considerable reluctance given its merits (and that there was no issue of affordability) I dismissed the enforcement application. I concluded that given the way in which the obligation had been drafted HL was not in breach of the letter of the order as his obligation to meet reasonable childcare costs only arose from the date that CL started primary education and breach of the spirit of the order could not fairly ground enforcement. I reserved any future hearings made by either party to vary the terms of the financial order to myself in the first instance.

5. Unsurprisingly my judgment led to WL issuing an application in Form A1 dated 19th November 2020 for (i) variation of the financial order of 1st June 2018 as it related to payments for pre-school childcare for CL; and (ii) a 'top up' order under CA 1989 Schedule 1 to assist WL in meeting the costs of caring for CL (HL being subject to a CMS maximum assessment of £1,098 pm). On 9th December 2020 WL issued a Form D11 Application Notice seeking an interim variation of the financial order to ensure (it was said) that WL could continue to meet her childcare costs pending determination of the substantive application.

6. These two applications came before me on 16th December 2020. I acceded in part to the interim variation application and ordered HL to make backdated payments for nursery costs of £517 pm from 9th December 2020 (being the date of WL's application) and £645 pm from 1st January 2021.

7. The remaining dispute between the parties was principally whether the parties should reemploy a nanny and if so whether the cost should be shared between them and in what proportions given that both were in well-paid full-time employment (HL disclosing a net income of £16,197 pm and WL a net income of £5,100 pm).

8. The parties' Forms H stated that together they had already incurred more than £15,000 in costs and estimated incurring a similar sum by the

FDR Appointment. It was therefore clear to me that the parties' expenditure on costs was already disproportionate to what was in dispute.

9. In consequence I exercised my case management powers under FPR Part 3.

10. Rule 3.3 states:

(1) The court must consider, at every stage in proceedings, whether non-court dispute resolution is appropriate.

Rule 3.4 states (so far as is material) as follows:

(1) If the court considers that non-court dispute resolution is appropriate, it may direct that the proceedings, or a hearing in the proceedings, be adjourned for such specified period as it considers appropriate –

(a) to enable the parties to obtain information and advice about, and consider using, non-court dispute resolution; and

(b) where the parties agree, to enable non-court dispute resolution to take place.

(2) The court may give directions under this rule on an application or of its own initiative.

(3) Where the court directs an adjournment under this rule, it will give directions about the timing and method by which the parties must tell the court if any of the issues in the proceedings have been resolved.

(4) If the parties do not tell the court if any of the issues have been resolved as directed under paragraph (3), the court will give such directions as to the management of the case as it considers appropriate.

11. These rules were considered in *Mann v Mann* [2014] 2 FLR 928 by Mostyn J at [25]–[28]. He identified where r.3.4 (then r.3.3) differed from the Civil Procedure Rule 1998 r.26.4(2A)[3] and, in particular, noted that the power under the FPR to adjourn so as to enable non-court dispute resolution to take place, while capable of being exercised on the court's own initiative, can only be exercised where the parties agree whereas, under the CPR counterpart, the court can impose a stay in favour of ADR whether the parties agree or not. Mostyn J suggested at [28] that the Family Procedure Rule Committee give consideration to deleting the words *"if the parties agree"* from (now) r.3.4(1)(b) so that it was put on the same footing as its CPR counterpart. This amendment has not yet been made.

12. More recently, in *Lomax v Lomax* [2019] EWCA Civ 1467 the Court of Appeal held (on appeal from *Lomax v Lomax (Referral to Early Neutral Evaluation)* [2020] 1 FLR 30 per Parker J) – a case under the Inheritance (Provision for Family and Dependants) Act 1975 – that in the civil context

3 If the court otherwise considers that such a stay would be appropriate, the court will direct that the proceedings, either in whole or in part, be stayed for one month, or for such other period as it considers appropriate.

the consent of the parties is not necessary for a case to be referred to Early Neutral Evaluation under CPR r.3.1(2)(m).[4]

13. Given that the costs of litigation were already disproportionate to the issues between the parties I considered that non-court dispute resolution was *"appropriate"* (r.3.3(1)). I therefore directed that WL's applications be adjourned until 15th January 2021 (i) to enable the parties to obtain information and advice about, and consider using, non-court dispute resolution; and (ii) where the parties agree, to enable non-court dispute resolution to take place.

14. I further directed that the parties' solicitors send me a joint letter by 14th January 2021 setting out the outcome of the parties' engagement in, or endeavours to engage in, non-court dispute resolution together with a schedule of the dates of any offers made and responses received (but not revealing the content of those offers unless made on an open basis).

15. On 13th January 2021 I was informed by way of a joint letter from the parties' solicitors that the parties had agreed to go to mediation in an effort to resolve the issues between them and a first session had taken place on 11th January 2021. The mediator had indicated that she would wish the mediation sessions to continue for at least the next two weeks and the parties were willing to do that. No further offers had been made since 16th December 2020 although it was expected that this was something that would occur as mediation progressed. WL had provided the mediator with information on the costs of employing a suitably qualified nanny to provide care for CL whilst she was at work.

16. The parties' solicitors therefore asked that the applications remain stayed for a further two weeks to 29th January 2021 and that I would then be provided with a further joint letter. I acceded to this request.

17. On 29th January 2021 I was informed by way of a second joint letter that the parties had attended two mediation sessions. I was provided with the dates of offers made and by whom (but not the content thereof). The letter further said that although it was not initially possible for the parties to reach an agreement in mediation, discussions had continued and that *"it now seems that it may now be possible for an agreement to be reached given most recent discussions and proposals"*.

18. The parties' solicitors therefore asked that the applications remained stayed for a further two weeks to 12th February 2021 and that I would then be provided with a further joint letter. It was said that it was hoped in the intervening period to be able to submit a draft consent order dealing with the resolution of the outstanding issues but if that proved not to be possible the solicitors' would be seeking to have the matter set down for a final hearing. I acceded to the request for further adjournment but said I would

4 Except where these Rules provide otherwise the court may … take any other step or make any other order for the purpose of managing the case and furthering the overriding objective, including hearing an Early Neutral Evaluation with the aim of helping the parties settle the case.

decide what should happen thereafter once I had received the further update.

19. On 12th February 2021 I was informed by way of a third joint letter that there appeared to be a *"broad level of agreement"* between the parties as to how the outstanding issues should be resolved, but there was disagreement on how an order to reflect the agreement should be drafted. It was said that the parties' preferred option would be for the issue to be dealt with by the court as a paper exercise so that each party submitted a draft of the order they would wish to see made with written submissions in support. Alternatively, it was said the matter could be set down for a short further hearing, although the solicitors were concerned about the costs of doing so, or the applications could again be adjourned for a short period of time to see if the drafting issues could be resolved. I was asked to advise as to how the court wished to proceed.

20. On 13th February 2021 I replied stating that I was very keen for the drafting issues to be resolved consensually if at all possible. I therefore said I would continue the adjournment for a further two weeks to 26th February 2021 in the hope that a draft order could be agreed before this date. If agreement had not been reached by that date then one draft order with the competing wording clearly highlighted and accompanied by concise written submissions cross-referenced to the competing wording was to be filed with me by 5th March 2021 and I would then determine the matter on paper.

21. I further asked both solicitors to advise their clients that (i) I was not bound to utilise either parties' preferred wording if I was asked to finalise the order; and (ii) either party may apply for an order that their costs of this exercise be met by the other and depending on how I determined the drafting issues in dispute I may well be persuaded to make such an order and summarily assess the same.

22. On 27th February 2021 and over subsequent days I received emails from both parties' solicitors which indicated that the parties were solely in dispute as to whether or not the order should (i) include an obligation that WL provide HL with copies of childcare employment contracts and invoices settled; and (ii) state that any childcarer employed should be in consultation and agreement with HL. Both parties subsequently modified their initial positions as to the precise wording they proposed. I was asked to determine this dispute on paper.

23. Both parties' solicitors agreed that (i) the parties were *Xydhias*-bound irrespective of my decision in relation to the issue I was being asked to resolve; and (ii) I was at liberty to adopt an alternative form of wording to that put forward by both parties even if this was in the form of a recital rather than in the body of the order.

24. Having considered the parties' competing submissions I determined the issue on paper on 5th March 2021 thereby finalising the order and bringing the proceedings to a conclusion. Both parties agreed to there being no order for costs.

25. I believe that my use of the court's FPR Part 3 powers in this case to encourage the parties to consider and enter non-court dispute resolution and my request for fortnightly updates assisted them in reaching settlement even though agreement was not reached in mediation but was reached thereafter between the parties themselves. My order took the matter out of the court arena and the inevitable focus on the next court hearing. It allowed the parties to maintain a direct dialogue rather it being conducted in writing via their solicitors (with the potential for polarisation and the inevitable increase in costs). It also allowed them to discuss with a third party and eventually agree a solution that worked for them as parents of their young child (rather than having one imposed) but, importantly, in the context of knowing that I was maintaining an overview of the progress of their negotiations.

26. Even though I ultimately had to decide a discrete issue on paper I am confident that adopting the approach I did led to a better, quicker and less expensive outcome than would otherwise have been the case.

27. I also consider that my use of the Part 3 powers furthered the overriding objective of enabling the court to deal with cases justly and in particular the obligation in r.1.1(2)(b) of dealing with the case in ways which are proportionate to the nature, importance and complexity of the issues; (d) of saving expense; and (e) allotting to the case an appropriate share of the court's resources, while taking into account the need to allot resources to other cases. My use of these powers was also an exercise of my duty as set out in r.1.4 to further the overriding objective by actively managing cases which includes at r.1.4(2)(f) *"encouraging the parties to use a non-court dispute resolution procedure if the court considers that appropriate and facilitating the use of such procedure"*.

28. Reference to FPR Part 3 was made in the Report of the Family Solutions Group (a subgroup of The Private Law Working Group chaired by Mr. Justice Cobb) dated 12th November 2020 (see Annex 10 C at p159-163). At paragraph 16 it was said [original emphasis]:

> **It would be helpful to gather data on the extent to which these duties and powers are applied.** Are there universal standards across the country or are differing courts adopting differing approaches? Concern has been expressed within our discussions and the wider PrLWG that the courts are not actively case managing in accordance with Part 3 of the FPR, and opportunities to resolve cases out of court are thus lost.

29. I therefore raised my use of the FPR Part 3 powers in this case with Mr. Justice Mostyn in his role as National Lead Judge of the Financial Remedies Courts. He asked that I record the same by way of a written judgment and that it be published on Bailii.

RECORDER ALLEN QC
5th March 2021

BT v CU [2021] EWFC 87

Neutral Citation Number: [2021] EWFC 87

Case No: BV18D07667

IN THE FAMILY COURT

Royal Courts of Justice

Strand, London, WC2A 2LL

Date: 1 November 2021

Before :

MR JUSTICE MOSTYN

....

Between :

BT		**Applicant**
	– and –	
CU		**Respondent**

....

....

Alexander Chandler instructed by Osbornes Law for the Applicant

Amy Kisser instructed by Mills and Reeve for the Respondent

Hearing dates: 7-8 October 2021

....

Approved Judgment

....

MR JUSTICE MOSTYN

The judge gives permission for this anonymised version of the judgment to be published. No publication or report of the judgment may reveal (1) the identities or residence of the parties or their children, (2) the schools of the children, or (3) the name of the applicant's business. Breach of this prohibition will amount to a contempt of court.

MR JUSTICE MOSTYN:

1. On 10 October 2019, District Judge Hudd made a final order at the conclusion of a four-day trial of the financial remedy proceedings between the parties. She ordered the husband (as I shall call the applicant) to pay the wife (as I shall call the respondent) £950,000 in a series of lump sums commencing with £150,000 on 1 November 2019, followed by four payments of £200,000 at yearly intervals commencing on 1 November 2020 and ending on 1 November 2023. A pension sharing order of 30% of the husband's pension was made. Tapering spousal maintenance in lieu of interest was ordered against the husband until payment of the final lump sum. The husband was ordered to pay child maintenance and school fees for the parties' two children aged 17 and 15.

2. The effect of the order was to divide the total assets of £4.75m in the ratio 58%: 42% in the husband's favour. The District Judge justified this departure from equality by reference to the husband's retention of the most valuable asset – a business providing school meals. The retention of this business by the husband was not controversial – both parties proposed it in their open offers. This asset predated the marriage and therefore to some extent had a non-matrimonial constituent. The shares in the company were characterised by the judge as having an element of risk and not comparable to cash in the bank. These two reasons justified the departure from equality.

3. In February 2020, the Covid-19 pandemic reached these shores and shortly thereafter the country went into lockdown. In March 2020, all schools were closed. On 27 April 2020, the husband applied pursuant to FPR r 9.9A to set aside parts of the final order. He contended that the arrival of the pandemic was both unforeseen and unforeseeable, and its impact had caused devastating financial consequences which invalidated the fundamental assumptions on which the final order was based. As a result, he claimed that he was unable to discharge his unpaid obligations under the order.

4. On 12 January 2021, Her Honour Judge Evans-Gordon directed that a hearing should be listed before a High Court judge sitting in the Family Court to determine the following preliminary issues:

   i) Is Covid capable of being a *Barder* event?

   ii) Has the applicant established sufficient grounds to set aside the final order, whether in part or in full?

Such a process is clearly permitted by FPR PD 9A para 13.8. This states:

> "In applications under rule 9.9A, the starting point is that the order which one party is seeking to have set aside was properly made. A mere allegation that it was obtained by, e.g., non-disclosure, is not sufficient for the court to set aside the order. Only once the ground for setting aside the order has been established (or admitted) can the court set aside the order and rehear the original application for a financial remedy. The court has a full range of case management powers and considerable discretion as to how to determine an application to set aside a financial remedy order, including where appropriate the power to strike out or summarily dispose of an application to set aside. If and when a ground for setting aside has been established, the court may decide to set aside the whole or part of the order there and then, or may delay doing so, especially if there are third party claims to the parties' assets. Ordinarily, once the court has decided to set aside a financial remedy order, the court would give directions for a full rehearing to re-determine the original application. However, if the court is satisfied that it has sufficient information to do so, it may proceed to re-determine the original application at the same time as setting aside the financial remedy order."

5. This provision permits the ground-establishment phase to be separated from the disposition phase. In my judgment, this is a sensible and useful procedure in a case such as this. Plainly, the nature of the hearing of the first phase is more substantive than an oral *inter partes* hearing for permission to seek judicial review, or for leave under s.12 of the Matrimonial and Family Proceedings Act 1984. As I see it, I have to decide on the material before me the primary factual question namely whether grounds for setting aside the final order have been established. If they have not, the husband's application will be dismissed.

6. The hearing was conducted before me without oral evidence. I received written and oral submissions from Mr Chandler and Ms Kisser of high quality, for which I am grateful.

The legal principles

7. The husband's application is, of course, made pursuant to the principles propounded by the House of Lords in the famous case of *Barder v Barder* [1988] AC 20. In that case, the alleged supervening event, the death of the wife and the children, was procedurally advanced by the husband by means of an application for leave to appeal out of time against the final consent order. Nowadays, the application must be made at first instance under FPR r 9.9A, which regulates procedurally the general power of set-aside found in s. 31F(6) of the Matrimonial and Family Proceedings Act 1984. This change of procedural route does not in any way relax the rigour of Lord Brandon's conditions which must be proved for a set-aside to be awarded:

Akhmedova v Akhmedov & Ors (No 6) [2020] EWHC 2235 (Fam) at [128], *CB v EB* [2020] EWFC 72 at [50]. Those conditions are:

i) New events have occurred since the making of the order invalidating the basis, or fundamental assumption, upon which the order was made.

ii) The new events should have occurred within a relatively short time of the order having been made. It is extremely unlikely that could be as much as a year, and in most cases it will be no more than a few months.

iii) The application to set aside should be made reasonably promptly in the circumstances of the case.

iv) The application if granted should not prejudice third parties who have, in good faith and for valuable consideration, acquired interests in property which is the subject matter of the relevant order.

To this list must be added a further condition namely that the applicant must demonstrate that no alternative mainstream relief is available to him which broadly remedies the unfairness caused by the new event: *Penrose v Penrose* [1994] 2 FLR 621 at 634; *Myerson v Myerson (No 2)* [2010] 1 WLR 114 at [35]; *J v B (Family Law Arbitration: Award)* [2016] 1 WLR 3319 at [34].

8. The new event(s) must have been unforeseeable. Whether an event was unforeseeable must be proved to the same standard as that required in the Queen's Bench Division when determining an issue of remoteness: *J v B* at [36] – [41]. The probability of the occurrence of the event must have been so small that a reasonable person would have felt justified in neglecting it or brushing it aside as far-fetched.

9. Once the applicant has proved all five conditions, he will have established sufficient grounds to justify a set-aside of the order.

10. There is at this point a residual discretion as to whether a set-aside should actually be ordered. In *Myerson (No.2)*, Thorpe LJ at [32] – [34] identified some further considerations bearing on the exercise of the discretion. In that case, the final order was by consent and the husband had agreed to an asset division which left him "captain of the ship certain to keep for himself whatever profits or gains his enterprise and experience would achieve in the years ahead". Thorpe LJ continued:

> "When a businessman takes a speculative position in compromising his wife's claims, why should the court subsequently relieve him of the consequences of his speculation by rewriting the bargain at his behest? [The husband] continues to enjoy control of the opportunities that go with it. The marketplace may take a pessimistic view of his future prospects. He may not share the marketplace view. Unusual opportunities are created for the most astute in a bear market."

Thus, the court is bidden to consider exercising its discretion so as to say to a businessman who has settled his wife's claim that, even if he satisfies all the *Barder* conditions, he has made his bed and must lie in it. As I read the decision, this discretion will only arise where the final order was made by consent and where the applicant is a buccaneering market trader. It is hard to envisage other circumstances where the discretion would properly be exercised against a set-aside once all five conditions have been proved.

11. In *Cornick v Cornick* [1994] 2 FLR 530 at 536, Hale J identified three possible scenarios where following the final hearing the figures used for the values of the assets changed substantially. She described them thus:

> "(1) An asset which was taken into account and correctly valued at the date of the hearing changes value within a relatively short time owing to natural processes of price fluctuation. The court should not then manipulate the power to grant leave to appeal out of time to provide a disguised power of variation which Parliament has quite obviously and deliberately declined to enact.
>
> (2) A wrong value was put upon that asset at the hearing, which had it been known about at the time would have led to a different order. Provided that it is not the fault of the person alleging the mistake, it is open to the court to give leave for the matter to be reopened. Although falling within the *Barder* principle it is more akin to the misrepresentation or non-disclosure cases than to *Barder* itself.
>
> (3) Something unforeseen and unforeseeable had happened since the date of the hearing which has altered the value of the assets so dramatically as to bring about a substantial change in the balance of assets brought about by the order. Then, provided that the other three conditions are fulfilled, the *Barder* principle may apply. However, the circumstances in which this can happen are very few and far between. The case-law, taken as a whole, does not suggest that the natural processes of price fluctuation, whether in houses, shares or any other property, and however dramatic, fall within this principle."

12. A final order in a case in Category (1) will not be set aside under the *Barder* doctrine, even if the shift in values has been massive, and even if it was the consequence of a major economic global downturn. This is because such a shift will have been a foreseeable consequence of the natural processes of price fluctuation. Major economic downturns are cyclical by nature. They may cause financial devastation, but they cannot be said to be unforeseeable or of a nature that invalidates the basis, or fundamental assumption, on which the final order was made.

13. A case in Category (2) is not a *Barder* case. It is a mistake case where the "new" facts are not new at all, but are shown to have existed all along, albeit unknown, at the time of the final order. A true *Barder* case is founded on new facts which have arisen since the date of the final order: *Judge v Judge* [2009] 1 FLR 1287 at [3]; *Walkden v Walkden* [2010] 1FLR 174 at [83]; *Richardson v Richardson* [2011] 2 FLR 244 at [80] – [82]; *J v B (Family Law Arbitration: Award)* [2016] 1 WLR 3319 at [50] – [57]. A set-aside

may be granted in a case in this category provided that certain conditions are satisfied (*ibid* at [57]). It is not suggested that the case before me falls into Category 2 and so I need say no more about it.

14. Category (3) is the sole true *Barder* case. To repeat: the five conditions must be satisfied and the new event must have been unforeseeable.

15. Cases falling outside Category 1 and inside Category 3 will be rare indeed. In case after case, it has been emphasised that the circumstances must be truly exceptional before a capital settlement can be reopened: *Walkden* at [80]; *Richardson* at [86]; *Myerson (No.2)* at [38]. To illustrate this rarity, consider the facts of *Cornick* and *Myerson No.2*.

16. In *Cornick*, the principal asset was the husband's shareholding in the company of which he was deputy chairman. The shares were quoted. At the time of the final order in December 1992 the shares were each worth £2.17. A lump sum order was made in the wife's favour which had the effect of dividing the assets almost equally. Following the hearing, the share price rose dramatically. The wife applied for leave to appeal out of time; this came before Hale J in May 1994. By then, the share price had risen to £10.04; this had the effect of leaving the wife with only 20% of the assets. The reason the share price had risen so much was because of shrewd management, the introduction of new products and the exploitation of the U.K.'s withdrawal from the ERM. Hale J described it as "the uniquely successful share of the last few years".

17. Yet the wife's application was refused.

18. *Myerson* had an even more dramatic set of facts. By a consent order made in March 2008, the wife received £11 million (or 43%) out of assets worth £26 million, leaving the husband with a 57% share. The principal asset was a shareholding in a single company worth £15 million, the price of an individual share being £2.99. The global financial crisis of 2008 then hit the husband's assets hard so that by December 2008, when the husband applied for leave to appeal out of time, the share price had fallen to 72p. This meant that the wife had 86% of the assets; the husband a mere 14%

19. By the time of the hearing in March 2009 the share price had sunk to 27p. Having regard to the husband's debts, this meant that his overall assets had fallen into negative territory: his net worth was minus £539,000, giving the wife 105.2% of the overall assets.

20. Yet the husband's application was refused. It is true that Thorpe LJ relied on the discretionary factors mentioned at para 10 above as well as the availability of an alternative remedy (statutory variation of the lump sum instalments). But it is clear that his principal reason was that the global financial crisis of 2008 was not unforeseeable and the downturn did not invalidate the fundamental basis of the order: see [26] – [31].

21. When assessing whether a new event was unforeseeable in a case where it is said that the event has caused a major shift in the value of the assets (as opposed to a case where the new event is the death of a party) I consider

that the court should principally focus on the economic impact of the event rather than its cause or nature. It sounds highly dramatic to plead that a business has been grossly impacted by the once-in-a-century global Covid-19 pandemic (as here), but *au fond* such a case is no different in substance to one where a business was devastated by the impact of the 2008 Global Financial Crisis. A reasonable but well-informed person may well have given in 2019 a very different answer to the question:

> "What chance do you see of a global pandemic arising in 2020 which has the result of wiping out this business's operating profit?"

to the question:

> "What chance do you see of a global financial crisis arising in 2020 which has the result of reducing this business's turnover by 10%?"

22. My answer to the first question posed for me – Is Covid capable of being a *Barder* event? – is "probably not", but, as always, it depends on the specific facts of the case, as Sir Jonathan Cohen pointed out in *FRB v DCA (No. 3)* [2020] EWHC 3696 (Fam) at [26] where he said:

> "In my judgment it is not proper for the court to accede to H's application to vary the quantum on macro-economic grounds. If H wishes to assert that there has been a fundamental change in his worth so as to justify a reopening of the inquiry, then it is up to him to provide prima facie evidence. It is trite to say that the pandemic has affected different sectors in different ways. Some, such as hotels and airlines, which make up part of the wealth of H and his family, will undoubtedly have been negatively affected but so varied are his interests that it is far from obvious that there has been a collapse in his global fortune."

This case

23. Following the initial lockdown in March 2020, the turnover of the business was hit hard. However, the business availed itself of the government's Coronavirus Job Retention Scheme ("the furlough scheme") which was introduced in April 2020, and up to 13 June 2021, had received £3.1 million from this source. In addition, it had taken a low interest Coronavirus Business Interruption Loan from the government of £460,000. The accounts show that between 1 January 2020 and 30 June 2021, which covers the Covid period, the net assets of the business increased from £939,000 to £1.2 million, and the cash at the bank increased from £830,000 to £1.8 million.

24. All pupils returned to school in September 2021. The furlough scheme ended on 1 October 2021. In her witness statement made on 15 March 2021, the wife argued that there was no reason why the business could not resume full trading immediately following the reopening of schools. The husband's response on 30 March 2021 was as follows:

"Contrary to [C's] assertion, the re-opening of the schools does not mean that my business resumes 'trading fully immediately.' Primary school income is down by 10 to 20% with no after school clubs or breakfasts and this seems to be the case nationwide. Eating in classrooms, as is now frequently the case seems to be less popular. Secondary school income is down between 20 to 50% with no break or breakfast services. Our labour costs are greater proportionately for less income and this will be the case until at least September. Schools still operate "bubbles" for year groups and we still have reduced school populations due to year groups being out. Contrary to what C says the company trading in December 2020 does not demonstrate a return to profit. In December 2020 we received income from schools for free school meals that we had not provided as schools depopulated. This source of income is no longer relevant as schools have returned."

25. However, the position since March 2021, when these gloomy predictions were made, has changed significantly. Primary schools are now offering school clubs and breakfasts. Secondary schools are offering break and breakfast services. Schools are not operating bubbles for year groups. School populations are not reduced due to year groups being out.

26. In the summer of 2021, the husband produced a cash flow forecast to December 2022, which suggested, if normal trading conditions resumed, that by the end of that month cash at the bank would have risen to £2.4 million. Mr Chandler was astute to disavow this prediction as speculative and inaccurate. However, the second footnote to the forecast states: "The company has lost 9 schools over the summer but has picked up 12 new units to replace – no real impact overall on business levels."

27. This did not suggest that turnover would be reduced once full trading recommenced in the post-Covid era. I therefore conjectured during Mr Chandler's submissions that there must be actual forecasts in existence which have at least an attempt at accuracy. Overnight, the husband created a document ("the husband's document") which surmised that for the 12 months beginning on 1 October 2021, there would be a 10% reduction in turnover compared to that for 2019, the last full prelapsarian year, and an 8% general increase in the cost of food supplies and catering labour. The document also surmised that in that period it would be possible to reduce administrative expenses by 25%. The result of the decrease in turnover and the increase in costs would be to reduce an operating profit of £734,000 to a loss of £206,000.

28. I emphasise that the husband's document is not an existing internal company forecast but was an overnight creation by him. I am surprised that the business has not prepared detailed forecasts of the anticipated future trading conditions.

29. I now set out in tabular form the numeric data derived from the accounts and the husband's document:

	A Y/e 31-Dec-19	B Y/e 31-Dec-20	C[1] P/e 30-Jun-21	D[2] Y/e (est) 31-Sep-22	E[3] change
Profit & Loss					
Turnover	16,639,369	9,799,693	5,260,216	14,975,350	-10.0%
Cost of Sales	(14,654,527)	(10,701,133)	(5,108,669)	(14,244,122)[4]	-2.8%
Gross Profit	1,984,842	(901,440)	151,547	731,288	-63.2%
Margin	11.9%	-9.2%	2.9%	4.9%	
Admin Expenses	(1,250,468)	(1,219,272)	(678,919)	(937,851)	-25.0%
Other Operating Income (Furlough)	0	2,156,278	950,713		
Operating Profit	734,374	35,566	423,341	(206,623)	-128.1%
Balance Sheet					
Fixed Assets – Tangible assets	196,913	129,179	127,453		
Current Assets – Debtors	1,664,745	1,102,667	1,003,098		
Current Assets – Cash	832,760	1,049,207	1,808,866		
Creditors less 1 year	(1,723,723)	(949,753)	(1,248,260)		
Creditors more 1 year	0	(406,334)	(452,333)		
Provision for Liabilities	(31,531)	(32,218)	(32,218)		
Net Assets	939,164	892,748	1,206,606		

Notes:

1. Column C gives the figures for the six-month period ended 30 June 2021
2. Column D gives the figures in the husband's document referred to above
3. Column E gives the percentage changes between Columns A and D
4. The cost of sales of £14,244,122 in Column D is calculated by taking 90% of the Column A figure of £14,654,527 and then multiplying it by the general 8% increase: £14,654,527 × 0.9 x1.08 = £14,244,122.

30. Although a downward shift in operating profit of £941,000 looks dramatic, and therefore unexpected, it is essentially a reflection of its functional sensitivity in circumstances where the business has always traded on very tight gross profit margins. As the husband's document shows, even small shifts in the wrong direction of its constituent elements can lead to a very large movement downwards.

31. I am not satisfied that I have been given a sufficiently plausible explanation to accept at face value the premises of the husband's document. If the gloomy reasons in his statement set out above are now not present, what is the reason for the asserted 10% downturn in turnover? The best the husband could do was to say to me that that's just what he thought would happen. He speculated that more parents are sending children to school with packed lunches, rather than with money to buy lunches from the cafeteria provided by the husband's business. This is not hard evidence.

32. I can accept that there would have been an inflationary increase in the cost of raw food and labour but whether it would be as much as 8% is pure conjecture.

33. But even if my scepticism is misplaced, and the husband's document is to be treated as an accurate prediction of trading conditions in the next 12 months, I cannot accept that the events that caused these unwelcome movements in turnover and costs of sale were unforeseeable or that they have invalidated a fundamental assumption on which the order was based. On the contrary, the relevant question when determining foreseeability is the second one set out at para 21 above. In my judgment, a reasonable person would have said in October 2019 that there was certainly a chance, which could not sensibly be ignored, that in the next year there would be an economic downturn which would have the effect of reducing turnover and increasing costs.

34. Further, it is absolutely clear that the basis of the order was that the husband would be retaining assets which were risky, and for this reason would be granted a greater than equal share of the assets. In her excellent judgment District Judge Hudd stated at para 27:

> "A value in a company is not the same as liquid capital. There is an element of risk attaching. There is no guarantee that the company will continue to perform at the same level but assuming the company continues to perform well, as it has done for 23 years, the husband will retain the value of the company to realise when he seeks to leave the industry on retirement. He proposes to retain the value within his shares. Both parties propose that he should retain all of his shareholding. I have to be careful to ensure that I am considering both the potential value to the husband but also the potential risk to him."

And at para 56:

> "This is a company that has gone from strength to strength through careful management but no doubt there is a competitive market ahead and the wife is not carrying any of that risk on the proposed structure for lump sum payments. It seems to me, on that basis, it is appropriate that any distribution should involve a departure from equality in the husband's favour. It will be fair to do so to give him a greater proportion of the assets to reflect both the premarital value and also the risk that is inherent in his retention of the company and that it is not pounds in the bank or a property."

35. Mr Chandler for the husband now argues that the District Judge clearly based her order on the ability of the company to produce sufficient profits to pay dividends to enable the husband to meet the lump sums. He refers to para 58 of her judgment where she stated:

> "I am satisfied that the company is able to release money at that rate. A net profit of £600,000 will be comfortably adequate to pay the £200,000 to the wife and around £175,000 or thereabouts to the husband

by way of dividends net of tax. Obviously, tax will need to be paid at 38.1%. However, looking at the company's accounts for the past five years, it has achieved that level of profit in four of those five years and across those five years, there has been a comfortable excess of sums that will be required to pay sums in that order. The company is financially sound and has considerable leeway in how it operates. It seems to me that there is always the option for finance if there are any cashflow issues, but I am satisfied, on the basis of the expert's opinion, that given the retained earnings that are in the company, there should not be any difficulty in realising those sums and the issue would simply be one of liquidity rather than one of a level of profits to enable those dividends to be declared."

36. In this passage, the District Judge was not categorically stating that the fundamental basis of her judgment was an expectation that the business would carry on generating the same level of historic profits so as to enable the lump sums to be paid from dividends. On the contrary, she recognised that the business was inherently risky and that there may not be profits sufficient to pay the lump sums, in which case the husband would have to look to financing solutions or to the deployment of the ample cash held in the company.

37. If the husband ran into difficulty in raising the lump sums from any source, then it would be open to him to apply to the court for a delay in payment of them. This is not an impermissible variation: see *Masefield v Alexander (Lump sum: extension of time)* (1995) 1 FLR 100 where Butler-Sloss LJ stated at 103:

> "…it is necessary to look at the purpose and effect of the application to extend time to see whether in truth it is intended to strike at the heart of the lump sum order or whether it is a slight extension (as was said by Sheldon J in *Gregory v Wainwright*) of no great importance, which does not go to the main or substantive part of the order."

Clearly an application for a modest extension of time to pay an individual lump sum would not strike at the heart of the order and would be, if granted, of no great importance, particularly if compensatory tapering periodical payments are being paid in the meantime.

38. I agree with Ms Kisser that if the facts of *Myerson* did not satisfy Lord Brandon's first condition, then it is impossible for these facts so to do. The downturn suggested by the husband's document, even if accurate, is a pale shadow compared to the devastation caused to Mr Myerson's business by the 2008 global financial crisis.

39. I am therefore satisfied that the husband has failed to establish sufficient grounds to satisfy positively Lord Brandon's first condition.

40. Although it is not necessary for me to go further, I confirm that Lord Brandon's second, third and fourth conditions are satisfied in this case.

41. It may be that the fifth condition is also not satisfied for reasons which I will now explain.

42. There are two possible routes of alternative relief open to the husband. The first is for him to apply for the order of District Judge Hudd to be varied or permanently stayed inasmuch as it is executory. The second is for him to apply for that order to be varied on the grounds that it is objectively a lump sum payable by instalments variable under s. 31(2)(d) Matrimonial Causes Act 1973.

An executory order?

43. In *Thwaite v Thwaite* [1982] Fam 1, Ormrod LJ identified two routes to extinguish the lump sum order made in that case. First, in a harbinger of the later case of *Barder*, the lump sum order could be set aside on an appeal out of time in reliance on fresh evidence which destroyed the basis of that order. Second, the court could refuse to enforce the unpaid lump sum order, as it was executory.

44. *Thwaite* was cited to the Judicial Committee of the House of Lords in *Barder* and is referred to in Lord Brandon's speech at page 20 on a different point namely as an authority for the proposition that the legal effect of a consent order derives from the order itself and not the underlying agreement.

45. The first route must now be seen as being superseded by the decision in *Barder*, which propounded a much stricter test for the grant of leave to appeal out of time. The first route in *Thwaite* did not incorporate the requirement of unforeseeability; nor did it have the one-year limitation period.

46. As for the second route, it must be strongly emphasised that in *Barder* itself, Lord Brandon observed at page 10 that the order under appeal was executory. Yet, fully aware of the decision in *Thwaite,* the Committee did not decide the case by reference to that doctrine. I agree with Ms Kisser that the Committee must be taken as having impliedly rejected this route as a legitimate source of relief.

47. I will nonetheless examine this route.

48. In *Thwaite* at page 9 Ormrod LJ stated:

> "Where the order is still executory, as in the present case, and one of the parties applies to the court to enforce the order, the court may refuse if, in the circumstances prevailing at the time of the application, it would be inequitable to do so: *Mullins v. Howell* (1879) 11 Ch D 763 and *Purcell v. F. C. Trigell Ltd.* [1971] 1 QB 358, 366, 367. Where the consent order derives its legal effect from the contract, this is equivalent to refusing a decree of specific performance; where the legal effect derives from the order itself the court has jurisdiction over its own orders: per Sir George Jessel M.R. in *Mullins v. Howell* (1879) 11 Ch D 763, 766."

49. *Mullins v. Howell* concerned the release of a party from an undertaking to remove some buttresses projecting from an archway mistakenly given by counsel at an interlocutory hearing. There is, of course, a general power vested in the court to discharge an undertaking: *Birch v Birch* [2017] UKSC 53 at [6] – [12]. *Mullins v Howell* says nothing about a supposed power to vary a substantive final order which happens to be executory.

50. *Purcell v F. C. Trigell Ltd* concerned a personal injury action where a defence had been struck out for failure to comply with a consent order which required a full reply to interrogatories. That strike-out was upheld in the Court of Appeal; the court refused to discharge the earlier interlocutory order requiring answers to interrogatories. Lord Denning MR stated, almost in passing, at page 364:

> "But there is no ground here so far as I can see for setting aside this consent order. It was deliberately made, with full knowledge, with the full agreement of the solicitors on both sides. It cannot be set aside. But, even though the order cannot be set aside, there is still a question whether it should be enforced. The court has always a control over interlocutory orders. It may, in its discretion, vary or alter them even though made originally by consent."

Again, this case says nothing about the existence of a power to vary a substantive final order which happens to be executory. The cases merely say that the court has power to control its interlocutory orders *inter alia* by not enforcing them.

51. Thus, *Thwaite* goes no further than to confirm the existence of an equitable jurisdiction to refuse to enforce an executory order if, in the circumstances prevailing at the time of the application, it would be inequitable to do so. Although the cases relied on by Ormrod LJ relate only to interlocutory orders, he pushed back the boundary of that power so as to cover final orders. But the reasoning in *Thwaite* does not, on any view, support the idea that there exists some kind of equitable power, not merely to refuse to enforce an executory order, but to make in its stead a completely different one. For this reason, I stated in *SR v HR (Property Adjustment Orders)* [2018] EWHC 606 (Fam), [2018] 2 FLR 843 that any application under the principle in *Thwaite* should be approached "extremely cautiously and conservatively", which, of course, was coded language expressing my doubt that the jurisdiction to rewrite (as opposed to mere refusal to enforce) existed at all.

52. I do not doubt that there exists a power to extend time to comply with an executory order or to stay its execution for a limited period, provided that the extension does not strike at the heart of the order: see *Masefield v Alexander* above. In that case, Butler-Sloss LJ cited *R v Bloomsbury & Marylebone County Court ex parte Villerwest Ltd* [1976] 1 WLR 362 at p 365 where Lord Denning MR said: "there is a very wide inherent jurisdiction, both in the High Court and in the county court, to enlarge any time which a judge

has ordered." In *Hamilton v Hamilton* [2013] EWCA Civ 13, Baron J at [33] held that the time to pay a singular lump sum could not be extended "by any significant period".

53. As for a stay, CPR 40.8A provides that

> "A party against whom a judgment has been given or an order made may apply to the court for … a stay of execution of the judgment or order on the ground of matters which have occurred since the date of the judgment or order, and the court may by order grant such relief, and on such terms, as it thinks just."

Although this rule is not replicated in the FPR, the same power is to be found in FPR 4.1(3)(g) which provides that the court may stay the whole or part of any proceedings or judgment either generally or until a specified date or event.

54. CPR 40.8A in terms grants a power to award a stay of an executory order, which may only be exercised where matters have occurred since judgment. It has been held that a permanent stay should only be awarded under this rule where the court would set aside the order under the principles in *Tibbles v SIG plc* [2012] 1 WLR 2591: see *Raja v Van Hoogstraten & Ors* [2018] EWHC 3261 (Ch) at [59] per Morgan J. *Tibbles* at [39(ii)] states that the power to set aside an order will only normally be exercised where there has been a material change of circumstances since the order was made or where the facts on which the original decision were, innocently or otherwise, misstated. This is similar to the *Barder* test, but omits the requirement of unforeseeability, and the one-year limitation period. I would go further than Morgan J and hold that a permanent stay could only be lawfully ordered under this rule, or under FPR 4.1(3)(g), if the *Barder* test is fully satisfied. Were it otherwise, there would exist a means of obtaining relief indistinguishable from that in *Barder* but without having to satisfy the rigour of the *Barder* conditions. I note that in *Benson v Benson (Deceased)* [1996] 1 FLR 692, Bracewell J applied the *Barder* test to a set of set-aside applications which included a *Thwaite* application.

55. Accordingly, it is clear that the court possesses power to enlarge time for payment of the lump sums or alternatively to stay execution of their payment, but in each instance for no longer than a reasonably short period. For the reasons given in the next section, these capital awards are not variable in their overall quantum under s. 31 of the Matrimonial Causes Act 1973 and so, the *Barder* doctrine aside, it must follow that there is no power to award a permanent stay of execution of the payments, let alone a power to replace the lump sums with alternative provision. To decide otherwise is to repudiate the binding precedent of *Barder.*

56. However, since my decision in *SR v HR*, there have been four cases which have rejected my doubts and which have held that the court has the power not merely to stay enforcement of an executory order, but to rewrite an executory final order to provide for something completely different to that which it originally stated.

57. In *US v SR* [2018] EWHC 3207 (Fam), Roberts J pointed out that *Thwaite v Thwaite* had been followed uncritically in *L v L* [2006] EWHC 956 and in *Bezeliansky v Bezelianskaya* [2016] EWCA Civ 76. She followed *L v L* and held that a power to vary an executory final order existed. It would be exercised where it would be inequitable not to vary the terms of the executory order because of, or in the light of, some significant change in the circumstances since the order was made ('the *L v L* test'). On the facts, she held that the *L v L* test was satisfied and varied the order.

58. That decision was followed in *Akhmedova v Akhmedov & Ors (No 6)* [2020] EWHC 2235 (Fam) at [154] and in *G v C* [2020] EWFC B35 (OJ). In both of these cases, it was held that the *L v L* test was not satisfied. In the latter case, the court held that the decision of the Court of Appeal in *Bezeliansky v Bezelianskaya* was not a binding authority as it was a decision refusing permission to appeal which had not been certified in accordance with the *Practice Direction (Citation of Authorities)* [2001] 1 WLR 1001 para 6.2, and FPR PD 27A para 4.3A.2.

59. The appeal from *G v C* was heard by Lieven J and is reported as *Kicinski v Pardi* [2021] EWHC 499 (Fam). The issue was whether the order in that case (a *Rose* order) should be varied to write into it an indemnity from the husband in the wife's favour in respect of financial claims made against the wife by the husband's aunt and uncle. On any view, that was a prohibited variation under the terms of s. 31 of the Matrimonial Causes Act 1973.

60. Lieven J accepted that *Bezeliansky v Bezelianskaya* was not technically binding but said that it carried for her the 'greatest weight' (para 29). In para 47 she stated:

> "On my analysis of the caselaw, the first question in deciding whether to exercise the *Thwaite* jurisdiction is whether there has been a significant (and necessarily relevant) change of circumstances since the order was entered into; and the second question is whether, if there has been such a change, it would be inequitable not to vary the order. For myself, I do not find the words "cautious" and "careful" particularly helpful. There are two requirements to the use of the jurisdiction and their application will ensure that the *Thwaite* jurisdiction is used with care. There is no additional test or hurdle set out by the Court of Appeal in *Bezeliansky* which is the case that binds me."

61. She held that it was not necessary to show anything more than a significant change of circumstances. It was not necessary to show that the change of circumstances had been unforeseen (and, presumably, unforeseeable): [51].

62. On the facts, she found that a change of circumstances had occurred and that it would be inequitable not to vary the order as sought. The husband was therefore ordered to give the indemnity. Her logic would undoubtedly lead to the conclusion that in this case, provided the *L v L* test was met, a permanent stay of execution of the payments could be lawfully ordered.

63. I have to say, with great respect, that I do not agree with these decisions. They appear to me to be in conflict with the binding precedent of *Barder*.

64. There is nothing within the terms of s 31 of the Matrimonial Causes Act 1973 to suggest that its strict curtailment of the power of variation and discharge is confined only to orders which have been performed. An application to set aside an executory order under the *Barder* doctrine is explicable as an exercise of appellate powers, now replaced by a specific rule permitting the power to be exercised at first instance. An application to set side an executory order based on fraud, or mistake, can be explained as a separate cause of action. These are surely the only legitimate exceptions to the statutory prohibition on variation of the amount of capital settlements.

65. In the nature of things the variation powers in s. 31 will apply predominantly to unexecuted orders. Some are variable; most are not. It is a carefully devised scheme which was proposed by the Law Commission (see below) and democratically enacted by Parliament. The *Thwaite* exception, as developed in *L v L* and the later cases, in my opinion drives a coach and horses through the statutory scheme.

66. If this route were available, then it means that many *Barder* cases, including *Barder* itself, will have been tried, and in most cases dismissed, applying a set of principles far more rigorous than those required under the executory order doctrine. This is because most *Barder* cases, including *Barder* itself, concern orders which are executory. It would therefore seem, if the proponents of the executory order doctrine are correct, that the entire litigation in *Barder* itself, all the way to the House of Lords, was conducted on a completely wrong footing.

67. The uncertainty surrounding the availability of this relief leads me to conclude that it is not realistically available to the husband for the purposes of the fifth *Barder* condition.

A lump sum by instalments?

68. The Law Commission report, *Financial Provision in Matrimonial Proceedings* (Law Com No. 25, 24 July 1969) is the key originating text for our current substantive law. At para 10, it stated that “it should be made clear that any lump sum awarded can be ordered to be paid by instalments”; it repeated this in its summary at para 17, and in its comprehensive summary of recommendations at para 115(1)(e). The draft Bill appended to the report provided in clause 2(1)(c) that the court could order that “either party to the marriage shall pay to the other such lump sum as may be so specified”. Clause 2(2)(b) provided for such lump sum to be payable by instalments. Both clauses referred to a lump sum in the singular, as do the notes to the clause on page 67. The draft Bill did not expressly vest the court with power to award a number of lump sums.

69. At para 89 the Law Commission considered the question of variation and said:

> "… orders for cash provision ought normally to be reviewable. But, here again, there must be an exception to this general rule. This relates to orders for a lump sum payment. Once a payment has been made it obviously cannot be cancelled or varied. If, however, the order has not been fully complied with it could be effectively varied and it is necessary to consider whether this should be permissible; **its importance is mainly, of course, in cases where a lump sum has been ordered to be paid by instalments. In our view variations should not be permitted**. An order for a lump sum of £5,000 payable by five yearly instalments of £1,000 is to be distinguished from financial provision of £1,000 per annum for five years. Apart from the different tax consequences, the former should not end on the death or remarriage of the payee whereas the latter would. **If a lump sum is ordered it should be on the basis that the payee is entitled to it here and now although, to soften the blow to the payer, actual payment may be spread over a number of years. In our view once an order for a lump sum has been perfected its amount should not be variable whatever may happen later.** This, of course, does not mean that a subsequent order cannot be made which may have the effect for the future of undoing the original payment. If, on a judicial separation, the husband had been ordered to pay the wife £1,000 and if the husband subsequently divorced her because of her adultery and was granted custody of the children, it might well be that the court would then order her to pay him £1,000 or some other sum. This would not be a variation of the original order, but a new order made in the light of the changed circumstances when a second occasion arose to review the financial position." (emphasis added)

70. Thus, the recommendation was that lump sums payable by instalments should not be variable as to overall quantum save in the (clearly uncommon) situation where a matrimonial cause for judicial separation was followed by one for divorce. The draft Bill provided for that in clause 9(4). As for the instalments of a lump sum, clauses 9(1) and 9(2)(b) provided that the court had power to discharge, vary or temporarily suspend an order under clause 2(2)(b). The notes to clause 9 on page 79 state:

> "Hence orders for lump sum payments (except in relation to the instalments or the security therefor) and out-and-out transfers are not variable at all and orders for other property adjustments are variable only if made on the grant of a judicial separation and then only in the circumstances stated in subsection (4). But all other orders are variable.
>
> **It will be observed that though the amount of lump sums will not be variable (the reasons for this are set out in paragraph 89 of the Report) the provisions relating to the instalments or any security therefor will be variable. A change of circumstances may make it just either to extend or to curtail the time of payment of the instalments or, indeed, to increase or reduce the number of instalments.** And after a number of the instalments have been paid it may be reasonable to reduce the amount of the security." (emphasis added)

71. The emphatic recommendation of the Law Commission was therefore that the variation of a lump sum payable by instalments could not alter its overall quantum. The timing and size of the instalments could be altered, but the overall quantum had to stay the same. A careful reading of the provisions in the draft Bill shows that the power to vary applied only to the instalments and not to the amount of the lump sum itself. This was a crucial feature of the new scheme which appears to have been overlooked in all the later cases which have considered the variability of a lump sum payable in instalments.

72. The Bill was enacted by Parliament largely unchanged as the Matrimonial Proceedings and Property Act 1970. Parliament must be taken to have accepted and implemented the prohibition on statutory variation of the quantum of all lump sums, whether or not paid in instalments, as proposed by the Law Commission.

73. A significant addition was made to the draft Bill at some stage during its parliamentary journey. Section 2(2)(c) as enacted allowed the court to make an order that either party to the marriage shall pay to the other such lump sum **or sums** as may be so specified. Why the legislators added the words "or sums" is not known; I have not been taken to Hansard. It would seem likely that it was to enable separate sums to be payable on separate occasions for separate purposes, in contrast to a single sum which, in order to soften the blow to the payer, is permitted to be paid in instalments.

74. In *Coleman v Coleman* [1973] Fam 10, Sir George Baker P considered these provisions. The husband had been ordered to pay the wife a lump sum of £2,000. In addition, there was a form of property adjustment order in the wife's favour in respect of a sum of money of £5,500. The wife later applied for a further lump sum. Her application was dismissed for want of jurisdiction to make such an award on a subsequent occasion.

75. Sir George pointed out at page 16 that the words "or sums" had been added to clause 2(2)(c) of the Bill during its passage through Parliament, and he quoted paragraph 89 of the report which I have set out above. At pages 19-20 he stated:

> "I think that the purpose of the words "or sums" must be to enable the court to provide for more than one lump sum payment in one order; indeed, that is what has been done in the present case, for there is an order for the payment of £2,000 and for the payment of £5,500, the latter being expressed by the registrar in his judgment to be "so that she may, should she so wish, acquire a capital interest in her home." Many examples suggest themselves – an order for a lump sum to cover expenses, as in section 2(2)(a) of the Matrimonial Proceedings and Property Act 1970, or for the purchase of the house or for furnishing the house, or in lieu of maintenance, or it may be that one lump sum is to be payable immediately and another by instalments. Then there are wives like the present wife who must have money at once for at least the deposit on a new home for herself and the children, but the final amount

> she should receive cannot be fairly decided until the selling price of the former home (owned by the husband) is known. At the present day that may be in a bracket of many thousands of pounds. This problem can be resolved within the section by requiring the husband to give her an immediate lump sum for the deposit and adjourning the question of the further lump sum (if any) until after the sale of the former home
>
> …
>
> Counsel for the wife submits that section 2(2) of the Matrimonial Proceedings and Property Act 1970 supports the view that the insertion of the words "or sums" in section 2(1)(c) must be for the purpose of enabling the court to make a plurality of orders. Were it otherwise, section 2(2)(b), which enables an order to provide for the payment of a lump sum by instalments of such amount as may be specified in the order. would, he submits, be quite unnecessary. **Although at first sight the meaning and purpose of section 2(2) of the Act is not entirely clear, it seems to me that it is merely a declaratory subsection, for on any construction section 2(1)(c) at least allows sums to be ordered on a first application."** (Emphasis added)

76. What Sir George decided was that pursuant to one single application, the court could order a number of lump sums and that it could further order that one or more of those lump sums be paid by instalments. Thus, for example, an order could be made providing that on 1 January the husband is to pay to the wife a lump sum of £5,000 and a further lump sum of £4,000 payable in four monthly instalments of £1,000 commencing on 1 March and ending on 1 June.

77. It is true that Sir George did not consider the question of variability of such an order. He must be taken, however, to have accepted the Law Commission's intention that the figures of £5,000 and £4,000 in my example could not be varied under s 9(1) but that under s. 9(1), 9(2)(b) and 9(7) there was a general discretion to vary the instalments of the second lump sum of £4,000 to, say, eight monthly payments of £500 commencing on 1 March and ending on 1 October.

78. Sir George further held (slightly surprisingly) that it was within the power of the court when dealing with an application for a lump sum or sums to order that, say, the husband was to pay the wife a lump sum of £5,000 on 1 January and that the application for a second lump sum would be adjourned to a later date.

79. Let me attempt to explain how the language of the provisions as enacted in the now repealed 1970 Act clearly achieved the effect intended by the Law Commission. (Where emphasis appears in the cited provisions it has been added by me).

80. Section 2(1)(c) provided:

> "On granting a decree of divorce, a decree of nullity of marriage or a decree of judicial separation or at any time thereafter (whether, in the

case of a decree of divorce or of nullity of marriage, before or after the decree is made absolute), the court may … make any one or more of the following orders, that is to say **…(c) an order that either party to the marriage shall pay to the other such lump sum or sums as may be so specified.**"

Therefore, the power to award a lump sum or sums derived from this provision, and this provision alone. But, s. 2(2) provided:

> "Without prejudice to the generality of subsection (1)(c) above, an order under **this section** that a party to a marriage shall pay a lump sum to the other party:
>
> (a) may be made for the purpose of enabling that other party to meet any liabilities or expenses reasonably incurred by him or her in maintaining himself or herself or any child of the family before making an application for an order under this section;
>
> (b) may provide for the payment of **that sum** by instalments of such amount as may be specified in the order and may require the payment of the instalments be secured to the satisfaction of the court."

81. This states that the order for the payment of the lump sum is made under "this section". Literally, this means section 2 as a whole but it can only be a reference to the primary power in s. 2(1)(c). But the order may go on to specify, in subsidiary provisions pursuant to s. 2(2)(b), that payment of "that sum" shall be made by defined instalments and, further, that the instalments be secured. Thus, the subsidiary provisions will specify the rate and term of the instalments making up "that lump sum" which has been ordered under s. 2(1)(c).

82. Section 9(1) and (2)(b) provided:

> "(1) Where the court has made an order to which this section applies, then, subject to the provisions of this section, the court shall have power to vary or discharge the order or to suspend any provision thereof temporarily and to revive the operation of any provision so suspended.
>
> (2) This section applies to the following orders, that is to say ….
>
> (b) any order made by virtue of section 2(2)(b) of this Act …"

The variation power therefore does not apply to the order under s. 2(1)(c) which constitutes the lump sum. Rather, it is strictly confined to the subsidiary provisions under s. 2(2)(b) allowing for payment of "that sum" by instalments in the amounts and periodicity there specified. Thus, variation cannot alter the quantum of "that sum".

83. This interpretation is not only the natural meaning of the provisions but is, unsurprisingly, entirely consistent with the stated intention of the Law Commission set out above. It would be surprising, to put it mildly, if the Law Commission had drafted the Bill using language which achieved the exact opposite of what it so clearly intended.

84. The Matrimonial Proceedings and Property Act 1970 was later repealed, and its terms consolidated within the Matrimonial Causes Act 1973. The relevant provisions with which I am concerned were transposed without material alteration as follows:

1970 Act	**1973 Act**
Sec 2(1)(c)	Sec 23(1)(c)
Sec 2(2)(b)	Sec 23(3)(c)
Sec 9(1)	Sec 31(1)
Sec 9(2)(b)	Sec 31(2)(d)
Sec 9(7)	Sec 31(7)

Plainly, the meaning of the original provisions did not alter on transposition.

85. Later developments have led me to conclude that the correct current position in relation to my hypothetical order in paras 76 and 77 above is that:

i) the two lump sums of £5,000 and £4,000 could be set aside under FPR 9.9A provided that the five conditions in *Barder* were all satisfied, and it was proved that the new event was unforeseeable; alternatively

ii) the date for payment of the first lump sum of £5,000 could be varied from 1 January to, say, 1 February under the inherent power of the court as explained in *Masefield v Alexander*; and/or

iii) Under s. 31(1), (2)(d) and (7) of the Matrimonial Causes Act 1973 the scheduled payments of the instalments of the second lump sum of £4,000 could be varied to eight monthly payments of £500 commencing on, say, 1 March and ending on 1 October.

86. On this analysis, there is not much difference between the variability of a lump sum payable by instalments and the variability of a series of lump sums. The timing of the payment of individual lump sums in a series can be altered under the inherent jurisdiction of the court as explained in *Masefield v Alexander.* However, the amount of the instalments cannot be altered. It is not possible later to vary the payment schedule to provide for the overall amount to be spread over a longer period in smaller instalments. In contrast, a lump sum payable by instalments can be varied in that way.

87. There have been a number of cases which I respectfully suggest have misread the relevant provisions and have assumed that an order under s 31(1) and (2)(d) Matrimonial Causes Act 1973 could vary the overall quantum of a lump sum which is payable by instalments. The cases are:

i) *Tilley v Tilley* (1980) 10 Fam Law 89, CA

ii) *Penrose v Penrose* [1994] 2 FLR 621, CA

iii) *R v R (Lump Sum Repayments)* [2003] EWHC 3197(Fam), [2004] 1 FLR 928, FD

iv) *Westbury v Sampson* [2001] EWCA Civ 407, [2002] 1 FLR 166, CA.

v) *L v L (unreported)* 13 October 2006, FD

vi) *Hamilton v Hamilton* [2013] EWCA Civ 13, CA

vii) *Myerson v Myerson (No 2)* [2009] EWCA Civ 282, CA

viii) *FRB v DCA (No. 3)* [2020] EWHC 3696 (Fam), FD

88. This is a formidable catalogue but in none of those cases was the Law Commission's report referred to, and in none, with the exception of *Tilley,* was a variation as to overall quantum actually ordered. So the statements are all *obiter dicta*.

89. *Tilley* is only reported in abridged form in Family Law journal. However, it appears that Donaldson LJ purported to extinguish the final instalment of £3,500 payable by the wife, on the ground that it should be treated as a quid pro quo for child maintenance that the husband ought to be paying, notwithstanding that the order stated that his liability for child support was nominal. The decision is extremely hard to understand from many angles. The Law Commission report was not referred to and the report does not reveal that any consideration was paid to the true construction of s.31(1) and 31(2)(d) of the 1973 Act. I do not consider that there is a clearly expressed *ratio decidendi* which binds me.

90. In *Westbury v Sampson*, Bodey J stated that variation of overall quantum under s. 31 Matrimonial Causes Act 1973 would be extremely rare. He stated:

> "57. Nevertheless, given the constant emphasis in the authorities generally on the need to uphold the finality of orders intended to be final, including orders as to capital, it seems to me that very similar considerations ought in practice to be applied under s. 31 as those laid down in *Barder*, at any rate as regards varying the overall quantum of a lump sum order by instalments (as distinct from re-timing or 're-calibrating' the instalments).
>
> 58. The re-opening under s. 31 of the overall quantum of lump sum orders by instalments, especially when made as part of a package intended to be final (and all the more so when ordered by consent following an agreement) should only be countenanced when the anticipated circumstances have changed very significantly, and/or for cogent reasons rendering it quite unjust or impracticable to hold the payer to the overall quantum of the order originally made.
>
> 59. This formulation gives a little more latitude as regards s. 31 than do the Barder conditions for the grant of leave to appeal out of time; but that must I think follow from the statutory requirement under s.31(7) that the Court is to consider "all the circumstances".

91. In *Hamilton v Hamilton,* however, Baron J did not adopt such stringency. At [43] she merely stated:

> "The Court is given the power to vary a lump sum [payable by instalments] and it stands to reason that that power must extend to quantum as well as timing."

And at [49] she recommended that:

> "Finally, in future, parties may consider that a recital at the beginning of an order which sets out the basis of the agreement in terms of a potential variation would put disputes of this type beyond doubt."

92. In the light of this recommendation, a practice has developed of framing what to all intents and purposes is a lump sum payable by instalments, as a non-variable series of lump sums. Thus, in this case District Judge Hudd stated in her judgment, at para 69:

> "My order will leave the husband with the full value of the company once the lump payments have been cleared in full. They must be cleared and I am quite clear that this is an order for a series of lump sums and it is not my intention that they should be susceptible to variation. It seems to me preferable for both parties that there is certainty."

Her order contained a recital that the parties agreed and declared that the lump sum orders should be considered to be a series of lump sum orders. The order itself at para 7 was headed "series of lump sum orders" and required the husband to pay the wife a series of lump sums.

93. In *Hamilton v Hamilton*, the order in question provided that the wife was to pay to the husband "the following lump sums", which were then set out. There were five lump sums payable over four years. Parker J held that, notwithstanding the way the liability was described, it was in reality an order for a lump sum payable by instalments. The wife sought a variation as to quantum; this was refused but some further time for payment was allowed. In the course of her judgment, Parker J held that:

> '…in every case where there is to be a staged payment then this is in reality a lump sum by instalments and that it is not possible to protect the payee by drafting the order as a "series of lump sums".'

94. In the Court of Appeal, Baron J held that this went too far; Parker J was wrong to conclude that every order for the payment of a series of lump sums over time is an order for a lump sum by instalments. However, Baron J went on to hold:

> "41. … Where there is a disagreement as to whether the terms of the order are, in reality, correct then the Court retains jurisdiction and must assess what the parties agreed against the objective factual matrix of what occurred during the relevant period. Ordinarily the language of the order will settle matters but, in the event of a dispute as to the nature of the agreement, the Court is entitled to look at the surrounding facts and circumstances which bear upon the terms as drafted. This investigation is perfectly proper because it is evidence of the stages that preceded the perfection of the Court order. To be clear, the test is objective as the court is not looking to assess the subjective beliefs of the parties rather it is looking at the objective factual matrix to interpret what was agreed in the light of the words used and communications that passed."

95. Baron J held that Parker J had been entitled on the facts of the individual case to hold that objectively the order in that case was a lump sum by instalments. The appeal was dismissed. The resolution of the appeal did not depend on Baron J's view that the overall quantum of a lump sum payable by instalments is variable. That view is therefore an *obiter dictum*.

96. Factually, this case is indistinguishable from *Hamilton*. Objectively, and notwithstanding the camouflaging language, this was a lump sum payable by instalments. If the award is a pay-out under the sharing principle, but spread over time to soften the blow to the payer, then it will surely almost always be a lump sum by instalments, regardless of how it is dressed up. If, however, there are different payments on different dates for different purposes, as described by Sir George Baker P in *Coleman*, then that arrangement will be a series of lump sums. Mr Chandler submits that the law should look to effect and not semantics; and cites Lord Templeman's famous aphorism in *Street v Mountford* [1985] AC 809 (albeit in a different context):

> "…The manufacture of a five-pronged implement for manual digging results in a fork even if the manufacturer, unfamiliar with the English language, insists that he intended to make and has made a spade."

I agree.

97. In my judgment, notwithstanding that the order in this case is to be characterised as a lump sum payable by instalments, it is not variable as to overall quantum under s. 31 Matrimonial Causes Act 1973. The overall quantum can only be set aside or altered under the *Barder* doctrine. Under s. 31 all that can be achieved is recalibration of the payment schedule.

98. I do not conclude that this limited variation power affords the husband an alternative remedy for the purposes of the fifth *Barder* condition.

Conclusion

99. The husband has failed to establish sufficient grounds to satisfy the first *Barder* condition. His application dated 27 April 2020 is therefore dismissed.

Postscript: anonymity

100. My original intention when handing down this judgment was that anonymity should be granted to the children alone. This was to reflect the increased emphasis on, and move towards, transparency in financial remedy proceedings. The Consultation Document on Transparency in the FRC dated 28 October 2021 has pointed out that had journalists or bloggers attended the hearing before me they would have been entitled, subject to any reporting restriction order made by me, to have named the parties and to have published anything which had not been disclosed under compulsion.

101. However, Mr Chandler in admirably succinct and lucid supplemental submissions argues that anonymity should be extended to the adult parties and that the rubric to this judgment should therefore prohibit disclosure of the identities or residence of the parties or their children; the schools of the children; or the name of the applicant's business.

102. The application before me was not the wife's application for financial remedies. It was the husband's application to set aside parts of the final order made on the wife's primary application. That is a significant difference. It cannot be said that any of the husband's evidence in support of his application had been disclosed under compulsion. On the contrary, all of that evidence was volunteered by him. Therefore, I consider it most unlikely, had journalists or bloggers attended, that the husband would have succeeded in persuading me to grant an order preventing a report identifying the parties or any of the financial details about the business. The only possible ground would have been that the parties came to the hearing with a reasonable expectation that their anonymity would be preserved. I discuss this below.

103. Mr Chandler argues that same principles of anonymity should apply equally to a primary application for financial remedy and to a set-aside application. I disagree, but will nonetheless address those principles. I accept that the current convention is that a judgment on a financial remedy application should be anonymised, although the decision whether to do so reposes in the discretion of the individual judge. Mr Chandler has cited the judgment of Thorpe LJ in *Lykiardopulo v Lykiardopulo* [2010] EWCA Civ 1315 at [45] and [79] where anonymisation is described as the "general practice" justified by reference to respect for the parties' private lives, the promotion of full and frank disclosure, and because the main information is provided under compulsion.

104. The move to transparency has questioned the logic of this secrecy. Almost all civil litigation requires candid and truthful disclosure, given under compulsion. The recently extended CPR PD51U – *Disclosure Pilot for the Business and Property Courts* -contains intricate and detailed compulsory disclosure obligations. Para 3.1(5) requires parties "to act honestly in relation to the process of giving disclosure". Many types of civil litigation involve intrusion into the parties' private lives. Yet judgments in those cases are almost invariably given without anonymisation.

105. I no longer hold the view that financial remedy proceedings are a special class of civil litigation justifying a veil of secrecy being thrown over the details of the case in the court's judgment. In my opinion it is another example of the Family Court occupying a legal Alsatia (*Richardson v Richardson* [2011] EWCA Civ 79, [2011] 2 FLR 244, para 53, per Munby LJ) or a desert island "in which general legal concepts are suspended or mean something different" (*Prest v Petrodel Resources Ltd and others* [2013] UKSC 34, [2013] 2 AC 415, para 37, per Lord Sumption).

106. The secrecy becomes even more difficult to defend when one considers appeal judgments. These are not anonymised, and this is so whether the

appeal is from circuit Judge to High Court judge or from High Court judge to the Court of Appeal. Hence, the appeal judgment of Lieven J in *Kicinski v Pardi* [2021] EWHC 499 (Fam), which I have discussed above, was reported in full without anonymisation.

107. Almost all financial remedy judgments of the Court of Appeal are given in full without anonymisation. I note that the judgments of the Court of Appeal given as recently as 2 November 2021 in the case of *Siddiqui v Siddiqui & Anor* [2021] EWCA Civ 1572 conclude with the following statement:

> "Sir James Munby's judgment was anonymised when published and the parties have requested that this court's decision should also be anonymised when published. Having considered the parties' respective submissions, we have concluded that there is no sufficient justification for the judgments above to be anonymised."

108. This divergence in practice, depending on whether the application is proceeding at first instance or on appeal, is impossible to defend. It becomes yet more arbitrary and irrational when one considers that, where during the interlocutory journey of a first instance application, there has been an excursion to the Court of Appeal, the judgment at the final hearing will often be given without anonymisation: see as an example the recent decision of Peel J in *Crowther v Crowther & Ors (Financial Remedies)* [2021] EWFC 88, where everybody and everything were named.

109. Mr Chandler has argued that anonymity of the adult parties and the children and of the name of the husband's business should be granted in this case. He relies on the convention which I have set out above. In principle, this argument should be rejected. The convention does not apply to a set-aside application. In any event, where it does apply, it is time for it to be abandoned.

110. Mr Chandler argues that naming the husband will lead to identification of his business and that its financial details as set out above at [23] – [36] would be of great interest to commercial competitors. I reject that reason also. Mere assertions of this nature do not justify the imposition of secrecy. Hard evidence would be needed before that argument could be accepted. A judgment on a petition under s. 994 of the Companies Act 2006 would no doubt contain much information about the company of interest to its competitors. But I very much doubt that that would lead to redaction from the judgment of the name of the company or of the identities of its members. The same standard of openness should apply to a financial remedy judgment. The desert island syndrome should be avoided.

111. However, Mr Chandler argues that there are two good reasons why I should depart from my initial intention and grant anonymity to the adults. First, he argues that naming the wife will inevitably be picked up at the children's school where she teaches, leading to a detrimental impact on the children's welfare. Thus, he argues, my grant of anonymity to the children may well be ineffective. I accept that submission.

112. Second, he argues that the parties in this case came to the hearing before me with a reasonable expectation that the hearing would preserve their anonymity. Although I have held above that reliance on the convention of anonymisation of financial remedy judgments should now be abandoned, I accept that it would be unfair for me to spring this change of practice on these parties without forewarning.

113. However, it should be clearly understood that my default position from now on will be to publish financial remedy judgments in full without anonymisation, save that any children will continue to be granted anonymity. Derogation from this principle will need to be distinctly justified by reference to specific facts, rather than by reliance on generalisations.

114. I have therefore anonymised this judgment and have revised the terms of the rubric, to which careful attention should be paid.

115. That is my judgment

Index